DIVINE SIGNS

Connecting Spirit to Community

H. L. GOODALL, JR.

Southern Illinois University Press

CARBONDALE AND EDWARDSVILLE

Copyright © 1996 by the Board of Trustees,
  Southern Illinois University
All rights reserved
Printed in the United States of America
Edited by Carol M. Besler
Designed by David Ford

99 98 97 96   4 3 2 1

"The Sacred" is reprinted from *Between Angels*: Poems by Stephen Dunn, by permission of W. W. Norton & Company, Inc. Copyright © 1989 by Stephen Dunn.

"A Spiritual Uplifting" first appeared in *Pudding Magazine: The International Journal of Applied Poetry*, no. 21, 1993, from the author's chapbook, *Getting the Body to Dance Again*, winner of the 1944 National Looking Glass Poetry Chapbook Competition, Pudding House Publications, 1995.

Library of Congress Cataloging-in-Publication Data

Goodall, H. Lloyd.
  Divine signs : connecting spirit to community / H. L. Goodall, Jr.
      p. cm.
  Includes bibliographical references and index.
  1. Communication and culture. I. Title.
  HM258.G664 1996
  302.2'22—dc20   95-38681
  ISBN 0-8093-2024-X   CIP
  ISBN 0-8093-2025-8 (pbk.)

The paper used in this publication meets the mimimum requirements of American National Standard for Information Sciences—Permanence of Paper for Printed Library Materials, ANSI Z39.48-1984. ∞

FOR SAN whose early investigation of spirituality and communication created the initial inspiration for this study, and who continues to provide the necessary eternal light

AND FOR NIC the fine son whose blessed innocence compelled me to answer his penetrating questions about what I really believe in, and with whom I have been privileged to experience—once again—how everyday imagination works on—and in—realities

With deep appreciation to all those who have shared our journeys, and who have given freely to us the immanent poetry of their presence and the transcendent joy of their experiences

Some people see things as they are and ask "why?"
I dream of things that might be and ask "why not?"
—Robert F. Kennedy

There are more things in heaven and earth
than are dreamt of in your philosophy.
—William Shakespeare, *Hamlet*

The most beautiful experience we can have is the mysterious.
—Albert Einstein

Contents

Preface	ix
Acknowledgments	xv
Introduction: Context, Imagination, and Interpretation	1

PART ONE: REALITY CENTRAL

1. Destination and Arrival	27
2. Boredom and Ecstasy	47
3. Difference and Possibility	73

PART TWO: PERFORMING COMMUNITY

4. Rapture and Ecstasy: Spirituality, Football, and the Accomplishment of Community	105
5. Immanence and Angels: Experiencing Parallel Worlds	136
6. Awareness and Imagination, or Altered States of Syntax as Communication Riddles	157

PART THREE: HIGHWAYS AND SURROUNDS

7. Vision and Reason, or The Strangeness of Instructions	179
8. Insight and Complexity: The Future of Unities	208
Afterword: Problematizing Spirit	229
Appendix 1: Power, Other, and Spirit	245
Appendix 2: Modern, Postmodern, and Spiritual Communication	248

CONTENTS

Appendix 3: Connecting Spirit to Community through
Imagination and Communication   252

References   279
Index   285

Preface

Nexus

What constitutes meanings in and for a community? How are those meanings suggested? How are they organized?

If we assume the answer to the first question is "communication," then probably the answer to the second and third questions is "through the intersections of public and private messages." Viewed as a social, political, and economic collectivity, "community" becomes an interpretive *nexus* constructed out of the symbolic, semiotic, and rhetorical materials of place and space; individuals and groups; race, class, and gender; homes and works; art, artifacts, and architectures; thoughts and actions; and perhaps a dozen or so other representational concerns.

Yet there is also something else required for the making of a community. It is something as mysterious and ineffable as the unknown within and as biologically necessary as air and water. It is something that is neither "some" nor "thing," and that exists in and between the intersections of persons and their meanings. These are the clues that begin to spell out that true connection between us and where we are, and between where we are and all the rest. This necessary something that is an ineffable nonthing is Spirit.

This book is about Spirit. Specifically, it is about how the everyday dualities or tensions in public forms of communication provide the raw semiotic, rhetorical, and symbolic materials for connecting ourselves to Spirit within the *nexus* of communities. It is about how the mythic narratives informing and guiding our sense of communities are shaped by struggles among Power, Other, and Spirit. And it is also about why interpretations of these intersections of meanings, messages, and connections

PREFACE

matter to those of us for whom the quest for community is inextricably linked to questions of human communicative purpose.

IMAGINATION

The presence of Spirit reminds us of questions of purpose. Human *communicative* purpose. *Communal* purpose. Writ large, "purpose" conjures up the singular vision capable of inspiring a shared social drawing of a communal map in ways that all map readers can recognize, differ about, and still use. As students of words or maps know, however, the vision for a communal map—however much its organization or sense of Order is shared—is never quite equivalent to the communal territories it purports to represent. Maps and words serve more as inducements to knowing, abstract guides to Being, suggestions for doing.

Getting from place to place in any community requires more than simply reading a map; it requires *imagination*. The act of imagining is spiritually significant because it connects what is given locally with what is represented ambiguously, universally. To imagine is to invite Spirit, to open one's self or one's community to broader possibilities for purposeful meaning and interpretation. This is true, I think, for all imaginative forms of reading or speaking purpose or motives into situations. Considered this way, Spirit is an invitation to intersections of meaning that connect us to purposes and motives larger, deeper, more subtle, more confounding than maps can contain. Perhaps the necessary ambiguity in map reading is a sign in itself, a sign of pathways into imagined worlds that acknowledge or maybe induce meaningful gaps between what we can do with words about territories and what words about territories do to or for us.

Imagination locates the *nexus* where meaningful communities begin.

SIGNS

One problem of studying the connection of Spirit to the work of community is how to make the mysterious and ineffable palatable and real. By nature, what we call "the spiritual" or "the communal" is *experiential*. Something extraordinary happens to us or to someone we know, and we explain or account for it with words and actions that are drawn from mystical or religious texts or contexts. We feel connected to something beyond ourselves; we feel connected to a sense of community. The narrative frame for the connective account relies on our ability to link local knowledge with mythic or ancient parables, allegories, metaphors, or stories. In this way, the local experience is read or interpreted as a *sign* of the universal, thus linking an extraordinary human experience with the timeless experience of being human.

But what if manifestations of Spirit—usually considered an *extraordinary* experience—were, in fact, *ordinary*, but were narratively or mythically *obscured*? What if part of the problem with communities falling apart was that our framing for those experiences was falling apart? What if the violent struggle between modern narratives of Power and postmodern fragments of Other had so confounded our ability to make coherent explanations for everyday occurrences that we were in danger of losing the vital narrative links between and among ourselves, each other, and our communities?

Communities are composed of linkages of persons and things. They are communicatively composed of our responses to signs and symbols, and to each other's uses of signs and symbols. Walk down any street in any town and your sense of "where you are" is largely informed by what you see and hear, and by the meanings you have for this semiotic surround. Familiar icons mingle with the unique; colors define and then mix with other colors, other icons, other surfaces. People speak to one another or perhaps shout across a roadway; there are mechanical noises, electrical hums, a presence or absence of animals and vegetation. Music plays softly or intrudes rudely. In the distance a basketball is being dribbled.

There is a unique sense of place that is formed not by where we are, nor by ourselves, but by the symbolic linkages of ourselves to where we are. These connections are mediated by signs, which in turn are mediated by our imaginative interpretations of their meanings—of their relevance. By what they suggest we need to do, or ought to be doing. Whether their purpose is to inspire commerce or reverence or laughter, our ability to interpret them as personally meaningful helps us to locate meaning in and for our communities.

Read this way, signs inspire a different take on these local maps. Perhaps our ability to make and interpret signs has to do with our need for direction, for purpose, for possibilities. As such, signs—just as any other form of human communication—can convey both empirical and analogic information. They can instruct us about where to turn or what

PREFACE

to buy, or they may be misspelled in ways that make us consider that which we may have previously ignored. In these cases, our ability to make and use signs as part of the human communicative apparatus only tells part of the story, the empirical story; what gets left out is the analogic, which is to say the relational, the connective, the mystical, or, simply, the *spiritual*. All that exists in between and around the edges of what we know and assume to be so, too, has a purpose.

Let me approach this *nexus* from another avenue, following the leads of other signs. Systems and cultural theorists in every field take for granted the inherent *interconnectedness* of life. The meanings of persons and things, we have learned, must be read together. So, too, our place in the galaxy is best understood as part of the whole, not a separate part but an integration. Atoms and stars, leptons and wild grasses, expressions of love and the flowspin of the Milky Way toward Virgo—all of these otherwise disparate elements and components and particles and waves move in some kind of sync that we do not always understand but are learning to accept. That we do accept it may well determine not only our survival but the overall outcome.

Humans are, as Kenneth Burke expressed it, "bodies that learn language" (1989, 8). We are the storytellers, *homo narrans* (Fisher 1988). Yet language and storytelling has too long been dissociated from its rightful place within the physical world, appreciated mostly for a very limited part of its instrumental capacities to point to, count, or categorize and define. That our capacity for language and our need to tell stories is taken for granted seems related to our belief that language stands outside of the world in which we dwell, outside of the communities where we are induced to know who and where we are, and what our daily speaking and reading are *for*. We seem programmed to acquire languaging and to use that capacity to link ourselves to each other and to our communities through stories, in much the same way as stars and planets are born to travel in a particular direction at a given speed.

But perhaps this narrow view of human communicative purpose, in light of human communicative and communal abilities, ought to be reexamined. Perhaps we are evolved sufficiently to perform that task now. That we are asking these questions may be a sign that we are ready, that maybe we *should*.

What I want to do is suggest a series of communal tensions that emerge from taking signs seriously, of reading signs as clues to a larger communicative mystery of which we are all naturally a part. Put differently, I want to enlarge considerably our appreciation for what "communication" and "community" can refer to and in so doing redefine how that connection works—or fails to work—within that framework. To accomplish this project requires challenging a wide variety of presuppositions about boundaries and representations on the maps most of us carry into the world, as well as to reframe many tenets of contemporary communication theories.

Reading this book on its own terms requires both an active imagination and the willingness to suspend disbelief, at least until the last chapter. In this way, reading this book is very much like hearing someone else describe their meanings for your neighborhood. You will undoubtedly disagree with some of it, raise objections, be entertained, be challenged, and, I hope, by the end or somewhere along the way, be persuaded that this neighborhood is large and complex enough for both of us. And that maybe, just maybe, we both *belong* here.

A note on writing and my use of actual footnotes. Textual construction these days is a complex matter. Writing the ineffable, or at least what resists empirical representation is hard; I have chosen to induce, to suggest, to puzzle, and to poeticize that which I otherwise have no writing strategy to deal with. To complicate matters even more, I make use of footnotes, the kind that really must be read as co-contributors to the meanings and inducements in the text. Some of my reviewers found the use of footnotes an annoyance, while others pointed out that my use of them here is more akin to hypertext in a computer program in that they offer a way for persons seeking further interpretation or definitional references to satisfy themselves. I might add that in some cases the footnotes also serve a *political* purpose, as sources of resistance narratives to read against the argument in the "dominant" text.

One additional caveat. This study is more of an *auto*ethnography than an ethnography, in that it relies far more on the world of my experiencing than it does on my experiencing Other's views of this world. For some of my colleagues and reviewers, this is a limitation. But I believe you will see how, when considering matters of this kind, the line between auto/ethnography is too easily privileged as a meaningful sign when the territory it purports to divide ceases to be.

Acknowledgments

This project came into being primarily because of the various influences of others, most notably Sandra and Nicolas Goodall. Sandra's serious study of alternative religions and New Age practices brought me into a world that most academics shun, and in many cases rightfully so. But within that diverse community there are, I believe, some truly gifted souls, a few rare individuals whose talents for reading signs and making meanings *are* deeply spiritual if not divine. I have come to believe that trained observers of the human condition—particularly of the human communicative condition—would do well to study their methods and learn from their insights. Nicolas's contributions to this book everywhere grace its pages in ways that are deeply mysterious and that perhaps only a father could understand.

I have also been assisted on many levels by a diverse group of friends and scholars who, although mostly skeptical throughout, nevertheless sent me materials, shared experiences, read drafts of chapters, told me straight out when they thought I was going too far or not far enough, and occasionally reminded me of how important, how close to heart and soul, this whole set of questions and meditations can be. In the spirit of collaboration (for which I alone own any faults or errors), then, I am deeply grateful to Eric Eisenberg, Lori Rosco, David Payne, Elizabeth Bell, and Mark Neumann of the University of South Florida; Patricia Geist and many of her graduate students at San Diego State University; Nick Trujillo of California State University at Sacramento; Janice Hocker Rushing and Thomas Frentz of the University of Arkansas; Steve and Lindsley Smith, also of the University of Arkansas and elsewhere; Stewart Auyash of Ithaca College; Mary Strine, Connie Bullis, and Jim Anderson of the University of Utah; Phil Glenn of Southern Illinois Uni-

ACKNOWLEDGMENTS

versity; Linda Welker of Xavier University; Lyall Crawford of Weber State University; singers and guitar players of the 1991 Alta Conference (particularly Larry Browning and Len Hawes); Peter Kellett of the University of North Carolina at Greensboro; Rita and David Whillock of Southern Methodist and Texas Christian Universities, respectively; Carl Lovitt, Claire Bateman, Chris Benson, and Art Young of the Department of English at Clemson University; the faculty and students in Speech and Communication Studies at Clemson University; Ron Moran, associate dean of the College of Liberal Arts at Clemson University; my graduate students in Advanced Organizational Communication; the anonymous church-sign makers in Pickens and Oconee Counties, South Carolina; my neighbors Mike, Martha, and Christopher Biggs; and the anonymous reviewers who encouraged the publication of this otherwise outlaw volume.

I also want to thank Southern Illinois University Press for its continued support of my work and experimental writing. Curtis Clark and Jim Simmons believed in this project as the culmination of my ethnographic "trilogy"; my production editors Teresa White and Carol Besler oversaw the general cleaning up and straightening out of the manuscript; and the whole staff at SIU Press offered me, at various times, encouragement, humor, insight, and support. For all of their efforts, this book is much better off, and I greatly appreciate it.

DIVINE SIGNS

Introduction: Context, Imagination, and Interpretation

> It is never possible to introduce only observable quantities in a theory. It is the theory that decides what can be observed.
>
> —Albert Einstein to Werner Heisenberg

Contexts and Change

Why do we need a book that connects Spirit to community? For that matter, why do we need a spirituality of communication?

Our time is unprecedented in human history because of the total collapse of all paradigms worldwide: social, environmental, educational, and spiritual. Poised, as we are, between ways of explaining ourselves to ourselves that have been largely discredited, and celebrating—however nihilistically—the critical and practical impossibility of constructing a Grand or Final Theory, we face the end of the twentieth century as two ends symbolically converging: the end of our Second Millennium and—all too often—the end of any hope for collective, democratic understanding.

Despite the predictable trajectories suggested by that possible symbolic convergence, this historical moment is also one in which authorities from all walks of life agree that "communication" is especially crucial. Professionals and academics are being called upon to articulate some new revolutionary "communication" breakthrough capable of teaching us how diverse peoples can learn to live together meaningfully without destroying each other and—in the process—the planet itself. The Enlightenment project for valuing the rational individual as the likely sponsor and eventual leader of organized democratic communities provided us with outlines for the outward behaviors necessary for making and maintaining Western, middle-class, (mostly) male-dominated, bureaucratic communities, but these behaviors and understandings do not necessarily translate into diverse global or even locally sanctioned virtues. This Enlightenment project also largely erased Spirit from any dialogue between Self and Other, and in so doing obscured the mythic and ritualistic foundations of sustainable communities.

INTRODUCTION

In popular as well as academic debate, the Enlightenment project continues to be challenged. New generations of theorists and researchers; artists and poets; social, organizational, and racial reformers; gender politicians and lifestyle advocates; environmental scientists, physicists, and literary critics have posited alternative ways of constructing realities capable of sustaining what we newly claim to "know" about the world and our place in it. These versions of the story seem to be pieces of a larger reality, but it is increasingly a reality that these honest, well-intentioned, and smart narratives themselves render even more disparate and disconnected because they remain accessible only to members of elite (and often warring members) of specific discourse communities.

Other possibilities for organizing and interpreting realities emerge from the teeming chaos of street level experiences, where the often contradictory and "senseless" events of everyday life do not accord with rational or scientific explanations of human behavior, and more often than not render the "authoritative evidence" irrelevant. One consistent and persistent source of critique for why this is the case concerns the absence of the "marginalized" Other—and Other cultures' dominant practices—from the world constructed by latter-day Enlightenment modernists for modernity,[1] an absence that robs our Western explanatory systems of any legitimate place—much less real importance—for alternative cultural practices, or for "inner," spiritual, religious, or even mystical experiences. We are, as a result, left adrift at an impasse between oppositional explanatory systems and cultures of explanation, themselves trapped in an urgent state of undifferentiated, frenzied transition. Too often within the academy, we cannot use our own theories or research findings to explain what is happening to us, within us, or just outside our doors.[2]

---

[1] For an extended discussion of this development, see Eric M. Eisenberg and H. L. Goodall, Jr. (1993); see also the excellent discussion of "modernism" and "modernity" in Harvey (1990) and Connor (1989). For a comprehensive account of the theoretical complications and implications of the postmodern challenge, see Best and Kellner (1992); for a more accessible account rooted in a dialogue about everyday ordinary—and extraordinary—experiences, see Ventura and Hillman (1992).

[2] An excellent account of "outward" public versus "inward" spiritual dialogics is found in Thomas Frentz (1993). In this provocative and inspirational essay, he recovers for rhetorical theories the thread of truth-seeking conversational activities derived from myth (imagination) and reason as an "interior" dialogue capable of creating heightened self-awareness. From Plato, through Kenneth Burke and finally to Julia Kristeva and C. G. Jung, this thread weaves itself into a consistent pattern: the out-

Introduction

In times past, academics could well afford to pass on the chance to build a brave, new, sustainable world. We have long been assigned a separate, protected cultural space—the metaphorical "ivory tower"—a necessary institution for collectivities of the overbrained and overemotioned, an overpass for eggheads under which run the truer highways and more important interstate commerce of "real world" traffics. This demonstrates, I think, how a cultural metaphor—in this case, a dumb cliche—not only can dominate, but exchange places with, the reality it (mis)describes. Regardless of the metaphor and the separation of academic and "real world" cultures it implies, we all live ecologically and materially intertwined on the same planet and within the same cosmos, and therefore it no longer appears that our *not* acting is a viable—much less ethical—option. After all, *not* acting is itself an action, and one that—following the second law of thermodynamics—only accelerates the rate of decay.

To meet the needs of the revolutionary change requires an edifying and democratic corrective. Our activities, both theoretical and practical, must be *edifying* in that we can little afford further criticism about our irrelevance to the present, however trenchant, politically (in)correct, or even funny it may be; the time to build a new world is *now*. Relatedly, to be effective, our collective road map must be *democratic*; it must capture the imaginations of large groups of people and must be anti-elitist in spirit, which, unfortunately, academic theory has *not* been in most of its scientific and critical incarnations. All this talk about cultural diversity over the past decade has been—just to cite one example—but a prelude to necessary democratic vistas of our collective futures, against which

---

ward world of appearances sponsored by Aristotle and dominant in Western intellectual thought for 2,500 years—a world in which "[masculine] truth [is] revealed through sensory and rational entailments of what credible [mostly masculine] people already do, know, or say"—is contrasted with an interior world dominated by a "chora" (Kristeva) a "pre-symbolic condition of language in the unconscious ... which is engendered feminine," and which is largely responsible for forms of resistance to domination through sexuality, escape, and madness. For Frentz, the "chora" is roughly akin to Jung's concept of the collective unconscious, in that the "collective unconscious is to the psyche what the DNA molecule is to the body—a genetic blueprint for development." And the journey to and into the collective unconscious—whether enabled by Platonic dialogue or analytical conversation that relying on the active engagement of imagination—what Jung called "transrationalism," is closely akin to the divine madness Plato associated with the search for, and speaking of, the Truth.

INTRODUCTION

we will—one way or the other—discover the degree to which we are in fact able *to organize* together.

A related distinction I bring to this book—and indeed many of my colleagues and friends bring to this project—is an emotional commitment to change. I remain hopeful, at times even idealistic, about the future. I have learned that the great enemy of change is cynicism—which we encounter everywhere among great thinkers—and which supplies the fundamental first obstacle to envisioning a more fully realized democracy and the enhanced role that a more complete understanding of communication might play within it.

Our time is right for a spirituality of communication because the narratives we have thus far used to organize and explain who and what we are about will no longer sustain us. Similarly, the "rational" communication practices we have employed to constitute our communities and build our world no longer seem adequate to deal with our problems. Something is wrong, and it seems to be inherently linked to what is missing from our lives, from our communities. We dwell in a *nexus* of everyday organizing limited not by human nature, but by a dominant narrative about the rational nature of human Being that does not fully account for our unique communicative abilities nor the role of Spirit in our lives. Historically, we have used communication to liberate ourselves from oppressive political forms of organizing while evolving toward a more democratic consciousness, so too must we now find meaningful practices capable of enabling our next step: using a democratic consciousness to enable an evolution toward an understanding of the purpose and role of communication in our evolving.

Communication as Practical Consciousness

What is the relationship between communication and consciousness?

It begins with the questions we ask. The British social theorist Anthony Giddens teaches us that one question should be at the center of any preoccupation with the relationship among institutions, communication, and social change: "How do we *go on?*" (1979, 56–57).

This disarmingly simple question captures the practical depths and theoretical surfaces of ongoing social and structural changes that communication must embrace as well as address: the effects of a global economy on downsizing, restructuring, and flattening hierarchies at work and in the family; the demands for cross-functional training in organizations and requirements for cross-cultural communication in global, mediated information societies competing in consistently shifting and heavily politicized world economic markets; the desire to reinvent governments within which must reside a new partnership between governments, corporations, and individuals for the long-term sustainability of our planet; the ability to refigure not just the role of information in the building of society, but the concurrent refiguring of our images of self and Others (as well as contexts) through mediated interplays of "real and "virtual" realities; and the hope—if hope can indeed prevail against the onslaught of the everyday—for dealing humanely with disparate political, racial, gender, and economic diversities on an earth dominated by weapons of destruction, images of everyday violence, and a penchant for spending more money each year on cosmetics than on education.

If there has ever been a relative time, or a cultural space, for the study and practice of communication to "make a difference" by turning "discursive consciousness" (e.g., the achievement of day-to-day routines) into resources for "practical consciousness" (actions that are accountable to the world that organizes and pays for them) (Banks and Riley 1993, 171–72), *now* is that time and space.

But how can we get there? Articulating questions is one thing, turning them into actions is something else again. Actions, after all, are not isolated responses we give to isolated questions but furtherances of or challenges to existing narrative frameworks that shaped the questions in the first place. For too long now we have been framing our central problems in global economic terms, viewing crises within communities principally through tales of economic woe, with our democratic salvation—if at all possible—only likely through the divine intervention of some golden capitalist god. In so doing, we have diminished the power of human communication to socially construct consciousness by according it merely clerical or technical status; we have forgotten that people must be capable of imagining a better world before they will act to build it. The call to human action is always contained in the *story* line, not the bottom line.

Communication, viewed this way, is the practical manifestation of consciousness. It is a consciousness that holds both the questions and the

INTRODUCTION

narrative frameworks that lead to answers and actions. To change that consciousness requires altering that which brings it into existence.

PRACTICAL CONSCIOUSNESS, IMPRACTICAL REALITY

I believe the stories we are telling ourselves about ourselves—our explanatory tales—and the ways we are encouraged to interpret our experiences through their meanings are seriously flawed and largely responsible for the current crises elaborated thus far. We have privileged a very limited view of what constitutes "communication" as well as what constitutes "reality," and at their intersection it appears that neither view is tenable or practical. *Put simply, the questions we are asking don't have answers within the contexts of the stories we have been telling.*

But there are alternative story lines available in the world. Lyall Watson, a biologist, offered many insightful lessons about the connections between communication and reality in his masterful book, *Supernature* (1973). One lesson involves the fact that in societies that do not draw distinctions between the natural (or "seen") world and "supernatural" (or "unseen") one, supernatural occurrences are not only reported more frequently but are also widely accepted as part of the everyday explanatory system. This observation is given additional support by the PBS special (and book) by Bill Moyers on "Healing and the Mind" (1992) in which detailed interviews with American medical scientists demonstrate the futility of maintaining Descartian distinctions about mind/body or body/nature separations, or of maintaining status distinctions that posit the "superiority" of Western versus Eastern treatments for disease. For example, within the Chinese culture, the map of the body is not drawn from a view of life privileged solely by the optical lens—muscles, organs, and blood vessels—but instead is understood and treated as a geography of energies and information that constantly communicate with each other and their environments, an ancient view of the nature of our natures that accords with contemporary physics. Citizens can select from Eastern or Western approaches to medicine and health, and many opt for a little of each because they learn that every explanatory system holds a piece of the larger puzzle. Moreover, the stories they tell themselves about themselves become part and parcel of their cures.

The central role of communication in our biological makeup cannot be ignored. The role of communication in our bodies as well as in all

Introduction

cultures is, as the philosopher Richard McKeon (1970) observed, "architectonic." It is the reality foundation of all explanatory systems, which is to say it is the "how" as well as the "what" of who we make—and believe—ourselves to be. Put differently, communication does not simply *structure* our perceptions of cultural realities "out there"; it *is* the summary "what" and cumulative "how" through which we bring those realities *into* existence *with* existence.

A second observation offered by Watson deserves to be quoted at length:

> There is life on earth—one life, which embraces every animal and plant on the planet. Time has divided it up into several million parts, but each is an integral part of the whole. A rose is a rose, but it is also a robin and a rabbit. We are all of one flesh, drawn from the same crucible.... [B]iochemical systems exchange matter with their surroundings all the time, they are open, thermodynamic processes, as opposed to the closed, thermostatic structure of ordinary chemical reactions. *This is the secret of life. It means that there is a continuous communication not only between living things and their environment, but among all things living in that environment.* An intricate web of interaction connects all life into one vast, self-maintaining system. Each part is related to every other part and we are all part of the whole, part of Supernature. (1973, 3–4; emphasis mine)

Taken together, Watson's observations define the need—at biochemical and poetic levels—to expand what we conceive of as "communication" to include the "all" of human (super)natures, those unseen and unobserved—but culturally significant—experiences we engage as part of the larger mystery of life. Again, there is a sense that something else is missing, something to do with how and why we communicate, something central to our communities that is at once central to our common quest. Although women and men of good will who have worked diligently within the methodological rigors of rhetorical and scientific approaches to communication to liberate it from cultural handbooks about social superstition, and given that the world they have inscribed is in fact already well inscribed and useful, the current problem is *not* with what we have "written into" our collective understanding, but instead what we have written out, ignored, marginalized, or left unsaid.

This book begins to articulate what has been so difficult to say for so long. Viewed within current debates in academic circles, it attempts to

INTRODUCTION

reestablish a place for the explanatory recovery of Spirit—for experiential and communal senses of spirituality—in our understanding of humans, humanity, and the role human communication plays in the cosmos. This debate has raged for a long time in allied disciplines such as anthropology, sociology, and the philosophy of religion, but as yet has made no serious inroads to the study of communication.[3] It advocates what I consider to be a "natural" connection between ethnographic imagination and access to previously marginalized or ignored spheres of communication and community.[4] And finally, it attempts to outline a way of experiencing and thinking about the new complexities of communication in our cosmos, an outline that has far more in common with the poetry of new physics and some of the beliefs and practices of New Age than it does with modernist but *un*enlightened if nevertheless "rational" world views.

Ethnographic Method as Experience, Imagination, and Communication

What does ethnography have to do with spirituality?

A book purporting to be an ethnographic study is a written form of cultural communication. It uses writing to evoke and to make sense out of a culture, where what is written is intended to be read as clues to a larger explanatory tale. Unless authored by an all-seeing, all-knowing God and rendered in the pure language of revealed Truth, the tale that is told by lesser humans is necessarily partial, sometimes partisan, always problematic. Like a map, even a very good one doesn't account for all of the territory.

Ethnography is always dedicated, therefore, to "knowing where *you*

---

[3] Some important exceptions should be noted. Gregory Bateson's *Steps Toward a Further Ecology of Mind* (1972) and posthumous *A Sacred Unity* (1991), Robert J. Branham and W. Barnett Pierce's (1980) account of "the ineffable," Connie Bullis and Hollis Glaser's (1992) recovery of the goddess myth for organizing, and Robert L. Scott's (1993) conception of the dialectic of communication and silence all provide insightful ways to expand the world of communication and theoretical explanations that inform this study.

[4] Paul Atkinson (1990) has authored a thorough account of textual construction in sociology that delineates the special role "imagination" plays in the writing and reading of all texts. For a parallel account that focuses on the texts of modernist anthropologists and the world views that inspired them, see Michael Manganaro (1991) and John Van Maanen (1988). For an earlier account of "imagination" in social texts, see C. Wright Mills (1959).

Introduction

are." It represents an attempt to account for the symbolic organization and meanings of cultural life surrounding lived experiences of a particular time spent in a particular place, where local knowledge inscribes localized space. It is the academic practice of professional poachers, persons who appropriate space for themselves and their words out of the raw materials of everyday life.

This is a bit ironic because an ethnographic study is generally designed not to be about "knowing where *you* are," but instead about how Others know where *they* are—in other words, how *they* live, work, worship, make love, make war, and innumerable etceteras up to and including how these particular Others understand their unique place in the cosmos.[5] Yet, to be able to enter into and move through the everyday traffic of "their" ordinary discourse entails a kind of closeness and intimacy that blurs every known border, and, in the blurring, eventually erases those borders almost entirely. It also calls into question the bifurcation of knowledge into "self" and "Other" categories, a distinction that denies a central role to the intervening Spirit that every ethnographer worthy of this intimacy well knows as the necessary guide to *any* knowledge of *any* culture.

ETHNOGRAPHIC INTIMACY AND EXPERIENTIAL OPENINGS FOR SPIRIT

I think this form of ethnographic "intimacy" and resultant "knowing" is commonly misunderstood. In the West—particularly in North America—no doubt because of the psychoanalytically and politically dominated discourses that shape and inform common interpretations of everyday meanings, the use of the term *intimacy* implies an immediate sexual context, at once and perhaps always charged with issues of power.[6] Although I am fully aware of the necessity and insight afforded

---

[5] A recent exception is the practice of "autoethnography," of the study of the self as the Other. For examples, see John Fiske (1990). Another way to examine the relationship of ethnography and the self is through the shaping influences autobiography has on what is observed, felt, or otherwise sensed in the field, and that gets embedded within ethnographic texts. See Judith Okely and Helen Callaway (1992) and chapters 5 and 6 of Goodall (1991).

[6] This is *not* to denigrate the relationship of sexual desire to intimate knowledge (see Nelson 1994), or what Plato envisioned as the "divine madness" that emerges from lust between two people that produces a dialogue aimed at Truth. Frentz (1993) argues that from a Jungian perspective, we often feel sexually aroused by someone destined to become a "soul-mate," thereby using the initial sexual intimacy to reach

INTRODUCTION

by these discourses, their meanings are *not* all of what I mean to evoke by my use of the term *intimacy*.

For me and for this study, *intimacy* is about *the location of deeply meaningful connections that are communicated (however ordinarily or extraordinarily) between and among persons, nature, and things*. I want to consider these connections *as* contexts for Spirit—as cultural and experiential frameworks that mysteriously enable individual, relational, and communal interpretations—and that serve as the intricate, and often overlooked, communicative handiwork for what most of us consider "meaningful" about a shared sense of a place, shared experiences, and the necessary intimacy with its peoples.

I believe that whatever we mean by "a context" is the intimate work of a historically informed, experientially based, culturally shaped, and dialogically argued-and-altered *mythos*, or *imagination*. Communication functions to connect what we imagine to how we live by joining awareness, intentions, interpretations, and actions in meaningful ways. Put simply, we imagine a world—or worlds—that we daily enter into as the taken-for-granted *contexts* for communicative action.

ETHNOGRAPHIC IMAGINATION AND QUANTUM REALITY

I suspect that some—if not many—of my socially scientific and rhetorical colleagues will consider the "imagined world or worlds" I speak of as "not real" or as "made up," in either case reducing the context for my argument to one roughly akin to advocating fiction as the true measure of fact. However, this is *not at all what I mean*. What too often passes for "fact" is, I fear, largely an nonrepresentational rhetorical invention of what is at best a partial, and highly partisan version, of "reality," one that is narrow and limited because of its inability to account for human action as an aspect of the *quantum* world that scientists since Einstein (as well as mystics before and since then) demonstrate to be our "true" reality at every conceivable level.

Deepak Chopra (among many others) calls the stubborn adherence to this "outworn reality" a "hypnosis of social conditioning . . . [to] a collective fiction we have collectively agreed to participate in" (1993). He

or enable intellectual intimacy, but also—at least as often, I suspect—confusing the two.

Introduction

maintains that there are inherited assumptions that limit our ability to fully comprehend reality (he states ten; for my purposes I will only use seven), assumptions that I find perfectly in sync with those I was asked to "inherit" by considering as "truths" in graduate school, and that still largely shape research and theory:

1. There is an objective world independent of the observer, and our bodies are an aspect of this objective world.
2. The body is composed of clumps of matter separated from each other in time and space.
3. Mind and body are separate, independent of each other.
4. Materialism is primary, consciousness is secondary.... We are physical machines that have learned to think.
5. Human awareness can be completely explained as the product of biochemistry.
6. As individuals we are all disconnected, self-contained entities.
7. Our perception of the world is automatic and gives us an accurate picture of how things are.

My aim is to challenge the "reality" of these taken-for-granted, "outworn" assumptions as they (dis)inform and undermine our experience and understanding of communication in contemplation, relationships, and communities. Following Chopra, a quantum approach to "reality" posits that:[7]

1. The physical world including our bodies is a response of the observer; we create our bodies as we create our world.
2. In their essential state, our bodies are composed of energy and information, not solid matter; this energy and information is an outcropping of infinite fields of energy and information spanning the universe.
3. The mind and the body are inseparably one, the unity that is me separates into two streams of experience, thoughts and desires and the experience of the body; it is in the union of the two that we are all meant to live.

[7] These assumptions are widely shared among theoretical physicists. For a popular elaboration in management science, see Margaret Wheatley (1992), and in physics see Fritjof Capra (1975).

INTRODUCTION

4. The biochemistry of the body is a product of awareness, beliefs, thoughts, and emotions that create the chemical reactions upholding life in every cell.
5. Perception appears to be automatic but in fact it is a learned phenomenon; if you change your perception you change the experience of your body and of your world.
6. Impulses of intelligence constantly create your body in new forms every second; what you are is the sum total of these impulses and by changing their patterns, you will change.
7. Although each person seems separate and independent, all of us are connected with patterns of intelligence that govern the whole cosmos; our bodies are part of a universal body, our minds an aspect of a universal mind.
8. Being is our essential state . . . and spirit is the expression of eternal Being.

What communication researchers and social scientists in general typically call "reality" is derived from mechanical—not quantum—assumptions. "Reality," the "facts of our empirical world," is limited to empirical and material manifestations in a world defined, informed, and unnaturally bounded by its observable features, rendered sensible and intelligible by the mediating language and logic influences informed by Western rationality (for an earlier critique, see Smith 1972). My aim is to investigate an alternative formation of what counts as "reality" by expanding our awareness of possibilities for interpreting the meanings of everyday "ordinary" and "extraordinary" experiences. Throughout most of this book I will refer to that alternative construction of "reality" as *another* "world" or as "parallel worlds" that must be imagined in order to be perceived and experienced; in truth *it is the same world* throughout, and all of us—even my empirical colleagues—participate in imagining it.

While I am challenging narrative authority, I might as well say that *all critical activity is the work of imagination*. Criticism is an intentional construction of an "Other" world in which what is critically analyzed expands previous borders of what is "known" by positing alternative realities formed by and through the critical activity or method. In this way, to entertain seriously the notion of a "postmodern" world is not very much different—except in the language details of *mythos*, of

Introduction

course—from entertaining seriously the idea that we communicate telepathically or with the dead, or that prayer reaches God, or that meditation or massage can alter our states of consciousness. Science, as critical activities rendered through explanatory narratives, should embrace not only what Gregory Bateson (1972, 1991) calls "the further reaches of human nature" but also the further nature of human reaching.[8]

COMMUNICATION AS DIALOGIC PATHWAY

To explore these contexts requires envisioning communication activities as *connective pathways* through which imagined worlds are symbolically and semiotically brought—urged—into *dialogic* personal, social, and communal existence. By "dialogic . . . existence," I mean two things.[9]

First, everyday communicative practices involve both real and imagined exchanges within one's self, with Others, with mediated Others, and with the many voices that make up our mediated realities in this increasingly virtual world. What we communicate—regardless of inspiration or ambition, regardless of media or medium—is *given* to—or given as a *response* to—someone, some imagined situation, or something else; hence, we are always "in dialogue" with our world or worlds.

Second, what we imagine is not fixed or static, but dynamic, interdependent, and evolving; it changes with new information and is altered by lived experiences that reveal, conceal, and comment upon the partial, partisan, and always problematic nature of the world we speak into and about. Without dialogue, the ability to know who we are and are becoming, much less where we are and where we are going, would be severely impaired.

This dual sense of the dialogic nature of human communication complements the intimate, connective function of communication. It enables us to move into and inhabit the imagined worlds we contextually engage. The complement is fully realized when our attention is drawn to questions of purpose and meaning both *in* those contexts as well as *because of* them. This is to say, at least initially, that perhaps our scholarly

---

[8] As "Seeker 1" on the information superhighway (another example of metaphor opening up imaginative possibilities for alternative worlds and communication constituting it) of Internet put it: "Tis an ill wind that blows no minds."

[9] The term dialogic is derived from a confluence of literary and rhetorical histories. See Bakhtin (1981), Holquist (1991), Goodall (1991), and Shotter (1993).

INTRODUCTION

appreciation for "context," "meaning," and "purpose" for communication action has prematurely been misunderstood as factual boundaries and therefore has not yet been read or interpreted instead as merely as *clues*. Clues, I maintain, to destinations and arrivals within a deeper interconnected quantum and spiritual mystery.

COMMUNICATION AND SPIRITUALITY

For some time now I have been interested in what a theory of communication would consist of—and say to us about us—if we began with the premise that humans are, first and foremost, *spiritual* beings, as something more than "a soulless jellital sack of behaviors suspended by a calcium skeleton and driven by something called cognitions" (Goodall 1993). Rather than examining communication as *merely* behavior exhibited by said sack, I have been trying to see communication in relation to *ultimate* purposes while learning to appreciate the spiritual human as a questing soul interested in experiencing and answering some fundamental, recurring questions: Who am I? Why am I (we) here? What am I (we) supposed to do while I (we) am here? What is this life all about? And so forth. Viewed this way, "intimacy" may indeed have common sexual and power articulations but seems more directly about establishing and nurturing close, working, imaginative dialogic relations that further our uncommonly spiritual natures and that build better understandings, higher consciousness, and better communities by aligning or at least loosely coordinating our communicative actions with purposes meant for Beings who communicate.

One definitional caveat. An admittedly irksome but necessary one. When I use the terms *spirituality* or *Spirit*, I am not using these synonymously with *religion*, nor am I negating the possibility of a linkage between these terms. While it would seem ridiculous to ignore the world's multiple religions and their deeply articulated histories in any serious study of Spirit or the spiritual, it seems equally obvious that to equate the two terms is both misleading and potentially dangerous. We are not, after all, latter-day Pharisees content to define legalistic rescriptions as the sum total of religious experience. Nor are we, at this end of the twentieth century, without local latter-day Pharisaic cultures.

My interest, therefore, is *not* primarily with the everyday psalms of evangelical performance or routinized church behavior, but is concerned with the everyday semiotic performances and communal behavior of churches as signs of evangelical psalms connected to a representational field of intertwined contexts for interpretation. It is also concerned with beauty shops as spiritual centers, gas stations, convenience stores, and Wal-Marts as resources for insightful transformation and change, as well as highways, parking lots, and environmental surrounds as material manifestations of a politics of spiritual—and Spirit—consciousness. Ultimately, I see all these experiences and meanings as the *intimate* nature of communicative connections, as existing imaginative dialogues between and among questing beings thrown into a *nexus* of parallel, and often conflicting, worlds.

Lived Experience and Experiential Living

How can that *nexus* be experienced, or written?

Most ethnographic studies record the lived experiences of the field researcher while he or she observes and participates in the daily activities of the local culture. This study is no exception, although a major part of the "lived experiences" encountered in this study exist in the *nexus* of self, Spirit, and Others. Similarly, most ethnographic studies are derived from transcribed field notes and/or journals kept by the field researcher during the period of study. Again, this study is no exception, although the inscriptions that formed the field notes were—and are—but partial accounts, because what is sensed cannot always be verbalized; the spirit of place is always revealed to its citizens in ways that conceal its ability to be shared in ordinary forms of speech or writing. Perhaps for this reason, imagined worlds are both ambiguous and empowering, they evoke the unspoken and invisible as if they aren't, and treat what can't be said as if it were perfectly obvious.

LIVED EXPERIENCE AS ETHNOGRAPHIC METHOD

All theoretical work, because it is inherently critical, evokes the work of the imagination on the lived experiences of everyday life. But what actually "counts" as lived experiences? The term *"lived experience"* (Jackson 1989) sums up a philosophical stance that values placing oneself in culture's way. The point of the fieldwork is not simply to live *with*, but to

INTRODUCTION

live *as*, the natives do. The idea is not to become a native (although that sometimes happens), but to learn *how one is one* so well that one can fit right into the mainstreams (and/or the margins) of cultural activity, performing what needs to be performed, taking for granted what should be taken for granted, and understanding what must be understood well enough to attain distinct personhood within a culture that is not specifically one's own.

To do this requires different skills in different places but seems to be governed primarily by an *attitude* more so than by a method (Anderson and Goodall 1994). It is an attitude born of diverse curiosities about, and recognition of, varieties of human Being, nurtured by a seeming natural desire and ability to take risks with one's identities, fueled by a philosophical appreciation for explanation combined with an existential desire to live in the domain of one's explanations, marked by a playful reverence for everyday communication as the localized site of constructions of realities, and sustained by membership in one or more discourse communities that sponsor this sort of life and work.

"Lived experience" is not, therefore, a method that derives its pleasures from summing up a precise set of procedures in a particular order. It is about *being there* (Geertz 1988), where "being" is experienced through loosely assembled routine activities mixed with the happenstance of accidents and daily human dramas, and *writing here* (Geertz, 1988), where "writing" refers to rhetorically informed, narratively sensitive, always experimental forms of expression dedicated to striking a delicate balance between outright representational accuracy or "realism" and evocative (sometimes provocative) "confessional" or "surrealistic" tales (Van Maanen 1988).

Nor is "lived experience" a fixed method that derives its textual authority from strict adherence to methodological forms. I don't want to rehash here the interpretive turn away from grounding field research in the philosophy and methods of essentialism, objective social science. Those arguments have been made *ad nauseam* elsewhere and are no doubt familiar to any reader of this book. Nor do I want to rehash my own or others' cases for narratives of lived experience casting reasonable doubt about the plausibility of any objective account, of *anything*. Again, those arguments are already part of our scholarly history (see Clifford and Marcus 1986; Connor 1989; Lyotard 1979; Rabinow and Sullivan

1987). Even if the issues are still not resolved, it has been my experience that repeating them does little these days to alter the mindset of any reader and does a great deal of damage to the otherwise productive mood of pluralism that should characterize any dialogue.

LIVED EXPERIENCE AND NARRATIVE RATIONALITY

The authority of an ethnographic text is *not* in the details of revealing the method but instead in the method of revealing the details. In a minor editing of Walter Fisher's schema for "narrative rationality" (1987), this translates to narrative plausibility (do the *details* of the story hang together?) and narrative fidelity (do the *details* ring true to our experiences?).

Given this schema, the textual authority of an ethnographic tale relies on a steady accumulation of rich, localized details that enlarge and render more universal—by which I mean more "connected" and symbolically complex—the story being told by the narrator about "being there." Perhaps it is in this sense that there is some narrative fidelity between ethnographic authority for a localized story and ultimate authority for all stories; after all, it is in the ancient wisdom books of the Talmud that proof for the ultimate authority—God—is always found "in the details." Again, it is not in the details of revealing the method, but the method of revealing of the details, that authority resides.

LIVED EXPERIENCE, THE SENSES OF BEING, AND EXTRASENSORY KNOWING

The authority of "lived experience" is based on the method of revealing the details, but it is also true that the method of that revelation—as well as what details are included or discarded—is a complex issue. Paul Stoller (1989) reminds us that knowledge in the West has been largely a matter of *optical* sense-making. We *see*, we have *insight*, we are *enlightened*; therefore, we *know*. Yet life is experienced through at least five or six senses, and outside the West where the framing narratives allow for it, more. However, when we talk in a language of combined senses— "the taste of ethnographic things" being Stoller's tongue-in-cheek contribution—we are often thought to be breaking the rules of (optical) rationality; as a result, unless we claim some immediate poetic license—a

INTRODUCTION

desire, say, for metaphor—or admit to being under the influence of hallucinogenic drugs, our rule-breaking performance is connected to a judgment of our sanity: we are thought "mad or bad" (Shimanoff 1980). Either we are crazy or dangerous, or both.

Additionally, if we advocate ways of knowing—contexts of interpretation—that fall outside of the traditional categories of "legitimate" scholarly inquiry (or that call those categories themselves into serious question, or that blur them), we risk our work being at first marginalized, then inevitably trivialized and ultimately ignored. Consider the *three decades* of serious work done on human communication at Esalen Institute under the direction of Michael Murphy (1992), or the many workshops and seminars done annually at Omega Institute by New Age or spiritual leaders that connect everyday activities with more profound life purposes. In both cases, realms of what may be termed "unordinary experiences" or "extrasensory experiences" that blur distinctions between knowing and being and that are nowhere found in the communication literature are routinely explored and reported.

Because these institutes ask imaginative questions that challenge existing academic wisdom in ways that often threaten the authority of university-trained researchers and theorists, intriguing research findings and a symphony of useful voices and life experiences are summarily ignored. Ironically, academic ethnographers traditionally seek out "exotic" cultures where these sorts of experiences and understandings figure everywhere into the realities they study. Even more absurd is the idea that validates this ignorance: Perhaps only as long as the cultures that contain these knowledge resources are characterized as hierarchically "primitive" or "pre-scientific," what members and leaders of these cultures claim to have experienced and know can be treated seriously.

In either case, knowledge claimed from combining the senses or knowledge acquired from unordinary or extrasensory experiences, while quantumly correct, makes traditional academics terribly nervous, probably because we are guilty of violating one of the deepest beliefs of the Order. By arguing for a body of knowledge that relies on adding new or combining sensual data we are, in effect, turning a well-ordered perceptual bureaucratic world quite literally upside down, rendering our limited body of knowledge into an expanded knowledge of the body (and cosmos), and turning the enterprise of scholarly storytelling into a newly chaotic, carnivalesque mess.

Introduction

LANGUAGE, ORDER, AND CHAOS

Once again, the story we have been telling ourselves about ourselves is the problem. The complex relationships of language, cosmos, communication, and culture are at the very heart of this controversy. As Peter Stallybrass and Aron White (1986) explain it, the localized site of this sort of sensory blending and fooling around with Order is a cultural performance representing a public form of social transgression. By privileging previously unmentionable parts—and rhetorical appeals—of the "lower" body not only "over" but in a messy commingling with the more sanitized "higher" reaches of eyes and mind, we are questioning not only the hierarchical authority, we are also calling into question the well-schooled world made known and knowable through the dominant language of vision. Put simply, if we can't "see" it—or if it confuses us when we experience it—it either doesn't exist, or shouldn't. Furthermore, if what we can't see but do experience *does* exist, then whatever "it" is lies beyond the reaches of (optical) rationality, in which case it isn't a proper subject for academic scrutiny. We lose an opportunity but preserve our pride.

This conservative state of academic affairs obviously irritates me. But rather than remain irritated, I have decided to try to act on my instincts, arguments, and experiences in ways that are in some material correspondence with academic integrity as it is commonly construed. To do this, I have here undertaken a study of imagination, spirituality, and communication *as* context and interpretation. I will show why this particular study simply would not be very convincing if it ignored connections between and among otherwise disparate phenomena, even if the form and content of the phenomena occasionally cross into territories usually left to mystics, poets, faith healers, business visionaries, and to musicians who all recognize (metaphorically and practically) that what happens *between* the notes is how the whole composition hangs together and makes the experiencing of it art as well as mystery.

Why Central and Clemson?

What is the relevance of this study to other communities?

When I have spoken about this project with family, friends, and colleagues, one consistent question is, "Why locate the study in Central and Clemson, South Carolina?" At first, the answer I gave was true to my

INTRODUCTION

opening lines but intellectually incomplete: I chose Central and Clemson (or maybe they chose me) because this is where I was dwelling while I was asking these questions. Writers are usually advised to "write what you know," and in my case that means "knowing where you are," which translates readily into "writing where you are." Also, I found something mysteriously compelling about the signs of social and material constructions in this place, something unspoken "into the between" of the ordinary, everyday routines of persons, nature, and things that drew me in, that could be, just maybe, articulated. Too, there was much mystery, metaphor, irony, paradox, drama, and comedy in and about the name Central that appealed both to the themes of this study and to my rhetorical nature. And Clemson—a carnival itself—was just down the road. How could I *not*?

Put differently, the central quest (see what I mean?) was one of composing a place. More specifically, the material of that composition had to be drawn from the organizing activities and artifacts—the material manifestations of this community—yet also had to suggest what I came to recognize—or at least to call—the "imagined worlds" that *connect* those manifestations to the persons and that give those who make lives here universal meaning and local relevance. These "imagined worlds" carve openings for communication out of otherwise open spaces *between* the actions of women and men, humans and nature. By the fact of their invitations to communicate, these spaces offer communal opportunities for interpretations of contexts, and—perhaps more importantly— they shape and ultimately define not only the *material* manifestations, but also the *imagined* possibilities, for relationships between self, Spirit, and Others elsewhere.

Hence the intellectual engagement. Theories of communication posit self and Other constructions—as well as senses of communities and cultures—primarily through interpretations of empirical, material manifestations of consciousness. This is to say that we "see" talk and activities, and deduce or induce from them what we name as the *substance* of relationships. But this is a material substance only. It is to make sense of the whole of a musical performance by attending only to the composition of its notes, or to view students moving between classes on a college campus as the material accomplishment of an education. What gets left out of our theories of communication is what lives in-between those empirical manifestations and their localized interpretations, or the "mu-

Introduction

sic" between the notes, the work of the insight on lectures and discussions producing the education. Put simply, what is missing is *imagination*, which, as I shall endeavor to show, is also to miss the *spiritual* basis for communication, relationships, and communities.

What I hope to do is teach the reader how to imagine possibilities for signs, for conversations, for inexplicable occurrences and underexplored emotions that can be useful anywhere. So, in a real sense, this book uses Central as both an ethnographic site and as a metaphor for envisioning or recognizing Spirit in the places you call home.

Power, Other, and Spirit: Cultural Myth and Western Interpretation

What is *Spirit*?

Janice Hocker Rushing (1993) makes an artistically rich, narratively compelling case for understanding Self, Other, and Spirit as characters in a larger Western cultural myth. Her argument is that Power (the "social manifestation of modern philosophy") articulates the "sovereign rational subject" as the core concept of modernism, challenged by Other (the "anti-philosophical adversary opposite of Power") through postmodern decentering and categorical deconstructions. Spirit is victimized by this struggle between Power and Other, although it "transcends opposition" by working "in" and "out" of—as well as "between"—both characters, thereby limiting Power by showing the *interrelations* among all things (e.g., "the One in the many"), and erasing the symbolically constructed separation—the taken-for-granted boundaries—between self (as the expression of Power) and Other (as the expression of difference). Hence, from this mythic (e.g., imaginative) perspective, contemporary theories of self and Others in communication must be understood as players in a larger cultural drama rendered as narrative myth, through and about which rediscovery of Spirit philosophically resolves these binary oppositions while repositioning "communication" as *the spiritual pathway* capable of uniting diverse communities (see appendix 1).

FROM MYTH TO CONSCIOUSNESS AND BACK AGAIN

The central idea—as well as the idea of Central and Clemson—may be expressed this way: What goes on in between the material manifestations of this place and the imagined worlds reflected and constituted by

INTRODUCTION

the spaces between, within, and among them is a communal consciousness that cuts almost invisibly across all activities. That these spaces for imagination tend to be ignored in the communication literature, that these lessons from the imagined worlds of everyday lives are absent from our conceptions yet everywhere present in our actions, interpretations, and meanings, offers a compelling intellectual reason for doing this study. If what we discover about ourselves, and about communication, is significantly altered as a result of recovering for theory what is evident in practice, then what is questioned here is far more than the explication of issues of organizing in a local community. It is, rather, a study whose radical purpose is clearly to question most of the assumptive foundations of twentieth century empirical communication theories. It is to begin to rearticulate what it means, ultimately, to be humans who communicate to make relationships and communities.

We are, as Kenneth Burke teaches us, symbol-users/abusers (1989). Yet we are also creatures whose symbols form the intricate architectures of perception and imagination. What we use symbols, or abuse symbols, *for* is not only informed by the material form of that architecture, it is influenced *by* it. Imagination provides the rhetorical basis for any connection of communication to the social construction of selves, others, relationships, and communities. On a practical level, what we imagine ourselves to be—alone or in the company of others—defines the boundaries of what we believe is possible. In turn, what we believe as possible defines the inner and outer reaches of what we construe, commonly, as our "reality." This is to say that we all imagine worlds that we then live bounded by; it is also to say that when we "commune" we dialogically enter the imagined alternative worlds—alternative, parallel realities—of others. When we put these two observations together we have what used to be called "synergy," something dynamic that expresses more than the simple sum of its definable parts. It is the creative tensions between imagined worlds—and between the connection of imagined worlds to empirical realities—that everyday communication mediates, substantiates, explains, quarrels with, justifies, comes to terms over, does science and fiction about, makes histories and politics out of, occasionally silences, and, perhaps—when viewed spiritually—merely *manifests*.

Central, indeed. Every sense of the term, more than a rose, this myth, this consciousness, this name.

Introduction

THIS PLACE AND OUR WORLD: INTERPLAYS OF TEXTUAL REALITIES

Beyond metaphor, however, one might wonder if Central and Clemson are generalizable as *communities*. Is a book about these particular places capable of generating ideas, even conclusions, about other communities? Other, *distinctive* places? Although this sort of question has a variety of answers in anthropology (see Gorer 1948; Verenne 1984; Warner 1952), Carol Greenhouse offers an answer with which I believe this study must closely identify:

> Specifically, a concept of culture as constituted by the logic of symbols and their connected meanings could be neither universally shared nor particularly unique. The human imagination is too varied, too responsive to private and public experience, to be so transparent or opaque. Thus I take a certain level of generalizability to follow from the concept of culture as the set of relations among ideas. Ideas—no matter how private or idiosyncratic—are *about* something or someone (to choose two out of many possible examples). Men and women may be solitary thinkers, in other words, but the fact of their thinking places them in a social, or shared, universe. (1986, 34)

I can think of no better way to demonstrate the truth of her assertion than by example. Consider the following passage, drawn from a recent book about Tuscaloosa, Alabama, and in this case, a particular barbecue joint located just outside of town:

> That is why I am drawn to Paradise, to the warmth and color that live secretly out in the dark of the Alabama jungle. Paradise has no structure; the moments when the self can dissolve come of their own volition, flapping across time like great lumbering bats, and suddenly overtake you. Of course there are the drugs, and of course there is the liquor and the groove of the pink hut that never stops. But those are ancillary to the true phenomenon. There is in the place and in the darkness of it, the darkness that lingers like a smell even in the daylight, an immanent invitation to abandonment. (Phillips 1994, 134)

At once this passage evokes a unique sense of place and a more or less universal experience that transcends that unique sense of place. It communicates to our imaginations from the author's lived experiences and the work of his imagination on them. And it valorizes an experience of

INTRODUCTION

place that calls into question the distinctions we otherwise maintain about the boundaries of self, imagination, Spirit, and world.

If I told you that what you have just read is taken from a novel, not from an ethnographic text, would this alter the value of its insights, its ability to evoke the universal from the particular? I ask this question because one obvious "problem" for some of my colleagues is that I make use of imagination in the construction of my ethnographic texts, including this one. Although everything in my books is true—true to my experiences—I do not privilege a separation between *mythos* and *logos*, or between what I perceive and imagine and what "counts" as reality. In my experience those categories are *naturally* blurred, thankfully. I believe, fully, that any science—just as any art—devoid of imagination is not only inhuman but also artificial intelligence and, given the high stakes we traffic in and for, practically useless.

The Point of the Purpose and a Clue for You

In a previous book I characterized the ethnographic experience this way: Every journey outward is also a journey inward; every study of Others becomes a study of the self (1991). The present volume extends that principle by concentrating on self and Others in *contexts* wherein the outward study of community becomes one with contextualizing one's *spiritual* self.

This ethnographic journey, then, is a community-based study that also seeks to be a contribution—and a challenge—to theories of communication. I will use data from the details of the former to construct tenets of the latter in a series of accelerated meditations on and revealed experiences about a seemingly disparate exotic place where experiences and events become increasingly connected as they also become symbolically and semiotically complex. Because I still believe in the detective metaphor to guide critical reading, the only clue I can offer is to pay attention to the details. Ultimately, they contain the whole story.

PART ONE

REALITY CENTRAL

Strange to find imagination as the ground of certainty.

—James Hillman

1

Destination and Arrival

> By *soul* I mean, first of all, a perspective rather than a substance, a viewpoint toward things rather than a thing itself. This perspective is reflective; it mediates events and makes differences between ourselves and everything that happens.
> We need to recall the angel aspect of the word, recognizing words as independent carriers of soul between people.
>
> —James Hillman

Take South Carolina #15 exit off I-85 heading up from Atlanta at the legal speed limit, pause at the stop sign at the end of the exit ramp, and—if you are prone to consider the meaning of such things—you see that you are now at a complex intersection of American culture. This place—this intersection—displays local histories, regional politics, and deep, dangerous—ultimately spiritual—conflicts. What are these stories? What is this place all about?

Intersections, like political elections, force you to look left and right, to make choices based almost entirely on what you imagine you see in the light of what you believe. To the right, toward Anderson, are familiar signs of God-fearing, gun-toting interstate existence. Here are the popular corporate icons to fast self-service gas to which are now attached square two-color convenience stores specializing in the open sale of sugar-coated, high-calorie nothings displayed seductively in brightly colored plastic wrap; cold no-deposit, no-return soft drinks and primary American beers in cans; multiple extra-strength pain relievers, caffeine tablets, and gas alleviators; NASCAR models, caps, and memorabilia; Confederate flags, Confederate flag T-shirts and pro-gun, anti-Clinton, kiss-my-ass bumper stickers; and public displays of criminal nicotine sold here at discount prices. Next door are the blessedly close reassurances of personal decay: faster, greasier, deadlier foods—fried antibiotic cow slathered with melted fat on bleached bread—slopped with special sauces or dressings, topped with chemically treated vegetables, served in cartoon-coordinated paper cups and bags. These are sources only of instant gut gratification for obvious needs that fast gratifying and plastic never fully satisfies, but that interstate travel or just the everyday velocity of life induces. And *yessir*, there are never-clean locked restrooms "For Customers Only" sweetly stinking in the rear, and a quarters-only pay phone stripped of local directories that has long served as a public ashtray and vomitorium outside by the loud highway, down at the inconvenient but legal edge of the property, where hearing and safety is severely, maybe purposefully impaired.

To the left—toward Clemson—is an authentic, perfect white southern mansion fronted by a small private pond and surrounded by a highly ornate iron fence and naturally intoxicating magnolia and oak trees. You can use it to momentarily imagine a gone world that probably never was, fill in the imaginary blanks with movie scenes and heavily accented dialogue, just as you always have. Across the highway from this white elegant elephant are two competing gas station/convenience stores, a new Wendy's, and behind them an unnecessarily long, somewhat ironic, curving drive up a man-made hill that leads not to another perfect white mansion but to an Outback Steakhouse, a Cracker Barrel restaurant/mini Southern country theme park, and an overnight inn of interstate proportions.

You have been here, we all have. If not this road, then some other one. If not this dream, then one you imagine as purely your own.

On the highway now—a four-lane blacktop upon which are painted huge orange tiger paws—continuous, fast, competitive traffic from elsewhere seems always to be going somewhere and doesn't pause at all for this admirable, astonishing view, as if this conflicted place, this intersection and all it suggests, only exists if you want it to.

You want it to.

Thrownness

All journeys outward really begin with an arrival, a destination, that happens within you. Maybe you come *to* something. Perhaps you come to a decision about your life, what it means, what it lacks, what it should mean, what it must—as of this moment—be about or directed toward.

Maybe its a decision about where you should live. Or work. Or whom you should be with. Or kiss.

Maybe you have just come to the end of something. The end of your personal rope. The end of an era. The end of a job. The end of a marriage. The end of your luck, or patience, or money. From this moment on, your arrival at the end—and you do recognize this moment when it occurs—opens before you the chance, the opportunity, for a new beginning. It is the work of the imagination; it has to be. Maybe you decide to stay in the same place or with the same person but to do things differently. Learn to think differently. Learn to act differently.

Or maybe not. Maybe you decide to move on. This, too, is work imagination urges upon you, an adrenalin rush and emotive sanction that moves within and through your body, taking you there. Perhaps there is an image you are drawn to live for, against, or just in. Perhaps there is nothing so much fixed, just the definitive, indescribable movement of time in your eternity, a movement that tells you, frankly, that what is simply will not do anymore, and that something else, somewhere else, maybe someone else—all as yet unimaginable and at the same time, in the same breath, entirely real—must now be the "it," the thing you are living for. This is the world you have always imagined, and so you enter it.

Martin Heidegger says that we are thrown into the world. Actually, he says that "Dasein" exhibits "thrownness," by which he means the soul ("Dasein" or "design") seems to be borne into a life already well under way, a journey that seems predestined, part of a world that is itself well under way and, perhaps, purposeful. This accounts for why one of the defining and enduring experiences of human Being is to suddenly, inextricably, feel lost, to not know what that seemingly predestined journey is all about, and, as a result, to sense that something important in our life *is missing*. This is often described in everyday talk as a feeling of "deep emptiness," or what the French existentialists have labeled *ennui*, while we are nevertheless busy living what we imagine, what we experience, as an ordinary or even extraordinary life.

There is nothing particularly new about this feeling of destinational loss. The world's great literatures from all continents are resplendent with similar experiences. For Dante, it happened "midway through the journey of life"; and certainly there is characteristic midlife emptiness that demands any quest for meaningfulness. Ditto for Siddhartha

Buddha and for Jesus Christ, each one offering testaments to their sudden callings—their sense of thrownness—while living otherwise ordinary lives. So, too, does the world's great music and visual art provide examples of this common moment and its extraordinary influences on and perhaps over us. Artistic work tends to thrive on the creative tensions between a lonely soulful emptiness and a hunger for some meaningful connection of us to the cosmos, disparate extremities whose direct experience will not be denied and whose work in and on our imaginations calls us, definitively, into Being.

Perhaps these feelings are simply cognitive problems. After all, psychoanalytic framing teaches us to think of such feelings, such metaphors, as expressions of "alienation" or "anxiety." Walker Percy (1983) described this problem as one of being a creature on a planet who knows just about everything about everything else but very little about himself. What we are alienated *from*, and anxious *about*, he says, is a loss of self, of a self "lost in the cosmos." It could be, he says and many psychologists agree, all in our heads. But Dr. Percy, wisely, I think, doubts it.

Or perhaps these feelings of loss are cognitive problems reinforced by behavioral maladies. Read this way, the usual culprit is bad behavior (we break rules or laws and suffer "guilt" or "depression"), or badly adjusted social behavior (we remain alone as a result of "failed interaction" or "communication apprehension"), or even "repressed childhood trauma" that emerges suddenly in the haunting of our dreams and then in an inability to function "normally" in the company of Others. In these cases, I think, where we read behavior as the only factual symptom, we too often follow the rules of misreading and thereby misinterpret that symptom as cause. It is akin to reading every other page of a novel *because* the fact is that read that way the page numbers can be said to be—explained as being—uniformly odd. What we are doing when we treat a narrative of absence as the anatomy of cognitively driven behavior *only* is to try to provide scientific answers to the known surfaces of pain, answers too often devoid of artistic imagination for problems that are themselves artfully (mis)rendered, answers for an empirical world that denies the possibility of a spiritual nature or of spiritual experience.

In the world of twentieth-century human communication, the loss of Spirit is painfully apparent. Driven by the modernist language and logic of machine and systems metaphors, our theories and research findings reveal the behavioral mechanics of human relationships and discuss families as systems of interlocking information created in and constituted by message, noise, and feedback loops. Thomas Moore (1994), working from the language and logic of a religious metaphor, offers this alternative:

> The heart is a mystery, not a puzzle that can't be solved, but a mystery in the religious sense: unfathomable, beyond manipulation, showing traces of the finger of God at work.... When we focus our attention on the soul of relationship, instead of on its interpersonal mechanics, a different set of values comes to the foreground. We are now interested in fantasy and imagination. We begin to see relationship as the place where the soul works out its destiny. We are not so concerned how to make relationship "work," because the soul point of view isn't ambitious in that way. It doesn't make love a life project. Instead, it recognizes the truth of a line from John Donne, that great poet of soul and relationship: "Love's mysteries in soules doe grow."
> Concerned about the soul, we don't ask why something has happened in a relationship, or how to make it better. Rather, we wonder about the soul's own purposes: "What is happening in the soul when we fall madly in love? What is the soul wanting in its fantasies of separation? What is this longing for deeper love, and why does it never seem to be satisfied?" With our focus on the soul, we won't feel the impossible burden of "doing" relationship right.... Instead, we may live through the mysteries of endings, crises, and turning points in love, marriage, friendship, and family, and submit to the life that is always germinating in them. (56–57)

Moore's views on intimacy reflect the intercession of Spirit into the mysteries of everyday relational "thrownness."[1] He also underscores the importance of root metaphors in the social construction of realities. If we begin our examination of the anatomy of relationships in a Western frame, we "see" behaviors and probe causal connections between them and "cognitions." We also learn to see the empirical bodily separation of self and Others as manifestations of material difference rather than as signs of deeper unities beyond the material manifestation of visible differences, or our spiritual "interbeing" (Goodall 1993). Perhaps most fundamentally, we reduce mystery to formula.

True to our metaphor, we act as if relationships can be "perfected"

---

[1] Moore writes that the superlative root in Latin for the word " 'intimacy' is 'inter,' meaning 'within.' It could be translated 'within-est' or 'most within.' In our intimate relationships, the 'most within' dimensions of ourselves and the other are engaged" (58). This view accords with Frentz (1993) on the misreading of Plato's interior turn for soul-ful rhetoric.

through information management and clockwork surveillance of everyday routines. Dissatisfaction, sadness, emptiness, longing, or *ennui* is logically akin to having a screw loose or a simple misalignment of the proper gearing. "Operating" our relationships and trying to "understand" or "deal with" our emotions, our passions, and our "thrownness" out of the foreign material of this bounded, mechanical language removes what is felt, intuited, or sensed from the logic of what is experienced. It denies any space whatsoever to the work of the Spirit, to any sense of spiritual quest, fate, relational poetry, or spiritual longing. "Making love" is reduced to "having sex," and dialogues are confined to the narrow space of "conversation" or "exchanges of information." Viewing relationships from this mechanical engineering frame trivializes "destinations" and "arrivals" by reducing their activities to coordinations of behaviors with behavioral goals, accomplishments of physical contact as fulfillments of bodily needs, and agreeing to live in particular ways as the directive work of having cognitive objectives. Finally, the narrative progression of this metaphor in our everyday relational lives requires us to engage the mythic struggle between Power and Other for the self's "control over" the Newtonian mechanics of our lives, worlds, and each other. The well-lived life is a life lived fully in denial of Spirit. The result is we die young and walk around as a well-preserved corpse who is content to follow the rules for behavior and thought and collect material commodities in exchange for our ethereal souls.

These current misreadings of our nature and purpose are further complicated by dominant scientific discourse in capital cahoots with the medical and legal establishment. If treating untoward outward behaviors through copious applications of social science discourse to our relation of self to the world doesn't do it, the therapeutic fallback isn't listening to the soul; instead, it is forcing the body to accept the occupation of foreign substances designed to militaristically manipulate chemical and biological change. Here we have more than a chemical solution to a biochemical problem; we have the cojoining of powerful social institutions and discourse that privilege treating (and paying for) a chemical and biological bases for just about everything that can go wrong with us, thus implicating a pharmacological answer for every problem.[2] The symp-

---

[2] Kurt Vonnegut, Jr. (1990) says that when we examine the ideology that determined how most of us actually lived, the twentieth century will become recognized as the "Age of Pharmacology." I think he may be right. Even consultants to organizations

Destination and Arrival

toms may disappear, the untoward behaviors may surrender or simply be held hostage to Thorazine or Prozac for awhile, but these outward changes are wrought at the expense of internal causes narcotized into temporary retreat but destined to reappear and reassert themselves later on. The body's need for stronger and stronger medications to treat the same recurring problems should tell us something more profound than the simple accumulation of chemical tolerances: The Big Picture is larger than this anatomical framing.

The institutional coordination of discourses drawn from medical, legal, and corporate powers dictating a pharmacological response capable of forcing behavioral and cognitive realignments is typically invoked when any sign of living *differently* is reason enough to re-bureaucratize the spirit through narcotic inducements. In the mythic narrative we participate in daily, difference is the domain of "Otherness" and produces signs of resistance to Power, to Order, to the routinized domination of bureaucratic sameness. That these signs of difference may be clues to deeper mysteries about Spirit or soul in a modern/postmodern society—to Dasein's feeling of thrownness—is seldom entertained, for acceptance of spiritual alternatives is beyond the ken of modernist mechanical eccentricity, and neither can Spirit's ethereal politics be easily located within the fragmented pragmatics of postmodern opposition. What is left out—what is lost in these formulations—is precisely what is wrong with this framing.

As a cultural critic, I am an unashamed deconstructionist. I have learned to ask questions of texts and social texts based on what Jacques Derrida (1976) calls "the presence of an absence, or the absence of a presence." So it is that when I confront a consistent cross-cultural language of "loss"—in this case, something that is being left out of an explanatory narrative as well as experiences for which no corporate language exists—I find instead hidden "opportunities." Perhaps that we can articulate these feelings of loss—these senses of incompleteness in text and social text—is evidence not just of absence, but also of a *presence of extraordinary awareness* whose time has come.

Put simply, I believe that from quite early on until and through the present time, humans—not all of us at any one time—evolve into a kind

---

these days offer the sage advice to schedule important decisions in the morning, the most "drug-free" time of the day for most employees (Deetz 1992). That is true, of course, only if you discount caffeine or nicotine.

of spiritual zone of awareness. This awareness of spiritual connections marks an evolution into an alternative consciousness—a kind of everyday awareness of parallel universes—in which questions about what we are supposed to do—indeed, questions about what we are supposed to be "about"—assert unequivocal influence. This zone of awareness occurs as a dramatic punctuation in the flow of one's life; it is experienced as "loss" because who you were before it happened, and what you thought your lifework was before it happens, *changes*. You literally find you cannot go on as you did. You have come *to* something, and you have come *to the end* of something as well. Here, indeed, is an "arrival," a full sense of "thrownness" that demands our attention, our contemplation, our action. Here, indeed, is the homeplace of experience that sums up all the smaller, seemingly less significant changes that have thus far only enabled our overall spiritual evolution.

So here you are. You have arrived. Now the question is: *Where are you?*

Reading the Ordinary as Evidence of Unordinary Experience

I am heading toward Clemson, South Carolina, on Highway 76 off I-85—a direct result of my turning left instead of right at the intersection—although my real destination is Central. A sign out in front of the new Welcome Baptist Church reads:

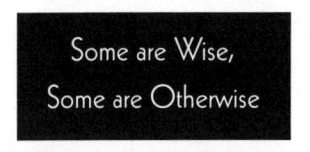

> Some are Wise,
> Some are Otherwise

Along my route I see other signs that further orient me to a sense of place. On the left is Denver Downs, a beautiful working farm owned by the Garrisons; to the right is a white frame house with a deeply red roof. A little further up the road is the huge Michelin plant; Boscobel Golf Course and Hacker's Heaven; a "World Famous" furniture depot; an outdoor buildings outlet; a scattering of modest homes, many of which feature boats and/or cars parked at angles in front yards; a place of business that is part bar, part fishing pond. Across the highway is a cellular phone outlet, another place of business that sells baseball cards, antiques, junk,

Destination and Arrival

and NASCAR collectibles; Mammy's Fish Fry; the Sandy Springs intersection with a gas station and convenience store featuring a sign welcoming you to "Tiger Country" on the right, and on the left "Ed's Meats and Things," another gas station, and convenience store; a train overpass that cuts across Three and Twenty Mile Creek, a brick home with a nice inground swimming pool in its front yard; Bill's Cafe ("Lunches. Dinners. Hotdogs 2 for $1 TOGOONLY"); the La France sign pointing to La France, South Carolina, and the La France textile plant, a large Milliken plant; some wholesale used car and truck dealers; a video poker casino; some gas stations, used car outlets, and $10 tire dealers; a strip mall with a Bi-Lo grocery, Revco drug store, Advance Auto Parts, A+ Rentals, and Jerry's Video rental fronted by a Dairy Queen and Hardee's; there is a fork in the road to Historic Pendleton, South Carolina, that I don't take, another convenience store called Jimbos, some open flood plain, the campus of Tri-County Technical College, another Milliken plant, a truck repair garage, two churches, fields of pine trees and a sign welcoming us to Clemson, a ballfield, the Old Stone Church and cemetery, the National Guard Armory, signs regulating football traffic to Clemson, the South Carolina Botanical Gardens, and Clemson University, and—finally—my local turnoff—this time to the right—toward Central.

    Central, South Carolina. Central, South Carolina, located in the westward end of the upstate region, an entirely ordinary small southern town. Archetypal, in fact.

    Central is midway between Clemson and Norris on Highway 93 (its main street), and consists of a baby blue water tower that says Central on it, a dual row of 17 shops and storefronts (hardware, antiques, hair stylist, cafes) on main street, across from which is the railroad that separates the town proper from the old Mill, a fire house, police department, EMS, and post office, a community baseball field, six Baptist churches, a Trinity Wesleyan church, a New Life Assembly of God, a Church of God, one Nation's Bank, an American Legion hut, Central Honda repair, Clinton's car customizing, a car wash, a day care, a Clock restaurant, a Plez U convenience store, a tax consultant, and a hairdressing salon named Mane Tamers, the Southern Institute of Pet Grooming, an elementary school, a cemetery, Central Plaster and Concrete, a building supply warehouse, a Teledyne affiliate, various apartment complexes, three service stations, a foreign car specialist, a drive-in pharmacy, Jerry's video rental and take-out pizza, a small private college, and various collectivities of homes.[3]

Looked at this empirical way—a place defined by the surfaces of its buildings and its conspicuous use of local terrain—Central is an ordinary town. *Entirely* ordinary. Maybe *too* ordinary.

But what does it take to be "ordinary"? Harvey Sacks (1984) teaches us that there is a lot of work involved in the "doing" of "being ordinary." Particularly in conversation. More particularly in conversations about what happens to you where you live, where you, as Heidegger expresses it, "dwell." He says, for example, that:

> a kind of remarkable thing is how, in ordinary conversation, people, in reporting on some event, report what we might see to be, not what happened, but the ordinariness of what happened. The reports do not so much give attributes of the scene, activity, participants, but announce the event's ordinariness of what happened, its usualness....
>
> This brings me to the central sorts of assertions I want to make. Whatever you may think about what it is to be an ordinary person in the world, an initial shift is not [to] think of 'an ordinary person' as some person, but as somebody having as one's job, as one's constant preoccupation, doing "being ordinary." (414)

Central, I will learn, prides itself on being an "ordinary" small southern town. Harvey Sacks would say, I think, that this is Central's preoccupation, its job, or, more properly, the preoccupation and job of its residents, those persons who imagine themselves living in its ordinariness, and who thereby constitute its ordinary existence and enact its ordinary meanings. To be seen, to be experienced, as "an ordinary small southern town," then, is *work*. It is the work of the imagination on the business of doing everyday life. And it is hard work. If it is done really well—if you learn how to make Central's ordinariness shape and inform your

---

[3] This is, of course, only a surface treatment of Central. The longer I spent here the more complex and problematic these surfaces became. For example, "collectivities of homes" is a descriptor that masks economic, social, racial, and class distinctions that are important symbols in many residents' everyday understanding of this place. There is not one "Central," but many, and the interconnection of the one with the many is both symbolically and semiotically relevant. Consider "Headtown." This is a residential area just behind downtown Central that was constructed for blue-collar workers by John Head, but today it also consists of citizens for whom the label "Headtown" carries fuller symbolic value: philosophically inclined students, drug dealers and users, New Age mystics, at least one Satanist, and several old-timers who remain here because "in their heads" it has never changed.

speech, dress, behavior, perceptions, attitudes, values, and beliefs—if you learn to "do" being an "ordinary small southern town" as well as you can, then its very ordinariness becomes your central preoccupation.

How do we "do" *preoccupation*? Ordinariness is a "preoccupation" in that—as Sacks points out—there is a tendency among persons to perceive the events, persons, and places in one's everyday life *as being* "ordinary." He teaches us to listen carefully to how we describe most of what happens to us as "the usual," and how, even in dramatically unusual circumstances, we begin our descriptions with how we thought "nothing special was going on *until*...." And even then, even when the most remarkable thing—the dramatic break in the otherwise ordinary existence of one's everyday life—is finally described, it is so framed by the experience of being ordinary that its very *unordinariness* is only understood by reference to the ordinary, to the routine, to the "usual" or "normal." "That is to say," Sacks says, "what you *look* for is to see how any scene you are in can be made an ordinary scene, a usual scene, and that is what the scene is" (1984, 416).

It is almost as if our imaginative preoccupation with ordinariness is a kind of linguistic and perceptual narcotic we take voluntarily every day, a way of routinizing—bureaucratizing—Being, so that what we pass around in exchanges of talk dulls down or tunes out the hard work of embracing the extraordinary possibilities otherwise available in everyday life. This narcotized, routine-induced habit of making experience ordinary is consistently reinforced by habits of speech that value phatic communion as a substitute for conversation, that express a common preference for giving simple answers to complex questions, that favor an easy exchange of cliches as replacements for the work of genuine human dialogue, and that strive very diligently to make us ignore everything that doesn't immediately conform to our already-in-place commonly shared understandings, experiences, or beliefs. As Sacks puts it: "The point is that it is almost everybody's business to be occupationally ordinary; that people take on the job of keeping everything utterly mundane; that no matter what happens, pretty much everybody is engaged in finding only how it is that what is going on is usual, with every effort possible" (1984, 419).

If imagination represents the *creative* potential for using communication to make connections and to spiritually evolve, I can think of no better summary for *constraint* than how we do the business of using phatic communion to frame everyday speech and perception. While it is "hard work" to do the business of being ordinary, the work that gets done is primarily one of defining limits, limiting possibilities, saying "no," drawing and continuously underscoring the lines and boundaries around the rules and roles that keep us mundane, that sum up the simple truths of an ordinary life, instead of accenting what might otherwise be seen as undefined, unlimited, unlined, unbounded, rule- and role-blurring experiences that open up the possibilities for interpreting the contexts of one's life. As the poet Claire Bateman once put to me, "Maybe phatic communion is what Jesus meant when he cautioned us to avoid *vain repetitions.*"

Think of imaginative alternatives for producing and consuming talk as resources for *creativity*. They help us enter the zone of awareness. They enable evolutions of consciousness. Sometimes born of a new metaphor or even a slip of the tongue, ways of combining and connecting otherwise disparate ideas challenge the invisible domination of the ordinary, the everyday, the mundane. But those of us who take risks in everyday conversation—who seek unordinary experiences—do so at the expense of being ordinary, and the costs can be very high. Unless you are a person who others see as "entitled to have their lives be an epic" (Sacks 1984, 419), conversational moves outside the ordinary are likely to be treated as, at the very least, pretentious.

Even more profoundly, "if you are going to have 'an entitled experience,' then you will *have to have* the experience that you are entitled to" (1984, 426). That is, a further constraint on creativity—the one beyond the yawning of phatic communion—is the social imperative—commandment—to live in the world you have envisioned and talked about, and *only* that world. So it is that even when you utter the opportunity for—or presence of—a previously unseen, unspoken experience or connection, your entitlement to it extends *only so far as* the routine boundaries of that experience or connection are *already* understood. The world you have imagined is one that Others will demand you inhabit. As the sign on Cannon Memorial Baptist puts it:

> Don't Pretend To Be
> What You Don't Intend To Be

Destination and Arrival

Consider my talk here, in these paragraphs, of spirituality and communication. Within a context of an ordinary small southern town—which itself exists as an articulation of ordinariness—which I have now—with the aid of Harvey Sacks—problematized. At each turn in my talk I bet your patience wears a little thinner. Spirituality, after all, is probably something you understand—or ask questions about—in a certain way. Ditto for communication. No doubt "saturated" as you are with media images (Gergen 1992), you have some understanding—at least some perception—of small southern towns. Certainly of ordinariness. But this frame-shifting (or is it frame-enlarging?) strategy of mine seems to break some rules for the proper order of scholarly discourse, for the making of an argument. An *ordinary* argument. Instead, one paragraph describes sights and signs along an otherwise obscure highway, the next discusses the wisdom of Heidegger.

Maybe these seemingly juxtaposed paragraphs offer two ways of saying the same thing. Of making interrelated connections. Asking *you* to interrelate *to* those connections. Similarly, I have described—in linear fashion—the surfaces of what you would ordinarily see along an obscure (Heideggerian?) highway on the way into and through Central, South Carolina, and then used Harvey Sacks's central thesis on the philosophy of ordinariness as the central, surface preoccupation of human communication, as if they are integrally connected. In this communication, in this text.

They *are* connected. I think that seeing the connections can open up a zone of awareness, a resource for theoretical and spiritual evolution, which are also connected. And having said that, I want to laugh. Talking like this makes me sound like a New Age salesman, or maybe a television evangelist on 'shrooms. *Lordy*.[4]

But I *have to* say it that way, at least here in the beginning, at the beginning where words don't just mean what they seem to and the mys-

---

[4] Although I make use of many New Age resources in this text, I feel obliged to point out that I have never considered myself a "New Ager." Perhaps I am too steeped in the social sciences to ever fully give up the healthy skepticism I've been reared on. At the same time, I think denying a place in our literature to New Age insights makes no sense whatsoever; science and criticism should always remain open to change. What I am after is a way of reading what I find intriguing and sensible in various New Age texts as spiritual pathways that open up alternative possibilities for interpretation, meaning, research, and understanding for everyday communication problematics.

tery is profound. This is the place for ambiguity to open the path to empowerment, the place where this mystery (always my subject) pulls me in. How to say it—how to articulate the unspoken connections, the message between the lines, the music between the notes—and the fact that we have trouble saying it, these are the initial clues to the questions being raised here, to the nature of the quest of this writing itself. The issue is what to say once you have arrived at the connection, knowing that what the connection entitles you to is not exactly what needs to be said about it. Put differently, how can you articulate arrivals—unordinary experiences—in ordinary talk? How can you speak to what lies between the lines?

How did I arrive in Central?

Speaking between the Lines: Signs and Experiences

I have lived here before. In a past life, or at least when I was a different person. From August 1974 to May 1977, to be exact.

I was hired straight out of my M.A. program at the University of North Carolina at Chapel Hill to be a temporary instructor of speech and director of forensics in the English department at Clemson University. I was twenty-one years old, and I was supposed to be here for one year, maybe two. I ended up staying three years, mostly because I was relatively harmless and entirely willing to be invisible. This is to say I was a likeable young guy in a nontenure-earning service position who taught his classes competently, coached a team that did well, and got along well enough with senior members of the faculty. I was a perfect candidate for ordinariness, for anonymity, invisibility. My life was lived between the lines of appearances, shaped by the invisibility and anonymity of my experiences, by the ordinariness of what I appeared to be, and to be doing. I left in May 1977 to continue the more obvious aspects of my journey elsewhere; fourteen years passed.

Clemson University prides itself on being an extended family, and because I was here before, my vaguer qualities and generally amiable nature regained me entrance through that family tie. It happened this way. Soon after our son, Nicolas, was born, my wife and I decided that we wanted to rear him (at least initially) in the South—closer to his grandparents—in a community that was small enough to inspire a sense of

Destination and Arrival

place and yet capable of sustaining the multicultural values and desire for cultural activities we share. As if moved by fate, the next month a job announcement appeared for a person with a somewhat odd mix of professional qualifications: Ph.D. in rhetoric (mine was from Penn State, 1980), teaching and writing in organizational communication (which I had been doing since 1980), and previous administrative experience building a new department (which I had accomplished at the University of Alabama in Huntsville, serving my last five years there as chair). I "knew" I was the person that was supposed to respond to that ad. I applied, I interviewed, one month later I signed the contract. I arrived at a sense of thrownness, and of destination.

No, this is not another Thomas Wolfe story. I am not consciously rewriting "you can't go home again," or anything like that, although I do admit that returning to this locale is returning to a piece of my spiritual home. But I never expected to find my past here, or to relive it. What I did expect to find was inexplicable, I only knew I needed to be here to find it. I felt, I think, like Binx Bollings in Walker Percy's *The Moviegoer* (1959); I knew I was "on to something," but I didn't know exactly what. Binx's first clues were Jews; mine were signs in front of Baptist churches, the contexts of those that live between their lines and that inspire the work of imagination.

SIGNS AS CONTEXTS

Signs provide contexts for interpretations of meanings. Or perhaps I should say signs *offer* the possibilities of contexts for meanings to engage. As such, signs are either evocative or representational surfaces that made practical the application of critical modernism and postmodernism. For me, the world we construct always has the equipotential for modern and postmodern interpretations.

Consider, for example, this week's sign outside First Baptist:

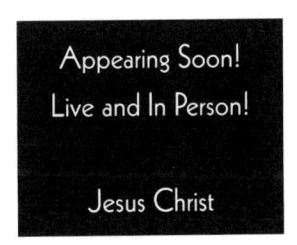

> Appearing Soon!
>
> Live and In Person!
>
> Jesus Christ

41

Now if you are a confirmed modernist—in this case, a fundamentalist Christian of Baptist oath—you are supposed to see this sign within the context of a particular context, within the range of a narrow, preferred reading: *Prepare for the Resurrection*. Given that this week is the week before Easter and this sign stands in front of a Christian church, the unwritten metaphorical subtext is already coded into the context of interpretation. The sign bears the mark of pure *authorial* intent. There is little, if any, tolerance for linguistic or referential ambiguity. And yes, Mary, there is a Truth because there is a God. Here is the mythic work of Power, of a modern alliance between religion and the self contained within a particular reading of history that legitimizes a particular code of conduct, that defines authority through revealed readings of a particular text, and that proposes that a belief in regulating outward behaviors and inward cognitions will have its final reward in heaven.

However, approached from a postmodernist perspective, this sign suggests a certain serious playfulness in its surface juxtaposition of popular and religious contexts: rock superstar slickness of style (re: Appearing Soon! Live and In Person!)—rendered in unabashed exclamatory concert glee—combined with a kind of immodest apocalyptic charm (if Jesus Christ appears at First Baptist live and in person, this Second Coming will happen in Central, South Carolina, and we are living at the precise localized site of Revelation).

Its ambiguities are necessarily strategic (Eisenberg 1984). You don't have to be a big believer to understand the context of the message, or to see it as directed at you. Because it announces itself with great authority, with unmistakable certainty, on a less than clear day of the soul you might be drawn to it. Recall the Steve Martin film *LA Story* about a Los Angeles fellow who takes direction from a particular sign along the Santa Monica Freeway. Who knows? This sign may be for you, Bud. If evidence of God is regularly found in burning bushes, voices from the sky, inexplicable visions, dreams, ancient artifacts, and sudden awakenings brought on by ethereal knowing, well, why not? Signs have always been read within the context of signs relevant to their times, and certainly today street advertisements fit that criterion. So, in a way, the ambiguity here works *for* the preferred reading, pulling in the boundaries of interpretive possibilities toward a historical and material subtext—to what happens invisibly in the reading, to what happens between the lines—that demands, albeit quietly, to be held accountable to certain truths.

And only to those truths. We travel so far out only to return so far back again.

Read this oppositional way, this postmodern sign becomes an invitation to enter the world of Otherness. It inverts the figure and ground of the myth of Power by narratively privileging what has been marginalized by the intentional text, by rendering the popular, the rock n roll, the celebrity Jesus culturally equivalent to the "high" culture seriousness and authority of Revelation. The postmodern oppositional reading of this sign thereby plays the Fool in the Kingdom of God, speaking Other truths, turning the right-side-up world of organized religion upside down and a little backwards.

But there are other possibilities in between the lines of this public scripture. Let's assume you are *not* a "believer," but more of a "backslider," as the Baptist culture puts it. Part of the coded subtext you could bring to the reading is the perception of the age-old semiveiled Christian threat: If you are not a certified saved person seated in church on Sunday when Jesus Christ returns to fulfill the prophecy, chances are very good that your personal eternity will be spent burning in Motel Hell. If you read critical theory via latter-day Marxists, this loud advertisement for a church service dresses up the Second Coming as little more than another consumable commodity, yet another experience to be purchased through routinized participation in a ritual ceremony, the precise value of the spiritual experience being roughly equivalent to the capital value of the offering dropped in the gold plate during the inspirational hymn. Hey mister, where's the T-shirt and coffee-mug shop, huh? More opiate for the masses. More reasons *not* to believe. Or at least not to believe in this version of faith, in this imagined construction of the Testaments, and of God.

There is at least one more interpretive possibility: Playing off the true superstar appeal of the death-into-life chapter of the Jesus Christ legend, this "appearance" may be a spiritual metaphor working culturally off of a rock nostalgia legend. Like the well-documented "appearances" of dead Elvis (Marcus 1990), this Advent indeed may be confined to the deeply desiring hearts and love-me-tender, love-me-true minds of the contextually faithful. But even within the lines of this interpretation lies the possibility that Elvis and Jesus might, in fact, be connected. Jesus Christ, Superstar. What if those who believe in Elvis—or for that matter, those who believe in Jesus—are exactly *right*? Or this: What if their individual communities of exact rightness are—unbeknownst to them—deeply, *spiritually*, connected?

Of course, this whole business of Jesus, of God, of Elvis, and indeed of interpretation, may be *hokum*. That too is a way of finding meaning(lessness) in the sign. A modernist might say instead: give me True Science. Or give me Market Capitalism. Or hey, just give me a fuckin' *job*. At some level, isn't the ability to spend time thinking like this—and to *work* at thinking like this—about possible connections between a church sign on the side of the road and matters of great importance, evidence only of my ability to think like this, of my social status and anxieties about its influences, my own preoccupations with making the world convenient for *my* beliefs? For *my* imagination?

CONTEXTS, OPENINGS, AND DIALOGUES

There is some truth in this counter claim, but not enough truth to carry it very far. I think there *is* more to signs than the words by themselves. "Words by themselves" must be what is meant by the expression "words taken out of context." But isn't to take words out of context also mean *putting them into* another one?

There can be no meaning without context. Yet, contexts aren't fixed and stable. They involve weaving together aspects of lived experience, making connections out of otherwise disconnected phenomena. Contexts are made up—or picked up—as we go along. To define a context is to make an opening where there was, just before, only a space between the words. A context offers, therefore, an opportunity to interpret experiences according to some framework, to some edges on the outerwork of meanings that can be fitted together in a particular way, so that the presence of the edges lends new meaning, new perspective, to what is contained by or within the frame.

I am, of course, already guilty of framing this discussion of context. But how could I not? Meanings, if not construed according to carefully articulated contexts—linguistically, grammatically, and rhetorically—nevertheless *inherit* them. Contexts are the spaces—the imagined spaces—between the lines.

Even if I could walk around believing this isn't so—even if I could walk around believing that a sign is just a sign, that a road is just a way of getting somewhere, that living in one place is pretty much like living

Destination and Arrival

in another, that living with one person is pretty much like living with any other person, and so on—that narrow locked-on flatness of interpretation itself would be possible rhetorically *only* by a grammatical context through and by which those linguistic interpretations, however plain, would be sentenceable. I cannot speak without speaking through the context of my interpretations. You just have to learn to read between the lines to see the complex work of ordinariness.

Here's what I think. To walk around locked on to one context is not to be open to the *imaginative* possibilities of life, which is practically equivalent to walking around dead. Binx Bollings was troubled by the overt presence of the waking, walking dead among us, and so I am. You see them, *everywhere*. These are people who dulled down to nothingness before their clocks ran out, who have nothing to live for and no place to go on account of it. They are Others who cannot imagine themselves otherwise. They may never be rich even if they have money, nor will they be poor without it; they occupy a kind of same even tedious maximum mediumness of existence, content to pass the time as if they were merely passing the salt. They exhibit absence, not presence, and what is most absent is a meaningful connection to living despite the obvious presence of life. In the poet/chef Jim Harrison's (1991) words, "they are not evolving, they are lapsed."

Without imagination—without Spirit—you add nothing to what is already here and feel like Being nothing while you are here. For without imagination, there is no dialogue with history, with religion, with literature, with music, with nature, with each other. And without dialogue, there is no reason to engage persons, places, and things in meaningful, creative ways, because, after all, the meanings of everything are already apparent and creativity is bullshit anyway. By this formula, life is full of meaningless bullshit, then you die.

I don't think so. In the most ordinary of places, in the context of the most ordinary of lives, the work of ordinariness is the work of lives connected by invisible, seemingly anonymous realities appearing, quietly, as simple open spaces between the lines. Here is the site of ordinary openness in the everyday. Which is to say, here is the site of dialogue, an opening for and arrival of Spirit in the everyday.

This dialogue opened by focusing, simply, on a sign, and on signs as contexts for interpretations of meanings, for musings, for reverie in and about the multiplicities available in the ordinary and the everyday. But I have also opened up *dialogues* as Spirit vying for presence in the wisdom and the otherwise of modern and postmodern days. My goal is to bring dialogue clearly into the discussion of what is envisioned, into the work of what is going on. To make that happen requires providing an opening, like the opening provided by the presence of the sign by the side of the road in front of the Welcome Baptist, Cannon Memorial, or First Baptist churches. We make dialogues into contexts by finding something to talk about when the open spaces surrounding what could obviously be said *are not enough anymore*. We make dialogues into contexts when we risk moving beyond the text, through the open spaces, into the extraordinary territories of spiritual connections to and within the everyday.

This, then, is a study of communication and spirituality as dialogue, and it begins with open spaces. Wide, open interpretive spaces. It is a study of everyday ordinariness as a dialogic context rich with interpretive possibilities for creativity, for meaningful connections, for imaginative engagements of the everyday as proper evidence of the Spirit in life. It is a study of openings offered by interpreting the invisible spaces between the lines in ways that render the lines visible and lives of the linemakers meaningful. And it is a study about the engagements of dialogue in the everyday read as resources for spiritual communication.

I admit that this whole study is a work of the imagination. *Intimate* imagination. It is how I understand and invoke Spirit in and on the ordinary, find Spirit dispersed across and into the territories of the everyday for the purpose of making poetic connections to alternative possibilities for Being, which is to say how Spirit communicates to and through us the potential for engaging the extraordinary in ordinary life. So, too, is this spiritual opportunity available to us in human dialogue, wherein angels carry our souls, our words and silences, back and forth between us.

Here we are, certain only of our arrival in Central.

Welcome to the mystery.

2

Boredom and Ecstasy

Everything is such as it is, not such as it is, both such as it is and not such as it is, and neither such as it is nor such as it is not. That is the Buddha's teaching.

—Mulamadhyamakakarika

It is, indeed, [the mystic's] success at just this sort of substantive communication that allows us to speak of, to learn of, and to participate in mystical traditions at all.

—Steven T. Katz

Many men go fishing all of their lives without knowing it is not fish they are after.

—Henry David Thoreau

Placing Central

Central is a place where—the townspeople will tell you—boredom happens. It is a place where boredom happens *regularly*. A modernist might see it as the influence of public architecture on public behavior (Sennett 1978). Admittedly, boredom seems built into the plain design of square buildings, the purposefully straight and mostly narrow streets and roadways bordered by ordinary signs and peopled by ordinary people. Even the grand presence of the downtown stand of old oak, maple, and gum trees—the apparent ecstasy of which in sleepy summer's midafternoon can just as easily be ignored—may be experienced as nothing more than the presence of tall trees, another context for a reading that opens up the imaginative possibilities of Central, of boredom, of ecstasy, and of talk that gets situated here.

MODERN CENTRAL

Modernists are always partially right; they have to be, a lot of America consists of their constructions. Viewed this way, boredom *is*—at least in part—publicly organized by the controls and constraints on public behavior found in the outward details of architectural designs. The absence of Central gathering place—a square, a courthouse, a park—is very unusual in the South and therefore becomes a defining absence here. But the architecture of this town did not evolve from some geographic middle made for public debate and discussion; instead, Central grew linearly along a railway line, and then multiplied itself laterally as main street begat side streets and back streets.

This is a town dominated by signs of working-class status and mill hierarchies, of residential divisions of labor and management, of the pervasive influence of clock time brought about by the proper running of the railroad. Life is measured here in years of work, in years of marriage, in the numbers of children and grandchildren and great-grandchildren, in church membership and days of uninterrupted Sunday school attendance, in physical and hierarchical distances between where one was born and where one ended. There is no local hospital, so birth and death often occurred at home, in local fields, or on local highways, and burial is held on familiar ground in the cemetery beneath the baby blue water tower and wide night sky, just a little elevated over the commerce and industry of Central's main street, where on its very everydayness forever passes by (as seen in this Cannon Memorial Baptist Church sign):

> Trials Are The Soil
> In Which Faith Grows

It is an American working-class town historically peopled by citizens who worked hard for long hours in mills or fields (or both) and then went home too tired for words and too busy for political discussions. It was also peopled by a constant railroad stream of Others who were mostly strangers, strangers who simply said "hello" and "goodbye," had a meal or two, told a story or two, gave a wink or two, and passed on through. Today, casual talk in Central is still housed primarily in restaurants, and is still initiated most often by strangers: they come in to ask directions and end up explaining, sometimes in great and intimate detail, the stories of their lives. But strangers do that. That is part of what makes them strange, a word we make to describe how they interrupt the everyday flow of ordinary consciousness.

Some towns are heavy with voices, others are not. Find yourself in LA, or New York City, or Atlanta, or Chicago (not Salt Lake City, however, which is the quietest big city I've ever experienced), and the streets are

Boredom and Ecstasy

filled with speaking people. Words are spoken, shouted, gasped, mumbled, or groaned; laughter intersperses with sudden bursts of applause; public space silence is either a result of bad weather or very bad intentions. Cities are places where Being is enacted as a verbal state, where the exchange of talk is part of a public evolution toward a larger public consciousness. Maybe talk isn't what makes cities grow, but it certainly does sustain them.

Small towns like this one often exhibit an absence of voice that is virtually deafening. Instead of overhearing someone give someone else a public piece of their mind, the more ordinary experience is one of quietude, of an overriding presence of what may be politely interpreted as "peace of mind," but which is often more indicative of having no opinion at all. When this is the case, as it often is in Central, what I find is a Central state of being all caught up in being Centrally bored. The railroad isn't what it used to be, the mill is shut down, all my friends and children are getting older, and talk of life seems suspended by the social organization of those well-measured deteriorations, dispersals, and endings.

Here is where the modern within us declines because our Centrals do not hold; here is where the visible and mechanical engines of our well-tended, well-ordered lives end up as Kenneth Burke put it "rotten with perfection," decaying anyway from within after a lifetime of outwardly maintaining them. Memories are not enough; like interest income due from a lifetime of investments on less money than it takes these days just to live, they never are. And interest in dreams—like the possibilities suggested by the stories of strangers—seem long ago to have dissipated.

These are the signs of public imagination's thoroughly modern end. Everything that rises up is used up, wears out, then breaks up and eventually falls down. Signs that were once new are now old, bent, pockmarked, gunshot, and red-rusted; they omit pieces of valuable information because the energy to renew or simply complete them is gone:

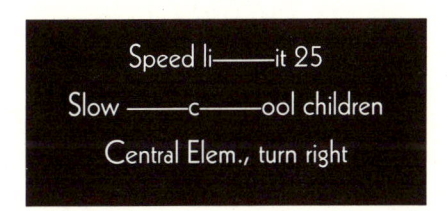

> Speed li———it 25
> Slow ———c———ool children
> Central Elem., turn right

REALITY CENTRAL

This is where a version of Central ends, an opening for boredom to happen regularly.

IMAGINING ZENTRAL

But Central is a many-storied story, and the modern tale is but one way of telling it. It is a way of making sense in a particular way, reading available signs as categorical symbols and the categorical symbols themselves as sums of dominant—and decaying—interests. Against this framing, let us explore—which is to say publicly imagine—an alternative sense-making schema. There are many to select from: Central as the localized site of alienated subcultures of artists, poets, and students; or as lower socioeconomic habitat of sadly undereducated and now disenfranchised workers who face a world they cannot comprehend much less work in; or as the quiet collectivity of elderly who are stuck in a past time and surround themselves purposefully with it; or of the Central Night Court dramas of acknowledging speeding, public drunkenness, family fighting, or lack of child support that cannot be remedied because it should not exist, but must be addressed, somehow; or of the topography of minimum-wage service employees who live mostly happy lives by following the lyrical teachings of popular country songs that also find their way onto local church (Cannon Memorial Baptist) signs:

> You Can't Walk With God
> And Run With the Devil

Viewed this way, Central is a pastiche of cultures, a patchwork crazy quilt of family sagas, an interdependent network of private lives and the social construction of meanings in public space. I could write Central this way—its all out there on view everyday, and ordinary if you imagine it that way—but I am after another kind of public reading. What I want to read lies in between the lines, in and around the silences. Think of this as Central Spirit.

Central as *Zen*tral, or better: Zen trail. I find evidence for this context in absences that if followed to presences, twist what is present a little bit askew. Where I have seen minimal words passed among persons in public places, I am now reminded of Lao-tzu's teaching: "He who knows does not speak; he who speaks does not know." Perhaps the public condition

Boredom and Ecstasy

of silent boredom that I find here actually is a sign of complete understanding of place, perhaps even of the cosmos. The citizens aren't speaking because they don't have to; they already know everything there is to know, speaking about it would only cheapen the general wisdom.

Carried a little further, this presumption of Zentral arrival explains many localized occurrences. One word answers such as "Good," or "Fine," or "No," are not preemptory responses but instead are Master Koans, meaning all of what is, as well as what is not, and therefore are utterances for serious contemplation. So too is the consistent inability among locals to hold conversations with strangers; when viewed from this Zen perspective this is clearly a sign of the stranger's lack of local knowledge as well as of the stranger's lack of learning to accept the presence of what must be taken for granted if the soul is to grow, and of the essential paradox of speaking. Or of the folding into almost every conversation some part of each person's family history; this could be a Zen echo of what Zhaozhou Congshen said: "What a long train of dead bodies follow in the wake of a single person!" And, of course, when the local citizens "go fishing," it is not entirely fish they are going for, which, no matter which perspective you bring to it, is still true.

But this direction for a local reading of public communication is stretching things quite a bit. Central is a mostly Christian—no, deeply Christian—town, a place of churches not meditation centers. If Zen is practiced here, it is probably practiced by accident. This fact doesn't negate Zen possibilities—for a Zen context transcends all religions by welcoming them—merely renders it less locally known, less locally plausible. It is an imaginative punctuation in the everyday, a dream we can learn from, but nevertheless a dream.

Being Public in Central: Grace and Graciousness

To attain public Being in Central—to be "in Central"—is mostly to enter stores and shops, a cafe, video store, post office, police station, or garage. It is to enter public places and ongoing streams of conversation that mix public business with public everydayness six days a week. Why six days a week? The sign next to a local restaurant explains it:

> CLOCK DRIVE-IN
> Always Closed Sundays

Perhaps for this reason—and for reasons that are drawn from a deep history of surface Southern politeness in social contexts—everyday public conversation in Central is almost always cordial without ever quite being friendly. The idea is to give and receive information *gracefully*, and at the same time to use that exchange to figure out who you are in relation to the Other person. Listen to these two sorority pledges at Clemson University as they converse over Diet Cokes at Hardee's in Central:

"Sooooo, let's talk about *you*?"[1]

"Wellll, my Daddy's one of the richest men in the upstate."[2]

"How *nice*...."

"Yes. Well. When I was twelve, my Daddy bought me a fine Thoroughbred racehorse so I could ride across our 5,000 acre farm."

"How *nice*...."

"Yes. And well, when I turned sixteen? My Daddy bought me a brand new red Corvette convertible so I could drive out to our farm from our home in Charleston to ride my fine Thoroughbred racehorse."

"Well? How *nice*...."[3]

"Yes. And well, just last month? Daddy bought me an airplane so I could fly from Clemson to Charleston every weekend, where I left my red Corvette that I can drive to our farm to ride my fine Thoroughbred racehorse."

(Silence, and an icy smile).

---

[1] The habit of inflecting the ends of sentences into questions is not solely a characteristic of Southern women's speech; many studies have demonstrated that women everywhere tend to display this performative style. However, in Southern regional idiom and performance, the power implications are different from other parts of the United States. Rather than reinforcing a "traditional" gendered subordinate role, the question-asking style reinforces the ability of the Southern woman initiating the questioning inflection to be "in charge." It establishes the conversational groundwork for important political and social agendas rather than signaling demur or the presence of personal uncertainties. When two Southern women engage in this style of speaking they are engaged in status combat—through the veil of politeness— over who owns the rights to lead the conversation, as well as who should be entitled to interpret its meanings.

[2] "The upstate" refers to the western region of South Carolina. "my Daddy" is a common reference to one's father; it is capitalized because it is spoken that way.

[3] Notice how the stress—or emphasis—moves backward in each conversational utterance for the listener? This indicates a sense of being "backed into a corner," from which the only way out is likely to be impolite. Watch out!

"Now tell about *you*?"

"Okay. Well, my Daddy's always believed in sending us to the finest schools."

"Is that right?"

"Yes. So I went to the finest boarding school in New England, where I graduated valedictorian of my class. I came to Clemson because this is where my Daddy, and his Daddy before him, came to school."

"And what did you learn in that fine boarding school?"

"Well for one thing, I learned how to say "How *Nice*" instead of "Fuck You. . . . "

So it is in this complex conversational sense that cordiality and politeness mingle with history, circumstance, and power. This exchange of energies and information represents a kind of organizing lesson, not so much about sorority sisters at Clemson (or sorority sisters *anywhere* in the South) but about the contexts for interpreting conversational style in this region: graciousness is laced—embedded—with the politics of class, race, style, and gender.

My colleague Pete Kellett explained this phenomenon to me one day as the historical replacement of "grace"—unconditional acceptance and forgiveness—with the veneer of "graciousness." In a postmodern culture still dominated by modernist inclinations and values for talk, what plays out at the surfaces is a complex intersection of deeper tensions. In a region historically established as a safe place to hold slaves, we now hold each other hostage to the politics of conversations, to exchanges of information that are always seeking socially higher ground. What appears to be "friendly" or gracious is, therefore, often deceptive, a way of seizing power or exerting control. We do this sort of thing when Spirit has been omitted from our lives, when—as Pete Kellett tells it—judgments of graciousness have replaced the communication of grace.

Judgments of status—like beauty—depend on who is doing the judging. Among the sorority pledges the game was played on a conversational terrain of wealth, family, status, and material possessions that was undercut by a crude, if gracious, put-down. What was guilty of being "Up," as Kenneth Burke teaches us, is socially corrected by what is "Down." Among working-class men at a local watering hole, however, status points are attained by the achievement of increasingly gross levels of lowness, to get "Up" by getting as far "Down" as you can, carnivalizing the everyday Order with extraordinary disorder and, when possible, outright chaos.

But deceptive friendliness is only one form of public talk in Central. Another common occurrence is less structured by social conventions of talk than it is by the visual organization of space. For example, strangers can walk down the streets without being noticed, as if—in Clifford Geertz's (1973) expression—you were "wind." If, as a stranger, you *are* noticed, you can be sure to be greeted and then quickly passed by, as if you only existed momentarily in a narrow range controlled by immediate vision. In these times, it is as if the necessity of a public greeting is inflected with a summary judgment of character. But this is probably true almost anywhere. It is a sign, a symptom, of what we obviously lack, which is a public sense of community.

In part, we lack it because we don't make public space for it, and in part we lack it because we cannot imagine ourselves entering the public zone of awareness any other way. Public greeting has become—through unimaginative ritualized practice—our common way of protecting ourselves from the imagined, unwarranted intrusions and judgments of strangers. So it is that in our heads we have the conversations with passersby we deny to—or avoid in—lived experiences, making of public space a merely imagined place, a virtual reality of our very own.

But not all conversations in public space are so empty, even if the general architecture of that space is linear, visually narrow, boring. The common alternative greeting a stranger or local receives in Central is best described as being "instantly friendly"—even instantly intimate—without ever fully passing through cordial or polite. For instance, you can enter the Plez U convenience store and receive happy, animated talk and the details of a stranger's love life in exchange for nothing more than your physical presence. You may be treated like a regular member of the community for whom the Others have singularly been waiting, and the conversation you have joined was, in fact, a long-standing conversation that has been in desperate need of your unique, prescient commentary.

The undercurrent of this kind of public talk is usually humorous, probably because any statement or question that can be interpreted humorously opens up conversational possibilities (particularly for the conversationally adept) and provides multiple openings for response (including the possibility of ignoring the humor, or depreciating its value). Like this:

"Still passin' for uggggly aren't you Jeff?"

"At least I'm passin'; you seem to have failed at risin' up to ugly, James."[4]

(Big shared laughter by both men that you join in)

The ability to "one-up" the put-down is an ancient form of public address, and one that combats boredom and everydayness (as well as points to and reverses the ideological class struggle) in the public sphere. What is spoken, as well as how it is spoken, is of major importance: it constructs our experiences and becomes the stuff of our public actions, our hopes, and our memories. Because I have read a bit in the classics, I can imagine this Central experience as being akin to a marketplace experience in ancient Athens or Rome, where almost everything that was rendered important was rendered important in public discussions, and where the meanings within the utterances were contextually complex.

So what *is* going on here? What is *really* being done—being rendered important—in these otherwise "ordinary" exchanges of talk? By simply imagining this curious analogy to ancient texts, and by making historical, communicative connections, what emerges for me are interpretive possibilities that set up the ethnographic agenda for this otherwise boring day in Central.

Yes, indeed, this is a modern boring place where ordinary conversations vitiate between graciously deceptive and overly friendly, and where status seeking and one-upmanship seems to dominate the surfaces of what gets talked about and exchanged. But this only underscores the ob-

---

[4] There is much that could be said about this exchange. One underappreciated and yet common form of address in the rural South is a negative tone or use of negative terms for otherwise complimentary statements, and vice versa. For example, you might encounter "you sure look elegant this morning" when you appear in public unshaven and clothed in rags, much in the same way as James is using "ugly" here to stand for a certain pleasure in seeing Jeff appear handsomely dressed. Contextually these utterances are understood to mean their opposites, or to point to meanings other than those presented in the talk. In James C. Scott's *Domination and the Arts of Resistance* (1990), the author points out that subordinated peoples typically use "ideological negation" as a form of resistance to whatever may be perceived by the dominant group to be "proper." In this case, the dominant group is an imagined presence and partner to working-class dialogue. Similarly, Richard Sennett and Jonathan Cobb (1972) argue that "public injury to one's dignity and standing as a person . . . is at the very center of class experience for American workers" (quoted in Scott, 112). To body forth "indignity" is to take an "off-stage performance of resistance" to center stage, thus placing—and culturally inverting the meaning of—the source of perceived ideological injustice in the public sphere while at the same time exerting control over it.

vious in the everyday. It fails to read these signs of public boredom as opportunities for engaging something more or something else, as signs of possibilities that emerge from, yet transcend, the ordinary. It is to confuse how "boring" gets done with what boredom means, which is to say, what Spirit arising through boredom prepares us *for* or is leading us *into*.

A different Zen, again.

Risking Boredom and Being Held in Suspense

Two friends visiting us shortly after we moved to Central agreed: "This is a nice, quiet, lush place, but don't you worry about being *bored*?" I replied, "In boredom is *opportunity*," a saying that caught even me by surprise, but through which I reached an awareness. I knew publicly at that moment something I'd always known privately, that I've always found that in those rare moments when nothing seems to be happening around me, and I am, in fact, feeling like the numb zero-sum of all the surrounding nothings, my experience is always one of suspense: *something is about to happen*. In this way, boredom sets the everyday stage for risky business.

I was happy, years later, to see my suspicions about the interpretation of boredom confirmed. Adam Phillips links the interpretation of boredom to the ultimate suspense, a feeling that protects us "from the impossible experience of waiting for something without knowing what it could be . . . [and, as such, represents a] diffuse restlessness, which contains that most absurd wish . . . the wish for a desire, [a state] in which hope is being secretly negotiated" (1993, 9).

Phillips, a child psychologist, argues that the key to understanding boredom is in our need for "being held"; in this case, being held in a suspended state of consciousness that is closely analogous to the moment before we surrender control, to the symbolic edge of letting oneself go—with the flow (absence of self-control), into the night (absence of self-involvement), into the arms of a lover (absence of self-sufficiency). In each case, the experience of boredom ("being held") balances a deep, risky desire for something to happen (the risk itself balances "going somewhere new" with the fear that in the getting there we risk "being dropped") with worry about doing violence to that risky desire (the delicate balance between the hope of realizing our desires if we take the risk and the corresponding fear that nothing, in fact, might happen if we do take the risk, and certainly will happen if we don't).

In these ways, the experience of boredom is similar to the experiences of initial kissing, being suddenly tickled, or—more primally—floating on water for the very first time. In each case, we are actively giving up the delusion that we are entirely self-sufficient—that we need to be always in control—and in general, that we are solipsistically concerned about ourselves. In each case, we learn "the pleasures of carelessness" that come from getting involved with someone else, from connecting our lives to the lives of Others—the places that Others live in, through, and within.

Viewed broadly, boredom may be a wellspring for community when communication is instrumentally and expressively linked to it. For example, the ability to alleviate boredom by telling stories creates experiential and symbolic commonplaces for audiences and speakers, which in turn serves as the bases for building lives that rely on each other. Ironically, for a self born to be self-sufficient, learning to rely on Others teaches us also to *worry* about each other and to worry about what might happen to ourselves as a result of *not* worrying about each other.

Boredom, it seems, reveals itself to be closely aligned with worry. When we worry, Phillips argues, we are busy stifling a dream, overcontrolling it, forcing what might happen into scenarios where we protect ourselves from the dream actually happening to us. He writes: "All of us may be surrealists in our dreams, but in our worries we are incorrigibly bourgeois" (23). So it is that when we lie awake at night worrying, "there may be a dream we are trying not to have" (24).

Why do we do this violence to ourselves? Why do we invite—indeed, *risk*—our desires only to worry about them? Phillips believes that boredom forces us to recognize that we must go outside of ourselves to grow, that we must learn to rely on what is mysterious, independent, separate, and potentially threatening to make our lives richer and more interesting. To surrender control is to surrender to the mystery of what it means to be alive, but to *worry* about what happens if and when we do surrender is to pay a personal penance to the fact that in addition to simply being alive, we may also be compelled *to live*. This is, I think, another important clue to how and why we "do" boredom as we do, and to what larger contextual meaning the lived experience of boredom serves.

Boredom sets free the imagination, the capacity for wonder, for possibility, for creativity, for freedom. It encourages us to live outside of ourselves, to engage Others, to make relationships more interesting and communities more satisfying. All the imagined directional arrows in the experience of boredom point outward, toward purposes that require speech, passions, and actions to be directed *toward*, which is to say relational and communal accomplishments. *To live* is to take the "here and now" *out there*, to bring what can be imagined as satisfying, as intriguing, as purposeful into a public space.

Spirit lives in possibilities. An awareness of Spirit tranforms ordinary boredom into extraordinary ecstasies.[5] When this happens, everyday highways and surrounds shimmer and glisten, there is a sense of our soul's movement simultaneously out of our own and into a new, older consciousness, a consciousness that connects what *seems* real with what *is* Real, with what has always been Real. Conversations move away from phatic exercises and become genuine dialogues in which the work is not in making words but in maintaining the surrender. Rather than concerning ourselves with Power, with gracious deception and status seeking, we seek instead awareness, arrival, insight, mutual growth, and intimacy. We recognize the quest *is* the destination, and understand that the sooner we have arrived at that recognition, the further we still have to go. Welcomed into the mystery of Spirit, we now *surrender* to it.

Surprisingly, when this happens, we find that what we have learned takes us back—this time differently—into the everyday.

Tracks and Possibilities

Central was christened because it exists exactly midway between Charlotte and Atlanta on what is now the Amtrak railway line (Allen 1973). Here is how it happened:

---

[5] In a pioneering work on the epistemology of ecstasy, Andrew Greeley (1974) writes: "Most social scientists are unwilling to take mystics at their own words. The psychotherapist says the ecstatic has experienced something 'rather like schizophrenia'; the Esalen psychologist says the mystic has been through a 'feeling state of heightened consciousness.' Such categorizing doubtless helps researchers to organize their work; however, in doing so they are paying little heed to what the mystic says happened. According to him, the experience is more one of knowing than of feeling. . . . [H]e knows something others do not know and that he did not know before. He sees, he *understands*, he *perceives*, he *comprehends*" (4).

Boredom and Ecstasy

> The town of Central had its real beginning with the advent of the Atlanta and Richmond Air-Line Company through Pickens County, September 28, 1873. It was on that date, according to a memorandum from Assistant Vice President William F. Geeslin, Public Relations and Advertising, Southern Railway System, Washington, D.C., that the connecting link in the line extending north from Atlanta and south from Charlotte through Central was completed and opened for operation.
>
> Since the village of Center was midway between Atlanta and Charlotte, about 133 miles each way, the Railway Company decided to set up its shops here and the place was called Central. Thus a town was born. (26)

If you consider how central the railroad was to the economic and social development of rural life in the American South in relation to how tertiary and nostalgic it seems now, you grasp one way to measure transformation and change as it happens to a small town. Where once the railroad prospered and shops, a hotel, a mill, a gin, churches, townspeople, visitors, and a way of life grew up prospering around it, now there are simply tracks that occasionally interrupt our passage from one town to the next, one experience to the next. In 1918 the state completed a dual underpass so that farmers en route to the Mill would not be unnecessarily delayed by passing trains. You can imagine how vital that legislation seemed then, against which how antiquated it would seem today. *Mills? Farms? Trains?* Language from another era, but still relevant to Central. Traces of its influences run deep in the blood, conversation, and culture as the evolutionary passage of this railroad way of life moves from empirical to peripheral realities.

Railroad tracks. Railroad tracks called the "Air-Line," a name chosen to reference the cushioned ride of its cars but also, from this vantage, a kind of ironic symbolic anticipation of a technology that would ultimately replace it. From Central to Anywhere, USA. Imagine the possibilities. How many family stories involve these tracks? How many people arrived here on them because they had come to the end of something in their lives, and here was the place to start over again? How many citizens were carried here by them to work the rest of their lives on them, or brought here to provide human fuel for the local industrial or agricultural machines that relied on them, or that used the very idea of them to dream of escaping into lives they weren't leading, or of escaping from the invisible real embrace of the lives they imagined they were doomed to lead? Or how about those persons whose numbers are never really known, but who contemplated the infinite possibilities suggested by the finite destinations of these tracks, who perhaps did so many, many times in their lives—probably most often late at night after the last long train whistle blew—only to find, perhaps because of that whistle and all it suggested, just enough of a reason, just enough of a dream, to stay here?

This is a poetics of railroad possibilities, admittedly shaped by absence as much as by presence. Its contours accord more to fragments of old movies and remembered conversations than to actual observation of lived experiences, because the past I want to evoke is one I never lived in except this way, a past that is for me, and for these citizens, at least as imagined as it is real.

Every September, over the Labor Day Weekend, Central is host to a communal celebration of railroads. This celebration is, in fact, purportedly one of the largest celebrations and displays of miniature trains in the United States. The diminutive status of the models somehow becomes one with metaphor. Men and women sporting engineer's outfits and caps converse about old trains, train experiences, and so forth, well into each night. Square dancing and the sale of hot dogs and soft drinks make the streets come alive, become a public space in which and through which dreams, histories, and citizens pass and intermingle, lives interact, connect, and become a center of shared activities that do not so much rely on shared meanings as they rely on the sharing of this experience, this weekend, this soon-to-be memory that itself will inevitably fade into a past, this past that will itself pass into its own unutterable afterlife. Boredom figures into this imagining as a rule figures into understanding the how of the known calculus for an available space.

Examined this way, noticing boredom is a lot like noticing the weather. Consider boredom as a cultural analog to what shapes the experiential context of summer's steamy heat—day after day of mid-90s temperatures accompanied by 90 percent humidity—or in the alternative contexts offered by the long cool rains of autumn and winter and spring. Weather. Or this way: Whether . . . ? Either way there is a connection between the atmosphere we imagine we live through daily and that which we become, that we enter, on account of it. The weather provides a context for interpretations of one's life, the meanings of it, the possibilities for it, what is absent in it and around it, what cannot be realized. Boredom, here in

Central, confronts the possibilities of the "whethering" as well as the "weathering" of these railroad tracks.

Boredom with Paradise

Boredom is not always alleviated by talk, any more than it is always the stage from which dreams of life are imaginatively born. Boredom can be enhanced by ritualized forms of talk, particularly those ritualized forms of talk that are so ritualized as to underscore the boredom that comes from putting up with them. Again, consider the inherent boredom that comes from participating in ordinary phatic communion, a ritualized form of address that substitutes cliches of recognition for displays of intelligence, and that daily diminishes the enlightening and transformative powers of public and private communication. Consider how many of these so-called ordinary conversations you have every day, ordinary conversations that go something like this:

"Hello, how are you?"

"Hi. I'm fine. And you?"

"Aw, pretty good. What's going on?"

"Same old same old. And you?"

"Yeah, me too."

[Long, somewhat awkward pause here]

"Well, we should get together sometime."

"Yeah, let's do that."

"Right."

"Right."

"Well, I gotta run. Shoot, I'm already late!"

"Yeah, me too. Bye."

"Yeah, bye."

Chances are good that this kind of conversation constitutes most of the public and many of the private conversations that you live through and in every day. We are in Central, but in this case a Central of the social imagination. Think of these ordinary conversations as something like the routine presence of railroad tracks in the rural South or as elemental properties of the local weather, together forming an atmosphere as pervasive and fundamental as "the way it is."

You may think of these ordinary conversations as *necessary conversations*, obligations of "being social" for the purpose of demonstrating that you are, in fact, a social being. Or perhaps you think of them as ritualized ways of enacting politeness when you encounter someone you know in the traffic of an otherwise ordinary day. If you ignored them—which you might prefer to do—you would be thought of as a snob, which, probably, if the truth be known, you are. Nevertheless, you may pass off or overlook the significance of this lackluster attempt at conversation as talk that really "doesn't matter," maybe because you know in advance what all parties to it are likely to say and maybe because, truly, what gets said during these episodes doesn't matter to you. These are just some tracks. Given that most conversations of a social nature on a daily basis *are* phatic communions, this means that most of what you say ultimately doesn't matter, at least to you and probably to others. They may be "just some tracks," but they are your tracks, and this is where you live.

If anything, phatic communion is a just another sign of boredom, *social* boredom. Boredom with each other. Boredom with the effort of saying something other than what will pass as socially acceptable, if meaningless, talk. Hey, who can do anything about the weather, huh? Because we are privileged to live in a country that guarantees us the freedom to say anything we want to say to each other, this form of social boredom, when considered within that constitutional context, is a kind of boredom with paradise. Boredom with the weather in paradise. Boredom with the tracks that run through paradise.

> What You Weave In Time
> You Wear In Eternity

Here is a sign (Cannon Memorial Baptist Church) that suggests we take seriously what we do in the everyday, not because of the everyday but because of where everyday actions take us. Read as a sign about the relationship of phatic communion to what our human ability to communicate is ultimately *for* may well be instructive. These regularized, ordinary, ritualized episodes of talk—this daily enactment of social boredom—are *dangerous* to our spiritual health. They are also dangerous to our personal evolution (relying on "old performance scripts," we fail to create new ones), to our capacities for building community (by spending most of our communicative time engaging in talk that "doesn't matter" in the presence of others, we fail to treat others—and public talk—as if they do matter), and to the communicative ideals of democratic society (without citizens who take what they say to each other seriously, the daily opportunities to enact citizenship are materially diminished). Phatic communion is dangerous in the way that ignoring the maintenance of the tracks—but still relying on them to carry the train—is dangerous to the train as well as to the areas the tracks and trains pass through, or dangerous in the way that ignoring the weather—particularly weather warnings about impending storms—is dangerous to those caught up in the storms.

By exchanging relatively meaningless phatic communication for genuine dialogue, we have given in—or maybe just given up—to the *velocity* of postmodern living (Baudrillard 1988). We say so little to each other because we are too busy to say anything else. We are too busy to get elsewhere to pause in the moment of where we are to say meaningful things to people who could be transformed into meaningful beings on account of it. Just too busy. Life is too fast, we're too busy. So we are bored with people because we only talk in boring ways when we are with them. We learn to say: "Sorry, I'd like to stay and talk, but I've got to go . . . " Yeah, *right*. The question is, if you did stay to talk, what would you say?

Again: what would you say?

One of the most dangerous aspects of engaging in phatic communion is that we lose the ability to make talk *inventive*. Creative. Fun. We "just talk." If our talk with others is conceived of as merely a kind of social obligation, our relationships become little more than contexts for obligations to be enacted in. We become, literally, bored with each other. And why not? We have not learned how to take talk—the fundamental building block of any relationship—and make it into the pathway for our mutual and communal quest. Instead, the path is reduced to a set of tracks, tracks of nothing more than overgrown mutual obligations. Tracks disconnected from the weather that envelops them, which is itself disconnected from a perception of how everything—weather, tracks, reality, possibility, talk, life—fits together. Here in Central. Here in Anywhere these lines, these paragraphs, can take you to.

Because phatic communion is dangerous to your communicative abilities, it is deadly to your spiritual health. Spirituality is realized—as well as deepened—through recognizing and expanding meaningful connections to and through each other, not out of avoiding meaningful contact with them. Feeling lonesome? Alienated? Frustrated in your life? Do you spend a lot of time engaged in mostly phatic communions? Perhaps the problem lies with how you *don't* talk to others, how you fail to seek out opportunities for dialogic connections, how you view social interaction as a just another sign of boredom instead of as gifts of speech that we offer to each other to engage our imaginations, to grow, to learn, to evolve, to further life's quests.

I'd rather receive a "How *Nice*" or even an "uggggly" than an "I'm fine, and you?" It would offer an opening, an invitation, a way out of the ordinary and the everyday. It would offer conversational salvation.

Boredom and the Tedium of Self

Phatic communion is a replacement for genuine dialogue because it begs support for a public self that does not wish to risk much but needs, desperately, to be recognized *as* a self. As a *questing* self. Even a *risk-taking* self. Or at least as a self capable enough at being a public self to risk the quest of surface friendliness.

Viewed this way, phatic communion may be understood as self-ish, Power-oriented communication. The goal is simply to be recognized, not to contribute. It is a social safety net, the bottomest of social lines separating the barely alive from the walking dead. In fact, it may be the fear of being treated as if one were dead—death here defined as the distinct social failure to *not* be greeted, to *not* recognize the self as a self in public—that keeps the loosely coupled threads of phatic communion weaving. This is, I think, the newly preferred form of social talk for a species in fear of vanishing, or at least one afraid of being somehow suddenly banished from the thin surfaces of clinical sociability it has retreated to. Phatic communion, read this way, may be a sign of a self in fear of impending victimage—from nuclear holocaust, from economic loss, from personal injury, rape, or violence, from an inability to act in one's own best interests, and so on—a self that feels itself always to be a potential victim.

Thus it is that many people, many selves, live lives between central boredom and border victimage. Good talk, real talk, a genuine exchange of views that actually matters to both parties could help, but this kind of help becomes increasingly impossible if it is not practiced, and practiced daily. To not practice dialogue daily is, I think, a sign of a self bored with itself yet content to be stuck with both itself and the boredom. Well, here we are *again*; might as well say "hi."

"Hi. How you?"

"I fine. You?"

"Fine too."

"Welllllll."

"Uh-huhhhhh."

"Byeeeee."

"See yaaaaaa."

Notice the absence of *verbs* in this performance of selves? Verbs typically connote states of being (here absented) or set up actions (here unsupported). Notice also the minimal wordage. Minimal wordage combined with an absence of verbs and elongated endings suggest selves bored not only with themselves but with each other, selves strung out on virtual emptiness. Yet, in this socially constructed complicity, there is empirical evidence that both parties are unwilling to let go of each other. That the surfaces of this lack of conversation will be repeated many times during an average day suggests a certain longing for something, as I said before, perhaps of the possibility of desire.

But for what?

Walker Percy asks: "Why is it that no other species but man gets bored? Under the circumstances in which a man gets bored, a dog goes to sleep" (1983, 71). Percy defines boredom as "the self being stuffed with itself" (71), and suggests that "the word boredom did not enter the language until the eighteenth century" (70).

The link between the chronicled entry of a term for boredom (which surely must have been experienced prior to that) into the *patois* of everyday life cannot be totally explained. Percy suggests five possibilities:

Question: Why was there no such word before the eighteenth century?

(a) Was it because people were not bored before the eighteenth century? (But wasn't Caligula bored?)

(b) Was it because people were bored but didn't have a word for it?

(c) Was it because people were too busy trying to stay alive to get bored? (But what about the idle English royalty and noblemen?)

(d) Is it because there is a special sense in which for the past two or three hundred years the self has perceived itself as a leftover which cannot be accounted for by its own objective view of the world and that in spite of an ever heightened self-consciousness, increased leisure, ever more access to cultural and recreational facilities, ever more instruction on self-help, self-growth, self-enrichment, the self feels ever more imprisoned in itself—no, worse than imprisoned because a prisoner at least knows he is imprisoned and sets store by the freedom awaiting him and the world to be open, when in fact the self is not and it is not—a state of affairs which has to be called something besides imprisonment—e.g., boredom....

(e) Is it because of a loss of sovereignty in which the self yields up plenary claims to every sector of the world to the respective experts and claimants of those sectors, and that such a surrender leads to an impoverishment which must be called by some other name, e.g., boredom?

(f) Is it because the self first had the means of understanding itself through myth, albeit incorrectly, later understood itself through religion as a creature of God, and now has the means of understanding the Cosmos through positive science but not itself because the self cannot be grasped by positive science, and that therefore the self can perceive itself only as a ghost in a machine? How else can a ghost feel otherwise toward a machine than bored?

(CHECK ONE OR MORE) (1983, 70–71)

Percy connects his question about boredom to a more generalized thesis about the strange absence of understanding of ourselves as humans as measured against all that we know, and all that we can do, out among the stars, lost in the Cosmos. Me, too. I prefer to focus on "human communication" as the primary vehicle for "self-understanding"—a move that, given Percy's other writings, I am convinced he would agree with, although not necessarily endorse—but otherwise the territories of our quests are identical.

Percy wrote in Covington, Louisiana. I write in Central, South Carolina. Aside from that obvious separation—and some other details—we are earthlings, carbon-based symbol-users, bodies burdened with souls, headpieces stuffed with saturated selves. We both seem to rely on where we are, and who we know—and certainly who we talk to—to engage and to enrich our imaginations. Philosopher-writers; he admittedly much better than me.

I suspect Walker Percy must have been bored, too. At least at times. How else could he write so convincingly, so knowingly, of that which he had not himself experienced? I know also, from reading about him, that he was a shy man who valued dialogue, he was an existential Christian and a fatherless son. He held great passion for language as well as deep curiosities about its uses in everyday life.

I would have liked to have spoken with him.

Boredom and Ecstasy

If boredom is a symptom—a sign—of the rapidly vanishing self, accomplished daily through phatic communion and experienced daily as general *ennui*, what is its likely cure?

If the cure for boredom is ineffably rooted in the psychic seat of desire yet bounded by the fear of actually satisfying the desire, how can desire be unbound from the fear that helps evoke it?

What is desire *for*, anyway? Certainly not its experiential accomplishment, for that is what we most fear, and that fear is what keeps us in a state of suspended estrangement from ourselves and from each other. So what can it be that we really want? What can be the vehicle, the way in the everyday, that goes deeper than desire and further than boredom, that avoids phatic communion and engages us in dialogue, that somehow can unify these complex dualities defining reality central?

Broader: is there some way out of the paradoxes and ironies of modernism that does not either condemn us to the eternal victimage of critical theories or crash us headlong, authorless, and fragmented into the aimless seductive high-velocity surfaces of postmodernism? Is there something, some way, some idea capable of connecting the individual self to the collective community that does not require either a colonizing or marginalizing of one over the other? And this: is there some way to experience connectedness, wholeness, communion, community, and cosmos that does not demand adherence to some consciousness guru?

Look to your experiences. What are they teaching you? Where is an opening for Spirit?

The longer I dwell in Central the more I know I seek ecstasy. I *desire* the experience of it. This must mean something. What is my desire for ecstasy about? What is ecstasy about?[6]

An ecstatic experience "transcends duality; it is simultaneously terrifying, hilarious, awe-inspiring, familiar, and bizarre" (McKenna 1991, 59). It is an experience that is, literally, *cosmic*. Terrance McKenna writes: "For a minded and language-using species like ourselves, the experience of ecstasy is not perceived as a simple pleasure but, rather, is incredibly intense and complex. It is tied up with the very nature of ourselves and our reality, our languages, and our imaginings of ourselves" (1991, 59).

Ecstasy is a *communicative* pathway, not an end state. The experience is not to be coveted simply because of how it feels or what it does (although that is generally the first clue that something new is happening to you) but for its questing ability to open doors, to create perceptual and meditative opportunities, to transfer information from one domain or sphere of lived experiences to another. Through the heightened communicative processes of ecstasy, traditional boundaries break down; what is

---

[6] The desire for ecstasy and its relationship to the construction of communities is detailed in Barbara G. Myerhoff's excellent account (1975). She locates ecstatic experiences within the framework of Victor Turner's concept of "communitas" (1974), or antistructure rituals in which "intense, passionate, and totally involving participation" enables an escape from the everyday self; communitas counters "routinized, mild, or mundane" everyday realities and experiences.

In her fascinating comparative study of Huichol Indians at Wirikuta and American youth at Woodstock, Barbara Myerhoff identifies essential and important distinctions in the organization of ecstatic experiences and their likely aftermath. For the Huichol, Wirikuta is a "real place, myth, and symbol" with clearly defined and commonly understood rituals for entry and exit; the experience is designed to be temporary, facilitated by a Shaman, peyote-assisted, and there is no attempt whatsoever to apply the ritual and spiritual bonds at the world they turn "upside down" at Wirikuta to the "right-side up" of everyday realities they must accommodate once they leave this spiritual place and journey home. By contrast, "hippies" at Woodstock attained an ecstatic communal and spiritual experience, but in an unstructured, spontaneous way. Mass ecstasy produced an unsolvable paradox when the participants tried to apply to everyday life what they had learned, and experienced, at Woodstock, a paradox that only deepened when their political and cultural goals for change conflicted with the need to organize for—and accommodate appearances in—everyday cultures.

Myerhoff points out that the lesson of this comparison is large: the trick to organizing experiences for ecstasy is the balancing of the need for order with an available, if temporary, antistructural parallel. (For an extension of this principle in the communication literature, see Eisenberg [1990]).

most often induced are senses of deeply spiritual collective connections, connections between and among persons, between and among persons and things, between and among persons, things, plants, and the cosmos.

McKenna, an ethnobotanist, is an advocate of using plants and drugs to attain access to the ecstatic pathway and has become, in recent years, a sort of guru of hallucinogens. While I do not dispute his testimony, I want to be very clear about two items associated with the term "ecstasy" in relation to McKenna's agenda. First, I do not believe—nor does McKenna—that the drug pathway is the only pathway to these communicative experiences. On the contrary. There are many paths, pysilocibyn (for example) offering perhaps the most dramatic and certainly the quickest route, but not necessarily the most fulfilling. A good imagination and some genuine opportunities for dialogue—for community-making—can bring ecstasies.

Second, the purpose of invoking ecstatic experiences here is to provide an experientially based linguistic channel, or metaphor, through which to re-envision the role of individuals in communication, communication in community, community in spirituality, and spirituality in the cosmos. To do this requires locating ecstatic communication as an experiential possibility or option within the ordinary and often boring terrain of the well-ordered, synchronous, heavily bureaucratized life. Genuine communication, when considered this way, is an alternative reality, often a parallel one to the known borders of the most ordinary, and the most boring, of days.

Think of it this way. Ours is a social terrain that depends largely upon the routinized accomplishment of ritualized surfaces seemingly indigenous to everyday cultural existence (think here of phatic communions). These enacted surfaces take up and largely define the purposes and meanings of our days; furthermore, in the daily enactment and reenactment we take ourselves further away from any alternative readings, or constructions that may challenge the authenticity, the performance, or the purposes of routinized existence—say, in this case, of a meaningful, connected, sacred and questing life. Put differently, the everyday accomplishment of living, while no doubt requiring hard work and great social coordination, serves generally to shape our surface performances as merely behaviorally correct, to distract us from purposes larger than surface social performances, and to render us, therefore, virtually senseless and meaningless. We are fit only for TV. Or workaholism. We don't recognize ecstasy because we have forgotten how to seek it. We ignore Spirit.

To seek it, to find an ecstatic pathway, requires challenging that dominant conception of life. It is to discover that not only is the ecstatic accessible *through* the everyday, but also that ecstatic experience *blurs* taken-for-granted boundaries that linguistically construct and linguistically separate persons from other persons as well as persons from other things. This is what makes ecstasy seem "bizarre"; experiences of worlds come together. However, the point of the blurring, the coming together of worlds, is not simply to tune us in to a world turned around but instead is to provide an opening through experience to alternative uses and nonlinear understandings of language and communication. These uses are taken from the same places as the uses of ordinary everyday experiences, but they are read differently, taken as signs rather than as advertisements, or as rich symbolic worlds rather than as the fanciful footwork of the imagination.

Ecstasy and Communication

Why learn to see persons and things this way? Why bother with ecstasy? Why not keep being medium cool, phatically correct, and TV-narcotized, just let the lines between and among us continue to run metaphorically along the culturally straight and narrow?

One answer: Because you *can*. As the education commercial puts it: the mind is a terrible thing to waste. So is our unique ability to communicate. We have evolved forebrains and communicative performances for purposes larger than the surface ability to tell entertaining hunting stories or engaging in restaurant put-downs. Perhaps we should begin to understand ourselves *through* our relationship to the stories we tell—the stories we can tell—as alternative ways of accessing worlds through communicative experience. *Homo sapiens, homo loquens, homo narrans*— how are these powerful defining capacities related experientially? How does the experiencing of them contribute to human evolution? To evolutions of consciousness? Of Spirit? What are evolving these capacities *for*?

Which brings us to another answer, a good reason for opening ourselves to ecstasies: because we *should*. I am taken lately by a commonly overheard instruction, repeated here as an example of a common expression of *ennui*: Get a life! Other commercially available versions of the same exasperation with the felt limitations of an overly bureaucratized, seemingly meaningless life are abundant but tend to center on the expression of a central complaint: "I have no life." Because I take seriously what people say, this sentence troubles me and yet offers a kind of hope. If more people are dissatisfied with performing the ropes of everyday experiences, if more people are feeling left out of whatever it is they feel life is supposed to offer them, and if more and more people recognize that where they live isn't what they want to be or even very much about who they are, then perhaps this overheard line is an overdue sign, and a sign of hope.

Communication has always been the human being's central tool for ensuring its survival. Communication has always offered us a way out of otherwise seemingly impossible, often otherwise impossible dilemmas: dilemmas of individuality, of community, of progress. At a time when we seem most reliant upon phatic communion for everyday talk, most dependent upon imagined scripts performed for us on TV, and least able to manufacture genuine dialogue as a means of envisioning alternatives, the idea of communication again resurfaces as the natural pathway out of our routinized, boring, even burdensome dilemmas of contemporary, postmodern existence.

Unfortunately, much of the work of this century's communication scholars won't help us. Our work has been primarily aimed at improving understandings and skills for *coping* with everyday life, not *altering* it. In part this is because most of our communication theorizing and research have been, in this century, derived from individual psychological models of interaction and sociological models of community envisioned within empirical and mechanical—not spiritual—views of humans' relation to each other and to the cosmos. Alternative uses for, and understandings of, communication and language in the everyday derived from unities of the sacred rather than from categorical, scientific divisiveness are virtually absent from our professional literatures. What we find in those literatures is the dominance of a desire to use communication in order to shape and control what we call "the rational mind" for a rationalized society that, in turn, we use to shape and control our understandings of, and uses for, *experiences* of the everyday.

We in the discipline of communication, are (as I mentioned in the introduction) sort of like the world of physics before Einstein, Bohr, or Heisenberg. Our most fundamental mechanical assumptions have yet to be challenged. We have yet to seriously question whether the rational world we understand we have constructed *is* the world or merely *a way of controlling what we see in it*. Instead of spending most of our time identifying and classifying what we narrowly call the "components" of (modernist) communication or isolating "findings" that depend on the deadening, soulless assumptions of a rather unimaginative world—the world of what is obvious and ordinary in the everyday—we might want to consider what lies beyond obtainable goals and routinized objectives. We might want to consider what communication can be "about" as well as "for."

We must consider an alternative to inquiry shaped by the interests of Power *or* Other, a way of opening our discourse—and our lives—to the unity of Spirit. In the Big Picture shaped and informed by ultimate purposes, amazing Grace, available ecstasies, imaginative Spirit, and a planetary need for communication capable making better relationships and communities, we must examine our profound sense of Being bored in relation to what we claim to know about that Being. Knowledge is about Power, and this may well be our Central problem. Are we so dedicated to control, to Power, to Self, that we have forgotten the pleasures—the ecstasies—of spiritual surrender?

Have we forgotten who we are out here among the stars?

3

Difference and Possibility

Communication as Quest

> The poet is he who, beneath the named, constantly expected differences, rediscovers the buried kinship between things, the scattered resemblances.
>
> —Michel Foucault

> Zen is the madman yelling: "If you wanta tell me that the stars are not words, then stop calling them stars!"
>
> —Jack Kerouac

I am a student of communication. I pay attention to how signs and symbols are used to construct messages by and for people. I ask questions about the hows and whys of persons' relationships with each other, their work, their families, their communities. I read signs, interpret symbols, conjure and argue meanings. I have come to understand "communication" as how we attempt to balance the constraints of secular forms—alphabets, grammars, rules, laws, borders, boundaries, and purposefulness—with our seemingly innate human desire for personal meaning, for creativity, for poetry in the manifestations of purpose. In terms of the work of my life this is my central mystery, the path along which evolves my journey, ultimately, my quest.

Part of my life has been dedicated to the formal, disciplined study of communication. Viewed this way, I have learned that communication is largely conceived of and practiced as a modernist invention,[1] as a way of celebrating speech, symbols, and signs as *influence*, as instruments of Power, as strategic ways of gaining control over Others and nature. I have

---

[1] The roots of modern Western rhetoric are generally attributed to Enlightenment philosopher-theologians such as George Campbell and Bishop Whately. However, these authors begin their treatises on rhetoric with Renaissance-like rereadings of the classic works from Greek and Roman cultures, specifically Plato, Aristotle, Cicero, and Quintilian. Given this lineage, "modern" rhetoric is both closely aligned with Western *rational* tradition and with the relationship of rhetorics of influence to politics of control.

also learned that this way of approaching communication is partial and problematic. For these reasons, the modern story about communication has been challenged by another account, another formal way of conceiving, or imagining, what "communication" is, how it works, why it works. This is the postmodern tale, and although it is composed largely in fragments, what "the postmodern" sums up as a social and aesthetic movement in the field of communication recovers a lot of what has been left out by the politics of modern suasive discourse. But the postmodern does so principally by mimicking—through oppositional tactics—precisely the best lessons of rhetorical influence found in modern political strategies of domination and control.[2] So it is that at the end of the twentieth century we have two large, competing narratives about "communication," each one offering partial and problematic accounts, each one vying for Power within our disciplines. Put a little differently, I have acquired the lessons of modern and postmodern influences, and both have helped me to appreciate how Spirit is victimized by the struggle, victimized by our traditional academic preoccupation of using communication to practice the politics of knowledge *about* communication and about what gets "counted" *as* communication.

Zen masters teach that knowledge as a language construction is a fool's paradise. Knowing is not knowing; the idea is to move beyond the uses and gratifications of words "to experience each moment without qualification" (Nisker 1990, 51). This statement rendered in this context is itself a paradox: "We now have *more* words about what is *beyond* words" (Nisker 51; emphases mine). Like the Zen realization of Kerouac's madman, part of our experience *is* words, and words about words, and words about the words about words. The difference should be not manifest in wordlessness but—as Spirit teaches us—in a certain *playfulness* about words capable of opening up possibilities.

I am also a student of contexts, an intellectual commitment that encourages me to read the meanings of words as communicative resources for what Clifford Geertz calls "local knowledge" (1983). This is a spiritual, as well as a political, problematic because local knowledge is always an intimately complex and contested social construction—from fool's paradise to serious argument to the playful interventions of Spirit—in-

---

[2] As Socrates demonstrates in the dialogue *Gorgias*, the summary effect is that one has to use rhetoric to defeat rhetoric.

Difference and Possibility

tersections for the dispersal of, and dialogue among, cultural values. Two semioticians, Robert Hodge and Gunther Kress (1988), provide the following instructive passage: "The site in which a text occurs typically contains instructions as to how it should be read and what meanings should be found in it. . . . Settings exert a coercive force on the meanings that can be produced or received within them. In practice, what happens is that specific categories of settings are socially classified as domains, sites where the specific meanings of specific groups can be expected to prevail" (68).

Read *politically* this semiotic statement states the obvious to anyone currently involved in the study of communication. It suggests that different social groups and situated individuals interpret the meanings of signs and symbols differently. The statement implies that signs and symbols created by dominant groups tend to organize public space for intentional, coordinated readings; it also says that when subordinated groups and individuals confront these signs and symbols—these hegemonic occupiers of what they perceive as *their* public space—members of these groups tend to perform readings that work *against* those dominant intentions. As Michel DeCerteau (1984) teaches us, marginalized groups use tactics to counter the hegemonic strategies of power elites; they "poach" a space for their own constructions of meaning by occupying (and inverting the intended meanings for) otherwise controlled public place. Here is where context becomes part and parcel of the modern/postmodern struggle over influence, and the ends of influence.

Read *spiritually*, all of the above is still true but a good bit askew. The quoted statement's obviousness encourages a far more radical commentary on our thinking about what "counts" as "local knowledge" within any community. After all, it is one thing to say that public space is "contested," but it is quite another to admit that part of what is being contested calls into serious question the whole meaning of context and interpretation as it is constituted by the community "regulars," in this case academic communicologists and citizens of Central. Similarly, it is one thing to suggest that marginalized and oppressed groups use their occupations and interpretations of public space tactically, but it is quite another to suggest that the ultimate purpose of that struggle may be to invite us *out of* that ceaseless polemic. Taken together, these two statements provide something else as well: an opening to imagine a pathway to reading signs and symbols—and to interpreting their meanings—that repositions communication as something other than an exchange of ordinary, everyday, secularized political performances, as the mere interchange of influence.

This may seem a somewhat heady introduction to a chapter about the semiotic organization of difference and possibility in Central. But I believe this explanatory lead-in and initial critique is necessary for two reasons. First, the conscious display and multiple interpretations of messages in any community are important pathways into its social imagination. That these signs and symbols *are* contested—that they offer radical maps of misreading as well as support what often passes among members of the dominant power elite for "common sense" interpretations—helps us to understand operational dualities that define not only power structures but also interpretive possibilities within a particular community. Second, when a community's public space is organized predominantly by signs sponsored by dominant religions and for-profit businesses—as Central is—oppositional readings suggest more than the presence of influential differences or the need for a critical stance on influence; they also ask questions about how these differences shape interpretive possibilities that may themselves be understood as quests for meaning, and for meaning that seriously alters what we think the work of communication "does" in the larger scheme of things.

Thus far I have maintained that a spirituality of communication operates as an interpretive framework the imagination visits upon lived experience through particular constructions of possible meanings found in and made for everyday communication. Hence, the "work" of "ordinary" talk—and its dominant form of public address, phatic communion—functions to secularize and otherwise downplay extraordinary or ecstatic forms of communication, experiences that use imaginative communication to mediate entry into a "higher" consciousness. Against those forms of commonly accepted conversational and organizational practices that coalesce to produce a kind of power struggle of public and private discourse, Spirit—working through the imagination—offers radical alternatives: genuine dialogue (including prayer, lovemaking, an open and free exchange of views, and meditation), creativity in relationships, expanded awareness of our communities and environments, teachings designed to promote insight and wonder, lessons that embrace extraordinary, holistic unities of Spirit and cosmos.

What is known and taught about communication is primarily the cul-

Difference and Possibility

tural territory of an academic power elite. This power elite consists of well-intentioned humanists and social scientists for whom "purpose" is textually reduced to pragmatic secular, gender, political, and material ends. It is a discourse community for whom the idea of "messages" constitutes mostly an empirical and theoretical center from which ordinary articulations of meanings and behaviors—meanings and behaviors within which are embedded cultural (rather than spiritual) codes—are researched, admitted into our scholarly literatures, and endorsed for pedagogical practice. Oppositional stances are encouraged insofar as they are *complicit* with the rules of Order; hence, postmodernists are admitted into the Game but doubted, and thus must "prove themselves" by rigorous exchanges of argumentation and debate, the very rational paradigm they seek to challenge. In the end we learn a great deal about influence and ego, advance our careers, and are deflected from the larger questions because the world we construct doesn't endorse them.

To advocate—as I am—an alternative approach to communication purposes, meanings, and behaviors not only incurs the responsibility to show what such an approach might yield, it also incurs an engagement with the struggle it seeks to transcend. There is no known formula for this sort of move into and yet against the constructions of influence on understandings. I cannot simply organize my research and writing according to known procedures. What I think I must do is to show what I am thinking when I am aware of where my imagination has been. In this way, I am making a text of possibilities and finding the lessons of experience in the materials of everyday life—the "signs," writ large—that evoke Spirit possibilities *when those possibilities feel like what it is that you should know,* senses of what lies beyond the senses that organize meanings beyond words yet through them.

Let's begin with two interrelated questions: What would a "communication study" of dominant signs and spiritual readings in Central look like? What implications might that kind of study have for communication theory, practice, and pedagogy?

Central Signs and Signs of What Is Central: Semiotics and Contexts of Interpretation

Consider the signs I see on the way to Clemson, passing through Central, from my home just outside of Six Mile. Turning right out of Issaqueena

Farms, I travel down a common rural highway that somedays invites me to experience this surround as much more than that.[3] To my left and right are scattered middle- and lower-middle-class country homes and occasional small businesses (Fresh Blueberries). The first sign I encounter is on a brick billboard in front of the all-brick Camp Creek Baptist Church:

> Life is Not a Rehearsal

This sign is interesting because it seems to work both for and against Christian beliefs. Read within the context of Jesus of Nazareth's teachings about one's reward for living the good life being a heavenly afterlife, this sign seems to suggest that either the afterlife doesn't really exist or that this life isn't a preparatory stage for it.

The curious paradoxes of this sign blend contextually into the surrounding physical countryside. Through them I find I notice the odd angles and bright colors of homemade houses and mobile homes (instead of the fine land or remarkable adaptability of all that has built here), the curious decay of relatively new cars (instead of the well-maintained older ones). I am also reminded at the end of this reverie of my most recent convenience store experiences with Norrisites whose patterns of speech were as confusing as these signs and noticings. They phatically communed a shared wariness that carried just beneath the slurred surfaces of half-hearted talk a "life sucks and you're in my way" attitude of opposition to all the forces of oppression that daily remind them only too callously of exactly who they are, an attitude that locks them just as exactly into a shared complicity with where they are. Even their acts of spoken kindness are bothered, overburdened, grudgingly uttered through a hard-edged vocal nastiness that destroys its own gift at the very moment of its giving. It is ordinary, everyday speech, the inherited result not only of sore economic circumstances and a failed system of public education,

---

[3] By this I mean I open myself to the full experiential mix of sensory possibilities, not just those offered by my eyes or my ears. For example, I have learned to distinguish the azure smell of dense ozone in the summer rain before a front moves in with the red clay presence that I breathe during the same circumstances in late autumn. I can also recognize fine distinctions among varieties of air as it brushes against my skin, each one alerting my body to further reaches of nature and my centeredness in it, from the seductive blue lightness of a cloudless daytime where drift—not purpose—is the real point of imagining, to the deep red focused mysteries of dusk when dusk itself requires total surrender, and the surrender itself envelopes an awareness of infinite boundless connection to the fields of nature, the reach of trees, the recognition that my soul, too, is fully at home out here among the stars.

Difference and Possibility

but moreover of an unfortunate cultural belief that *this is* all there is. Here is the flip side of the dominant narrative about the empirical nature of reality and the role of communication in it, the social construction of a dangerously unimaginative underside of our culture, of our world.

I continue driving down a mile-long hill past more homes that rise up on either side like sentries to meaning, one with a rusted '55 Chevy in a run-down frame garage dangerously close to the road, another with a swimming pool larger than the house, which itself overlooks a dark pond. To the left now is what is ironically referred to as "Cateechee Beach," a county dump next to a low river, a place where a dirt road drops you into potholes the size of meteor craters and a sign posted at the end reads: *No Way Out.*

I drive by this off-road opportunity, cross the river bridge, and head up the steep hill past the water treatment plant. I am in Cateechee proper, another tiny dot on the local map that never quite makes it to an *Atlas*, a dwelling place organized as a mill village on the county road to Norris, a bit larger place that shares the same ignominious unmapped fate. I've never ventured out of my car here, not only because there doesn't seem to be a good reason to but also because there are some places that—if you've been ethnographically around as long as I have—silently announce themselves as wanting no part of me or my business, as if there is a sign visible only to my wary extra-sense that reads: *Off Limits.* There is a broken-down gray barn with a sign for used furniture, then the Cateechee Cafe—a dark little concrete block place that seems to change owners regularly at the end of every third month—and another large brick Baptist church on the right that doesn't sponsor a road sign, which is very unusual but entirely fitting within the other absences that sum up the numb feeling of this place. Up the road a little further, past a very nice pasture and field of well-tended horses, is a sign fallen from a tree several summers ago, never yet resurrected. It rests half covered with brush, horse manure, and kudzu in an abandoned field next to nothing much on either side; the sign says, "Future Site of Cateechee Park." Uh-Huh. To the right is a sign for the elementary school that reads: "Central Elem." and points down another county road. In my darker moments I wonder if the abbreviation of that sign reveals a deeper cultural truth: elementary school (or for that matter, any school) *eliminates* all possibility of imagination. This thought stays with me longer than I want it to but disappears as I cross the railroad tracks and enter Norris.

REALITY CENTRAL

Norris is known to me only as Norris. Unlike the welcoming signs that mark entrance to Six Mile ("An Old Town of New Ideas"), or Central ("Home of Central Wesleyan College" and a list of civic clubs and churches), or Clemson ("Home of Clemson University"), or even the self-congratulatory, beauty-contestant-sponsoring Liberty ("Home of Miss South Carolina 1986, 1987, 1990"), Norris announces its name and that's all. Poor people often do that too, as in, "I'm Norris." Not even a "hello." I turn right at the BP gas station and head on to Central, passing a post office, two "family-style" restaurants, an evangelical temple that also is a floor-covering business. Sometimes, even when things are obviously *not* what they seem, they *aren't even not* what they seem.

Hidden behind a long row of very tall, very handsome pine trees is the pristine campus of Central Wesleyan College. According to the history provided by Mattie May Morgan Allen (1973), Central Wesleyan was organized as a grade and missionary education school and has a fine music department. Graduates of this institution are described this way: "Central Wesleyan's sons and daughters are teachers, ministers, and missionaries, both in the States and foreign fields" (64). I do not enter the campus proper on this day, but I have been there before. The students look like they are fully prepared to enter the world imagined in Mrs. Allen's statement.

THE INVITATIONS OF SIGNAGE

Central proper sponsors many signs that coalesce to produce a coalition of Fundamentalist Christianity mixed with Republican Common Sense, a state of Being driven by Guilt, laced with Fear, and framed by Capitalism. Here are a few examples I've collected over the months I've been here:

| Worry is interest due in advance of trouble. | If you were arrested for being a Christian, would there be enough evidence to convict you? | If your Christianity won't take you to Church, Will it take you to Heaven? |

80

Difference and Possibility

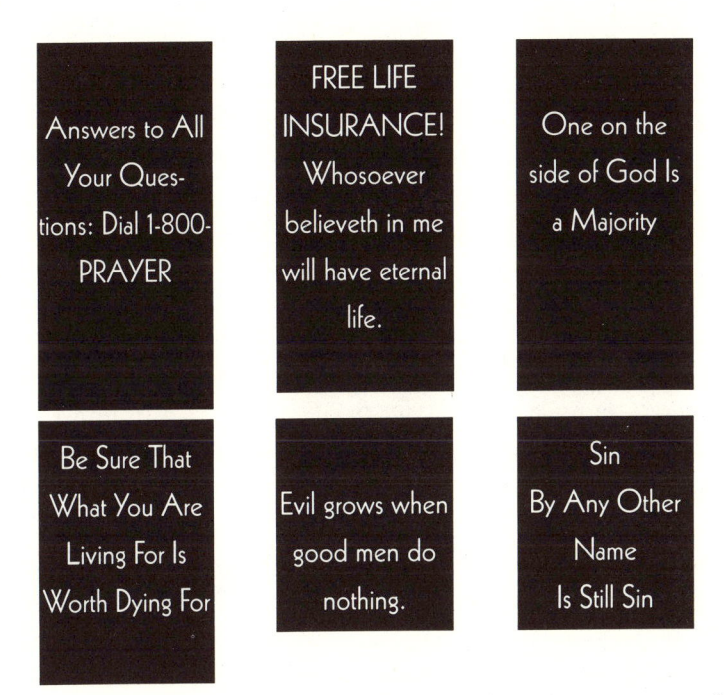

Answers to All Your Questions: Dial 1-800-PRAYER	FREE LIFE INSURANCE! Whosoever believeth in me will have eternal life.	One on the side of God Is a Majority
Be Sure That What You Are Living For Is Worth Dying For	Evil grows when good men do nothing.	Sin By Any Other Name Is Still Sin

    I like to pay close attention to signs, to the imaginative work—through interpretive possibilities—of states of Being and directions within communities. Maybe this "preoccupation" (Burke 1989) with signs arises out of my own boredom; maybe it is just me being an ordinary college professor brainwashed by his reading in communication, semiotics, and cultural studies. Or worse: Maybe it is just the sorrowful existential bleating of a middle-aged, middle-class, boom-generation white boy searching for what may be spiritual experience *anywhere* outside of proper, dutiful religion, wherein one must learn to accept dogma and bow to authority, tithe, and agree to participate in every (for Christians) Sunday morning and (for most Protestants) Wednesday night. At any rate, paying attention to details and entailments of signs seems these days to be my peculiar—if oppositional—calling.

    Or perhaps signs serve as clues to something because in this age of consumer capitalism and hypermarketing, most of us learn early on to eyeball them for great deals, smart shopping, or for the vague idea that if we are good enough and pay enough attention to the right signs, that somewhere, somehow, someone will offer us a bargain on precisely that item—or that dream—we most dearly covet. Here—on State Road 93 in Central—is signage advertising a real steal of a deal on a Sears lawn tractor; here is another one for a discount on a Sunbeam gas grille; over there is yet another one for leasing a new Lincoln; yesterday I saw one occupying the same cultural space that announced a dream trip to Jamaica. Into this corporate mix, over there in front of the Cannon Memorial Baptist Church of Central, is one now promising me safe passage to a place called Heaven for nothing more than the price of that dutiful prayer.

So much about these commercial and Christian signs is constructed out of the same rhetorical stuff. Their appeal is a buy-in to something we otherwise can't afford or don't know enough about or are afraid we simply cannot live (eternally or materially) without. They offer a better life, or at least promise a way to make the life we lead a little bit easier. They all offer resources for personal fulfillment, pleasure, and happiness. Sometimes they are true, prices are reduced, but they never tell the whole truth, such as what it *really* "costs" you. They are signs of difference that are supposed to make a difference in our lives. And sometimes they do. All that is really required is communicative entry into the imagined world they create and sponsor.

Signs compete with other signs for our attention, for our time, and for our dollars. Should I work overtime on Sunday to afford the new car or go to church to save my soul? Do I dare bet on which ad offers more of the whole truth, or at least offers the truer promise: a cheap trip to Jamaica or a passage to a place called Heaven? Because they compete with each other—often brutally—and because they offer resources for happiness that may or may not be true, that may or may not work as advertised, or that may cost us more in the long run, we consumers have upped the ante on what a "good sign" should or must do, what a "great sign" should induce in us, and even how signage in general should conduct or behave itself in public. In our culture, we have taken the potential influence of signs so seriously that we have made *laws* about them. Truly, you can go to prison for putting up a "bad sign"—known as an "illegal" one—and you can pay a hefty fine for advertising "falsely or in a misleading way," the interpretation of which depends on more that what appears before the eye, doesn't it? I mean, don't our dreams intentionally mislead us? By which I mean "lead us into" a world we imagine can be true, against which the ordinary, the everyday, the boring, and the phatic is compared?

Nevertheless, signs must *supposedly* be true (or at least capable of *some* truth), but moreover as modern and postmodern consumers we

Difference and Possibility

doubt the truth of everything and just want these signs to *entertain* us. If you think about it, a truth that is entertaining puts truth in a somewhat different context than a truth that is plainly spoken. We expect signs to capture our immediate attention and be capable of lengthening the lapse time our eyeballs spend perusing the offering and shooting messages to our brains. Because we live life at velocity speed, because there are so many advertisements vying for eyeball appeal, because we grow weary instantly of that which smacks of what we have already seen, and because we seen just about all of it before anyway, we have very high thresholds for excitement and very short attention spans. The seduction must be quick. Maybe even dirty (but ambiguous enough not to be "illegal"). At the very least *cute*. Like these:

> If you stretch the truth
> Watch out for the snapback

> There is no right way
> To do the Wrong Thing

SIGNS AS COMMUNICATION

Signs are serious invitations to interpret their terms, their inducements, their visual displays as cultural and material evidence of something that matters, something that influences, something that communicates to and in a community. Road signage is a naturally occurring discourse—a local part of this Central text—and part of a larger contextual quest to locate and make meaningful relationships between ordinary, everyday communication and the possible presence of extraordinary human spirituality. And I do this purposefully, willfully, with the intention of rendering visible—and sentenceable—that which may otherwise simply be passed by, overlooked, ignored, misunderstood, disconnected, or just left unsaid.

All forms of spiritual study—indeed, all forms of communication study—share an inherently interpretive foundation: we read into texts signs of life's meanings through metaphors of language. Read the Tarot or the Bible; throw the I-Ching or arrange the crystals; contemplate a Koan or open a channel to a past life; study cognitive dissonance, organizational communication, or American culture—the doing of research is all about finding analogical parallels between lived experiences and the relevant scriptures, between the meanings of signs and interpretations of truth.

Why is it that we want to resist—just say NO—straightforward sentences—and ultimate purposes—like this one?

Why is it that the study of real signs on real roads that speak to real people in reality Central must first be justified as a context for interpretation before it may proceed as an interpretation of a context? I could say that we like to fuss up the advertisement, which is our way—our academic culture's way—of gaining the necessary attention, of making it palatable, or of rendering it cute. Or I could say that my responsibility as an interpreter includes providing a relevant context for the interpretation, a way of reading my lines as signs of what lies between and around them, a way of connecting my concerns to those of my discourse community, the communication faithful.

Like the make-happening of any rhetorical magic, this sorcerer must possess the right cantation and combination of charms. I must have the central Juju, in which silences induce a sense of mystery and passion. I must conjure the symbolic spell to envision for the audience the deeper, truer world that lies parallel and unspeakable next to our verbal own, making productive use of the silences between words that make up at least half of their meanings and that live within what is spoken as a clue to what cannot be spoken at all, but can only be *experienced* through that ineffable inner ear. Here is the place, then, for the proper work of enchantment.

Call it reading signs, or offering opposition to the power signs have over us. Call it reading contexts for interpreting differences out of what ordinarily passes for similarities, for what passes—for that matter—as merely ordinary, for what might be seen as simply collegiate high jinks because of an overall presence of boredom.

Signs of Difference

An academic researcher must be guided by the presence of critical inquiry—of doubt—whereas faith depends largely on an absence of doubt. However, in my experience most academic researchers eventually come to a position they will defend as fervently against alternative interpretations as any true believer. Similarly, the most fervent true believers I have met tend to provide accounts of their lives in which they came to what

Difference and Possibility

they believe after a period of serious doubt and rigorous searching. Perhaps the difference is less a matter of practical experience than it is a matter of professional arrogance, an inability to accept—much less to sponsor—diversity, and convenient myth. All truth, it seems, is *revealed* truth. Who gets to call the revelation is a matter of authority.

Yet here is a sign, this time in front of the Cannon Memorial Baptist Church, that must be read against a deeper source of interpretive difference:

> No man is too good not to be saved,
> No man is too bad to be saved.

This issue is *salvation*, salvation of the present person and of the eternal soul. But salvation is a term that cannot stand alone, that bespeaks an interpretive domain of religious context. Many modern academics, tracing our intellectual heritage to the Enlightenment, see in this sign evidence of two sources of ignorance.

First there is an ignorance of science, of the known facts—the verifiable empiricality—of life. Where is the soul, exactly? Where is Heaven? God? And so forth. Notice that "science" is nowhere in the verbiage of this sign; it is part of a context that lies between the lines, that constructs the borders this message with an inherited attitude borne of deep historical and philosophical divisions. For many of my colleagues, this context is enough to render most signs of this ilk—as well as churches—lowly and invisible. Beneath perception. Not sufficiently true enough to be take seriously, except perhaps as a sign of commercial architecture. This is because we do not see what we cannot believe in. Recall Harvey Sacks's observations about seeing the ordinary—what we believe *should* be there—even in the face of evidence to the contrary. And when the contrary is pointed out to us, even then we see it only in the context of a bounded understanding.

Second, the use of the antiquated sexist noun "man" provides additional testimony to ignorance, in this case culturally sanctioned gender ignorance, or ignorance of "political correctness." For many of my colleagues, the words on this sign sponsor an outdated system of patriarchy that instantly condemns the Christian religion—a religion that sacrifices women and women's spirituality to the ideal of a man-God and that marginalizes women who seek the priesthood, women as heads of households and families, women as an equal source of divine connection—to cultural limbo, if not spiritual Hell. For many of my colleagues, this context and its attendant interpretation is enough (even without arguments about science) to render this sign—as well as churches—houses of oppression, houses of suspicion, places for dis-ease.

But there are many academics who do not discount the claims of religion—and specifically the message of this sign—simply because it violates a personal dedication to secular and scientific causes. For us, perhaps this sign is worthy of critical attention precisely because it *is* inflected with these uneasy readings for the self, because it does render problematic a certain ambiguity that otherwise lives in our routine experiences of the everyday. To raise questions about Christian patriarchy, to raise questions about what is embedded in particular public uses of language, to see religion and science as co-present resources for humane understanding and improvement rather than as warring opposites of some vain continuum—these are important questions, questions not easily shucked off or pshawed away.

This sign reminds us of our incompleteness, of our inherent ambiguity, and ultimately of our humanity. It makes us feel uncomfortable. Gives us religious dis-ease. Maybe it even makes us angry. It suggests the ability to raise questions about salvation is also to call forth the need for salvation, maybe from asking questions like this. But there is more to this sign—and I am speaking here of the words on this sign—than the idea of salvation. "There is no (wo)man too good . . . there is no (wo)man too bad . . ."

DIFFERENCES AND POSSIBILITIES

Good and bad. Right and wrong. Fact or fiction? What would you say to these dualities? What do you say to the construction of these terms as opposites? Perhaps this sign is saying that they are not, in fact, opposites. The good (wo)man is not good enough without the presence of salvation; the bad (wo)man is only bad so long as salvation is absent. Dualities intertwine and mutually converge; after all, we live in a modern and postmodern world. The bad can be good and the good be bad; appearances are not necessarily realities, nor are realities necessarily *all that can be* made real.

Difference and Possibility

This, then, is a sign about possibilities. Now we have it. It is a sign about salvation. *Of course.* But it is also a sign of the possibility of salvation confounding what you take for granted. Good *when* actually bad, bad when *actually* good. Up when down, down when up. Possibilities of diverse unities. And possibilities for spiritual questions about Unity.

Here is the dialogic context capable of engaging spirituality within (rather than against) empirical realities, the simple rebuttal to scientific scoffing that posits possibility, experience, and imagination as powerful sources of counterevidence, an expression—in the form of invisible questions read into (and against) the intentional meanings of a visible sign—of the presence of spiritual mystery in the empirical, in the everyday, in the ordinary. Here is an empirical, everyday, ordinary sign that—because it engages you, because it induces you to ask these questions—is a sign about possibilities that transcend the empirical and the everyday by the act of uniting them. Here is a sign that does what it says, and induces what it does in *you.*

DIFFERENT SIGNS

I surrender to wonder. I surrender to wonder *regularly.* I wonder about possibilities. I wonder about the lives of questions possibilities induce. Possibility, after all, is a form of imagined communication, an inroad to ecstasy, a way of personally engaging what might be, or what might happen, as if it *was* or *is* happening. To engage possibility—to pose those questions—is a way to make up a waking dream—or to wake up a making dream—and to move it along. And, just like a dream of life that is embedded within our lives, it is also to suggest that the linear narrowness of the empirical life is simply not enough to sustain us or our planet.

We spend our lives imagining possibilities through which we ask dreamy questions and out of which we move into the personal darkness of sleep to continue in the most private way the quest that in daytime is only partially fulfilled and nowhere nearly understood. We take signs—and signs of signs—with us. The sign we read as a "sad" smile, interpreted as a sign within the context offered by the slowly crossed leg and deep sigh that came with it (or was that just a question posed at the edges of interpretation, a gesture made real or just made up?) that reminded us of some "forgotten" passage snatched from a late summer text from years ago (what *was* the name of that novel?), or maybe a social text that grew out of simple boredom sometime yesterday when we were thinking about the answer to a question (why would I be dreaming of *that*?) that itself seemed to live inside the imagined scenarios of a previous night's sensual pleasures.

So intertwined is our ordinary life with this extraordinary one that it is often hard to separate them, to say for sure where this text ends and that context begins, to know for sure which resource for interpretation is more or less real. I mean, *are* we such stuff as dreams are made of? Or are our dreams such stuff as we wish we were? Put it this way: have you ever surrendered to your dreams, to your bliss, to your imagination—to your favored, hidden interpretation of a context, of a sign you thought *for sure* that only you read in that way—only to find it real, to find it shared by someone else who, too, only thought it a possibility? Of course you have. We all have. We all do. So what is going on then? What if she does have a voice like tousled sheets? How did we come to think that? To dream that? What is being communicated? What is being interpreted *as* communication? How does *that* happen?

Maybe we are surprised in these circumstances because we have been asking limiting questions about communication all along. I mean, what is existential about raw categories for behavior? Where does the existential life—the lived experience of the everyday—cross over into the inner realm of the outwardly symbolic? Where do signs of what *might* be become evidence of what *is*? And how, my friend, do we make that happen? Or better yet, *why* do we make that happen?

What if these signs are signs of something else. Something else *entirely*. What if our capacities for imagining, for asking, for dreaming—for not seeing our lives as merely a bored exchange of routinized behaviors—should be understood as all of one piece? One large, cosmic piece. As integrally, deeply connected? What if our capacity for wonder, for envisioning, for experiencing nature, for interpreting meaning through signs—through the most mundane, the most everyday, and the most ordinary of signs—is a reminder of who we *really* are? And who we really are is found in asking the larger questions, in accepting our real connections the ineffable territories of the possible, to understanding ourselves to be fundamentally godlike beings, spiritual beings, not "behavioral sacks suspended by calcium skeletons and driven by cognitions" to behave for each other in a capitalist void until death. What if we are spiritual beings for whom life's purposes—life's inner connections, life's

Difference and Possibility

meanings—are found in "what might possibly be" rather than what merely *is*?

Again: we are such stuff as dreams are made of. Or: dreams are such stuff as we are made of.

If this is so, what can a definitional statement—a disciplinary sign—like this one (Goodall 1983) mean:

> Communication is any response to a message

Depends on the context you bring to the interpretation, don't you think? That context also reflects the presence of clue—a clue that was only partially understood—within that moment of my own evolution. So it depends—the meaning of that definition—just like the meaning of a sign, on its reading, which is to say on the local context of its revelation.

Communication as Sign

Communication is how we imagine a world and call it into existence. Communication is how we create reality and the possibility for multiple realities, by which I mean how we construct *perceptions* of those imaginings through acoustic and visual exchanges of symbols, as well as how we point to, argue about, and discuss the existence, characteristics, and meanings of what we have created. Our ability to do that—to treat this simulated virtual surround we call forth and treat as consensus "reality" as if it were "real"—is a response we are making to what Gregory Bateson (1991) referred to as "the further reaches of human nature."

I have an audio-video system at home that accomplishes pretty much the same thing. My receiver-amplifier includes something magical called "Pro-Logic Stereo Surround Circuitry," and with the assistance of a television monitor, a CD player, and five loudspeakers it creates the impression of a live performance in my living room. So "live," in fact, that you wouldn't even consider Memorex. So *perfectly* live that no living band *ever* sounded this good, and if I could afford a bigger screen monitor I would never need to suffer the stale popcorn and wretched imitation butter of the local movie theatres again. The appeal of my system is not to "mimic" reality—for that is, these days, pretty boring—but to *exceed its limitations*, to invite us into a world imagined by state-of-the-art engineering, acoustic science, and visual artistry.

I draw this human-technology comparison for two reasons. First, I want to point out that what we are willing to symbolically purchase or buy into—whether it is a communication theory or an audio-visual system or a 4th of July sale or a relational possibility or spiritual message about our place and purpose in the universe—that symbolic construction must do something *more* than simply try to mirror reality. Its promise must *exceed* reality (or realities') limitations. Its performance must render the mirror metaphor mundane if not entirely banal. Richard Rorty's (1979) finely tuned refutation of philosophy as a mirror of nature gets most of this but leaves out the *communicative basis* for imagining worlds that, once articulated, become the virtual surround of our sensibilities and that press us, once living in and through them, to imagine even finer possibilities.

Second, because we are always actively engaged in bringing these imagined realities into existence through media such as language or technologies such as Pro-Logic (and sometimes even succeeding: witness a strong, loving relationship, a team-based organization that actually works, or an advanced audio-visual system), we ought to understand communication as a way of reaching for possibilities—reaching for *peak experiences*—rather than limiting explanations to a view afforded by the exchange of routinized behaviors, from the mirroring vantage of its baseline mimicry.

To do this would mean *not* reducing the meaning of human communication to the serial firing of neurons or to counting the number of blinks a particular thought produces in the generalizable human eye. The cognitive foundation of communication, as it is generally studied now, consists primarily of the transference of behavioral logics to cerebral contexts. Cognitive social scientists observe, categorize, and measure the movements of brain waves in relation to the movements of overt behaviors previously observed, categorized, and measured; the result is a way of explaining how one set of movements is related to another. This is called "doing science." But in fact it is narrowing the scope of science to dealing with a very limited context for interpretation.

Another problem is that this sort of work doesn't improve how we teach speech to those interested in learning something meaningful about it, or account for why this very sophisticated understanding doesn't matter very much at all to people who use communication in everyday life, which is just about everybody. To be fair, most advanced

Difference and Possibility

theories of *anything* don't enjoy much popular or practical currency. But whereas some of my colleagues see that last statement as a justification for their work, I prefer to see it as a sign that something is wrong. Any move that exchanges the meanings and complexities of communication to gain a surface map of the human mind and body parts—and greater methodological sophistication for the mapping—seems kind of fun, but as the justification for state funding and human support, mostly unreasonable and certainly unsustainable, at least to me. It may be "science," and no doubt it is difficult work, but simply being able to do hard science well doesn't strike me as a good enough reason to believe that is all there is—or should be—to understanding and improving communication. Particularly when the questions—the hard questions, the questions most scientists don't ever like to ask—remain largely unaddressed, despite the omnipresence of signs and clues and lived experiences to the contrary.

No, this doesn't mean that everyone involved in cognitive and behavioral approaches to communication study should abandon what they are doing, take a turn toward Spirit, and follow some spiritual path. In fact, I think the work they are doing *is* work that must be done, and probably by *them*. What I am saying is that there ought to be room enough at this discussion for some new evolutions of old alternatives, some revisiting of questions about communication and life's meanings.

I am more than a little reminded here of a scene from Monty Python's *The Meaning of Life*. At a board meeting of the Very Big Corporation of America the topic for discussion becomes the marketing of "the meaning of life." A committee report is read about the two essential issues involved in this project: (1) the number of hats being worn and (2) the influence of invisible energy fields that affect the development of one's soul (in ways contrary to Christian doctrine) by interference with the *foci* of one's guided self-observations, a fact of life that serves to remind us of "man's unique ability to be distracted from spiritual matters by everyday trivia." At the end of this report there is a profound silence, then another board member asks, "What's this about *hats* again?"

Indeed.

Zen and the Experiencing of Communication

Enough grousing. Allow me propose an alternative. A Zen of Communication alternative that recognizes the point of learning is beyond all explanations, just as the lived experience of Being has more to do with surrender than with knowledge.

I must begin with three interrelated, uneasy questions. These questions are derived from a view of communication and communication research as "mystery" rather than as "problem" (Goodall 1991). They are also given here in service of my quest to link communication and spirituality (Goodall 1993). But even if one or none of these two premises is necessarily shared, the following questions ought to be raised.

First: Why Should the Goal of Communication Theory and Research Be Explanation of the Phenomenon Itself?

Karl Marx, for example, argued against that objective over a century ago, suggesting instead that the end of philosophy should be social and political action. One could argue that as a result of taking Marx's ideas into the streets of Petrograd, millions of people eventually died, and even more were reared only to be ignorant, undernourished, paranoid, politically incorrect, and existentially miserable; but really, that is quite a stretch. These *postmortem* abuses of his theoretical work are precisely why Karl Marx was no Marxist, and, in seeing how they developed before he died, said so, publicly.

By analogy, blaming Marx for Marxism is akin to blaming Kenneth Burke for every negative influence of symbolic inducement and abuse associated with television advertising, sexually seductive and supposedly Satanic appeals in heavy metal lyrics, lies rendered as "shorthand terms for situations" that constitute negative political campaigning, symbolic sacrifices and victimage wrought by serial killers, and maybe even the savings-and-loan crisis, which was, after all, a perfect example of a twisted identification with a Master Trope. Given attributions of his theories to these very real, history-shaping outcomes, Burke would probably not want to be considered a Burkeian either.

So the point here is *not* to suggest that explanation is an unworthy goal for communication study. It is to suggest that it is only *one* goal, and not necessarily the most *important* one. For a social scientist, explanation precedes *prediction* and ultimately contributes to *control*. That is fine, if your goal is to predict and control. It's modern; it's about Power. For a historian, explanation is important because it establishes one's voice as an authority to speak for an event, period, persons, or movement.

Difference and Possibility

This too is laudable, if the goal is to become an authoritative spokesperson for such events and persons. It's modern or postmodern, but it's still about Power, either as the power of the rational self or the power of the marginalized Other.

However, for a person interested in awakening or deepening paths toward spiritual growth for oneself and within one's communities and learning how to care for each other while finding ways to sustain life on Planet Earth, explanation misses all the important points; it is like trying to play baseball with Pictionary. Or to experience the joy of love by reading the definitions for the words *joy* and *love* in *Webster's*.

Second: How Do You Explain That Which Is Essentially a Mystery?

Why, really, would you *want* to? For a Christian, the purpose of common prayer is communion with God, not the explanation of the prayer process. For a Zen Buddhist, meditation is practiced not for the purposes of explaining Ultimate Reality but for personal enlightenment as to its meanings in one's journey.

In part this is why I conceive of ethnographic studies as mysteries. The idea is not to come away with the twelve things that can be said about a culture but to have an *experience* of culture in a way that can be evocatively, provocatively communicated to others in ways that encourage new members to enjoin the search and provides a resource for those already on the path to continue the dialogue, and *that* purpose deepens the mystery. At the ends of our journeys, I doubt if anyone of us will regret not having come up with better explanatory definitions, or for that matter, will sigh resignedly over a failure to predict and control a study; I suspect that for all of us life sums quite differently than that.

(The irony for this project is trying to define and explain myself while arguing that definitions and explanations are not what I am after. Considering the alternatives—abandon writing as a form of scholarly expression or write without concern for providing a coherent framework—I believe I am stuck with this particular irony and might as well just say so.)

Third: Why Should We Treat the Nature of Communication—Which Defines How We Live and Work; What We Think, Speak, Listen for, Read and Know about What It Means to Be Human—As If It Was Equivalent to Any Other Phenomenon We Can Name?

I have never thought that describing or accounting for communication is pretty much the same thing as describing or accounting for rows of soybeans, or herds of cattle, or even the behavior of suns and moons among the planets and stars. Nor is it reasonable to suggest that with this sort of thinking all I am really doing is privileging the human (I don't) over other life forms and forces.

What I *am* pointing out is that communication is the *primary experiential source of all lived and imagined connections* to all life forms and forces, as well as to how, why, and what we know about them. "Communication"—even within these sweeping, heroic formulations—remains a problematic term. It refers, obviously, to all forms of verbal, nonverbal, written, and visual responses to situations and actions, as well as to the meanings we attribute to the actions themselves. But I also think "communication" refers to felt or intuitively sensed impressions, to the meanings of silences, to activities of the will including—but not limited to—those associated with perceived or sensed outcomes; the experiences of foresight, insight, and aftersight; the illimitable, seemingly surreal worlds that dreams and altered states of consciousness bring to us or adjust us into; and all forms of bodily, extrasensory, and biological feedback. Communication, thus summed up, is virtually equivalent to the holistic realm of human experiences in and with the cosmos, and certainly to the full effable and ineffable range of experiencing *being* human.

The study of communication, too long held a prisoner of the most obvious and everyday waking consciousness, too long guarded by the disciplinary police who march lockstep to modernist (or postmodernist), categorical, mostly spoken, mostly male, mostly white, definitively scientific or humanistically sanctioned constructions of a limited empirical reality, must, as these totalizing narratives are consistently exposed as incomplete and in some cases false—and in other cases singularly politically motivated—newly explore the holistic breadth, depth, and width of human communication's potential reach.

To do this requires liberating ourselves from unnecessary assumptive and definitional bonds of our own narratives, and to expose to experiential doubt our own self-imposed, self-monitored experiential repression. This repression includes, but is not limited to, the methodological and expressive dogmas that suggest we can't—at least not in a "proper" scholarly fashion—access or write about *what we actually live through*; when confronted with this problem—an idea we can't tame—we should

Difference and Possibility

simply negate it as a scholarly resource by either marginalizing or erasing it, rendering it institutional only when fully narcotized and bridled, as one might escort—albeit in a kindly, if somewhat condescending manner—an insane relative into a white-washed and readily awaiting mental hospital.

Communication as Disciplined Imagination

In the spirit of breaking out of our disciplinary hospital, I offer the following observations about the study of communication:

Communication Is the Work of Disciplined Imagination, As Is the Scholarly Pursuit of Its Clues.

Communication—considered experientially—is how we engage the imagination and act on what we find there. It is the imagination that shapes what purposes we communicate for and about, because the world we live in and through is largely an imagined place: it depends for its construction on symbols, signs, and images, and is rendered sensible through narrative contexts for interpretation. Consider a few of our disciplinary constructions: How else—but through the imagination—would we know we are "in a relationship," or understand the relationships we experience? How else—but through the imagination—could we envision change in relationships, organizations, or communities? What power would speech have without recourse to the conjured worlds of words? Or of words that shape and structure the experiences of community? Without imagination, how would we believe (or not believe) that our blue planet has a nameable place—if not a special one—in the Milky Way? Put simply, *without* imagination, what *possible* story would our lives tell?

Given these premises, the idea of a "disciplined imagination" is an odd turn of phrase, a bending of "imagination" around the rather rigid sign of "discipline." Yet I think the two are necessarily connected in and through communication. Communication is the work of "disciplined imagination" in every sense: since antiquity, to communicate has required acquisition of the knowledge and practices of grammar, logic, and rhetoric, whether pedagogically or experientially indicated. Each of these foundational disciplines supplies ways and means of reading and making signs through manipulations of symbols, and greater and lesser degrees of sophistication in usage and effect are attained by disciplined practice.

Yet the work of communication—by which I mean its singular symbolic power to create; to maintain; or to change perceptions, interpretations, and the actualities of human realities—relies on imagined contextual strategies and symbolically constructed worlds in which those strategies make signs of perfect sense within contexts of their own making. From the contexts of imagination come narratives of dialogic designs, sensuous rhythms that inspire bodily action, and occasionally, the masterful deep poetics of something that moves us—in our imaginations—to a heightened sense of awareness, an experience of sacred unities, and opens the course for meaningful actions.

Viewed this way, "knowledge" is at best a secondary concern, not the logical foundation from which we construct something called "the real world," but more of a supporting narrative motif in the experiencing of a well-imagined life.

Knowledge Isn't the Source or the Method or the End Result of Engaging Mystery; Experience Is.

To focus narrowly on the production of knowledge as the dominant sign of scholarship—as the dominant sign of what communication is *about* and how we should understand it—is to ignore that the house of human dwelling is primarily *experiential*. We live *not* in order to know, but in order to go on living. We learn so that we can do, so that through the doing we may evolve. We don't know *why*, but if we are lucky we learn to know *how*. We dwell in a house made of the senses wherein thought resides, Spirit longs to thrive, and communication connects us to the All of It. The Big All of It. To Life Itself. That is the part we must *imagine* and do.

Viewed this way, our discipline's overt concern for knowledge about communication attained through methodological sophistication represents the privileging of what can be said about acts and conditions of human communication as a kind of knowledge substitute for direct experience. This is roughly equivalent to a turn away from richly imagined and realized lived experiences and toward varieties of disciplined symbolic playfulness, a turn taken in the overall road that will eventually remind us that all we have done is taken a particular turn, not necessarily the right one. To talk seriously about knowledge—or of methods of arriving at knowledge—*over* the experiences of communication is to have fun with symbols out in the open air, wherein the actual experience of communicating about communication itself pokes a kind of irreverent fun at what is being talked about by simply being present and unaccounted for in the talk itself. Imagine that!

To suggest that knowledge *requires* methods to ensure warrantable knowledge is to sidestep the issue by diverting attention from the question, kind of like producing a belly laugh at the moment of real challenge. If experience is the issue, knowledge is a necessary—but seriously insufficient—sign of its realization. To know is surely one kind of experience, but knowledge of communication is an experience that has stepped away from its source and is therefore removed from its objective; it is a way, perhaps a preference, for talking about—or around—that which is desired.

Beliefs about Communication Are Relatively Unimportant; Interpreted Meanings Focus on Practices.

Most scholarship in the discipline of communication, as well as in disciplines claiming knowledge of communication, focuses on the squiring or warranting of beliefs.[4] This formulation establishes a causal relationship between the establishing of facts (i.e., knowledge) and the development of warranted beliefs: knowledge is sought so that beliefs can be founded on firmer empirical ground. Skills are then identified as the warranted pathways for doing or performing the "right" or "correct" beliefs, thereby completing this tediously belief-burdened circle: we teach students to perform communication skills according to the dominant beliefs we have established (e.g., imagined) for the purpose—primarily for *accomplishing* those beliefs.

Yet the connections between our beliefs and the world of actual practices widen as our scholarship narrows. Compare basic textbooks on

---

[4] Jennifer James (1992) teaches us that the reason "common sense doesn't become common practice" is because beliefs get in the way. As an anthropologist she uses the history of human cultural transformations (e.g., hunter/gathers into agriculturalists, agriculturalists into industrial revolutionaries, industrial revolutionaries into information/technology/communication denizens) to document her assertion that those who fail to adapt to change because their beliefs get in the way become "boiled frogs." Disciplinary knowledge also fails to evolve if beliefs about what "is" knowledge similarly fail to respond to new resources for cultural practices.

communication with the actual practices of persons, and chances are very good that you will agree that a great deal of what is important and real gets completely left out. Why is this? I think it is because the mechanical, canonical engines of scholarship—of warranted modern knowledge that sustains the misbeliefs while proposing that the postmodern challenge is, in fact, a challenge—are firing on only half the cylinders, if that many. We know—and even readily admit, and in some cases try to justify—that all but the formal study of preaching and the occasional sly scholarly digs at base evangelism are included within the spiritual dimensions of human communication, leaving out just about everything that would locate the spiritual in the everyday, say in relational, group, or public communions.

Like basic skills or the performing of actions, beliefs about communication are necessary—but incomplete—signs of communication. They define—provide an interpreted context for—what we can talk about, like this: An *action* is what we do. A *practice* is what we do regularly and for a reason; practices are purposeful accomplishments of actions. A *skill* is how we learn to repeat actions and practices. A *belief* is what we think about why we are, or should be, acting and practicing as we do.

Of the four ideas represented, the only the *practice* manifests itself as a fully realized context for interpretation. Only a practice constitutes—brings together—all the available resources of signs: the doing of actions, the mechanics of skills, and the purposes associated with beliefs are contained within and around practices.

We could argue about these definitions, serve up counterexamples and supporting testimonies and bring in wonderful quips and quotable quotes, and spend many afternoons returning to these offerings as if they were scriptures from which we were to interpret ultimate meanings. We would, under these terms, accomplish a kind of communication study, and I fear this is more or less how sanctioned communication study is done. But would we accomplish "communication?" Would we be furthering our life quests? Would we be engaging our journeys in ways that enrich how we progress? Would students of communication understand and practice communication as a resource for engaging the meanings of signs and symbols in everyday life, learn to organize themselves and their understandings through their communication relations with others, and to see those communication experiences as integrally connected to the experiencing of mystery, *or* would they learn merely stand at once

Difference and Possibility

in critical remove from all they experience—and from their own experiences—able only to name and argue about it and them?

Communication Suggests and Opens Imagined Paths with and through Which to Encounter, Involve, and Complicate the Dialogue of the Everyday, As Well As to Find, Appreciate, Surrender to, and Negotiate Differences in the Everyday; However, the Aim of Communication Practices Should Be to Continue Dialogues in Order to Find Unities, Not to Reach Consensus.

There are multiple worlds in even the most routinized places, and certainly beyond them. In this way, Central is a metaphor as well as a place, and the experiences I am recording and interpreting here are signs of dialogues everywhere, not just here. It does not so much matter *where* you are, but *how well* you are where you are. After all, to "know" and "be" where you are should connect you to all the circuits of life, as well as to the Spirit of its circus.

For these reasons, my aim is not to come up with a central meaning—a consensus construction of Central's reality—but instead to enjoin the multiplicities of the everyday worlds I find here, adding my voice to the overall mix, offering my perspective to others. I do not believe that the citizens of Central and its environs should be able to read my words and say, "By golly, he got all of it, didn't he!" Instead, I hope they will read it and find both their worlds and ones they never before recognized represented here. From these beginnings, dialogue surely continues.

Neither do I feel that this study of Central should only be construed as a study of Central, South Carolina. The questions raised here are the same questions that are—or that should be—raised anywhere. Central, as metaphor, should be read more simply as a sign.

There Are No Coincidences; All Forms of Communication Are Signs of Connections.

In a world of causes and effects, the idea of coincidences is an oxymoron, which is, ironically, also to say it is unscientific. So it is we treat the oddities, the slips, and the strangeness of everyday experiences as if they were abnormalities rather than symptomatic of what we should be paying attention to. We dismiss the inexplicable without elevating it to the status of even a simple question: why? By acting this way, we leave out pieces of our own puzzles and then wonder why things don't make sense or work out the way we plan. We also learn to treat the whole of experience as a series of partial screens, *terministic* screens, to borrow Kenneth Burke's language.

The more we ignore or leave out or forget to connect to, the more we feel fragmented, left out, or disconnected. And to this unified set of diverse conditions, we neither bring nor pose any new questions (or for that matter, any old ones); we just continue to search for unutterable answers, continue to see life as problem instead of as mystery.

What should these new questions be about? Perhaps we need only to look at what we have so long been discarding, the pieces of the puzzle left lying on our common disciplinary and experiential floor. Knowledge and beliefs have too long been central in our study of communication, and skills dissociated from ultimate purposes and everyday life quests are centrally implicated in our current dilemma. We have too long prepared students to be critics, scientists, and politicians, and too little prepared them to be people on the planet Earth. Practices, disciplines, and living here now—the *interdependent experiential realities of communication*—offer important clues to this mystery and could serve as the organizing locus of communication study and practice.

We have certainly discarded, perhaps lost, any sense of Spirit in the everyday communication experiences. Since the advent of scientism, any mention of nonempirical realities and ultimate purposes have been severely scoffed at, dismissed through demonizing discourse designed to denegrate—and to exchange—the dignity of human Being for the currency of human Knowing. Pieces of our common puzzle—perhaps very big pieces, if not the shape and meaning of the puzzle itself—must, I think, somehow be recovered.

Which brings us, finally, back to the realm of experience. *Personal* experience. *Lived* experiences. The experiences of speaking, of listening, of organizing, relating, surrendering, dialoguing, communing. And these experiences represent just a start. From here we can imagine experiences of communication that have yet to be articulated much less understood, or in some cases, experienced: communication through meaningful silences, communication through sensual pleasures, communication with nature and into the stars, communication through felt presences (even angels) and perhaps into other as yet unlanguaged worlds. To get there we must learn to ask more new questions about everyday occur-

Difference and Possibility

rences, to get more deeply into life's mysteries by way of our passage through Central.

One last sign, this time an imagined one:

> You are now leaving the
> town of Central
> Please hurry back!

Do we ever really leave behind signs of what is Central? Maybe we just forget, for awhile, where we have been, or what our arrival here is ultimately destined for.

PART TWO

PERFORMING COMMUNITY

There is a "revel" in revelation. Waiting in the word is the notion that stillness and solitude are not the only ways to the sacred; that self-knowledge may sometimes have more to do with "reveling" than with the meditative lotus position or the prayerful kneel. One implication is that the sacramental has also to do with intimacy and community—and with a community intimate and daring enough to revel together.

—Michael Ventura

You're the tradition, the years, the true center. Holy Smoke, man, you're *football*, or a *church*.

—Barry Hannah

As you drive from Central toward Clemson, a distance of a mere
two miles, the highway w i d e n s to accommodate
four lanes,
obviously in anticipation of something BIG. . . .

You pass Jerry's Video, an independent church, some houses, a futon factory,
the 93 Fish Camp, a turnoff to the major residential subdivisions along
Issaqueena Trail, a Hardee's, an Ingles Food Market/Revco Drug/Advance Auto
Parts/Dollar Store strip mall, an auto care facility with stacks of used tires, and a
long stretch between more subdivisions, a GUNS & PAWN store, an abandoned
music store, a BI-LO Grocery/Colombo's Pizza/Greek Catering strip mall, the
plowed site for a new Winn-Dixie Grocery Store, a Red Dot Liquor Store, and then
the Highway 123 Overpass.

You are entering Clemson

From this point forward the landscape is dominated by
Tiger Paws
painted on the highways, signs for football parking and stadium access, and an
NCAA Division I
college campus whose tallest building, indeed whose largest
structure—a structure that makes it the third largest city in the
state on football Saturdays—is a football stadium known locally
as
Death Valley.

This is a sign of S P I R I T
you cannot—and should not—fail to read as a
symbol

Because it changes everything.

4

Rapture and Ecstasy: Spirituality, Football, and the Accomplishment of Community

> The ethnographer is a little like Hermes; a messenger who, given methodologies for uncovering the masked, the latent, the unconscious, may even obtain his message through stealth. He presents languages, cultures, and societies in all their opacity, their foreignness, their meaninglessness; then, like the magician, the hermeneut, Hermes himself, he clarifies the opaque, renders the foreign familiar, and gives meaning to the meaninglessness. He decodes the message. He interprets.
>
> Hermes was a trickster: a god of cunning and tricks. The ethnographer is no trickster. He, so he says, has no cunning and no tricks. But he shares this with Hermes: *he must make his message convincing....* The ethnographer must make use of all the persuasive devices at his disposal to convince his readers of *the* truth of his message, but treating these rhetorical strategies as though they were cunning tricks, he gives them scant recognition. His texts assume a truth that speaks for itself—a whole truth that needs no rhetorical support. His words are transparent. He does not share Hermes' confidence. When Hermes took the post of messenger to the gods, he promised Zeus not to lie. He did not promise to tell the whole truth. Zeus understood. The ethnographer has not.
>
> —Vincent Crapanzano

> In a novel, a house or person has his meaning, his existence, entirely through the writer. Here, a house or a person has only the most limited of his meaning through me: his true meaning is much huger. It is that he *exists*, in actual being, as you do and as I do, and as no character of the imagination can possibly exist. His great weight, mystery, and dignity are in this fact. As for me, I can tell you of him only what I saw, only so accurately as in my terms I know how: and this in turn has its chief stature not in any

PERFORMING COMMUNITY

as a human being. Because of his immeasurable weight in actual existence, and because of mine, every word I tell of him has inevitably a kind of immediacy, a kind of meaning, not at all necessarily "superior" to that of imagination, but of a kind so different that a work of the imagination (however intensely it may draw on "life") can at best only faintly imitate the least of it.

—James Agee and Walker Evans

There are symbolic dreams—dreams that symbolize some reality. Then there are symbolic realities—realities that symbolize a dream.

—Haruki Murakami

At Clemson we have a style of football played radically different from anything on earth.

—John Heisman, Clemson football coach and founder
of the football tradition at Clemson, 1903

In order to get the real thing [the advertising agency head] wrote the museum of Natural History in Chicago, asking for a plaster of Paris cast of the imprint of the Tiger's paw. "The imprint was changed to a print, tilted about 10 degrees to the right and presented to the Clemson committee...." "The plan was to use the paw on football helmets, schedule cards, bumper stickers, as a pocket patch on blazers, painted on the football field and basketball court, and, in many cases, to replace the 'O' in the word Clemson.... Now the gospel had to be spread.

—Bob Bradley

Prelude

> Nothing is Too Great or Too Small For God to Attend
> —Highway 93 signage, Cannon Memorial Baptist Church, Central, SC

> The Kingdom of God is within you.
> —New Testament Gospels

It's early Saturday morning in Clemson, South Carolina, a.k.a. Tiger Town USA, and we are here as witnesses several hours in advance of the Rapture.[1]

---

[1] At the outset I think it is wise to admit to a political problematic that will necessarily involve how this metaphor—and this piece—is constructed and interpreted: Is

Rapture and Ecstasy

Knowing the event is near, most of this small town's 9,000 permanent residents and 17,000 students choose to sleep late, most of them to sleep off Thursday and Friday night's full revelry while a few strange, anxious angels rise early to coach Death Valley into an appropriate stage for an advent of miracles.

Death Valley is a major spiritual stage disguised as a major college football stadium, an altar upon which is annually conducted a deeply communal search by individual souls for something far greater—but yet somehow contained—in the ecstasy of a competitive sport. Forged out of white concrete and black steel and tinted glass, fully electrified and over-wired for megawatt stereo sound and computer-generated color graphics on the scoreboard, two gigantic arms define one of the largest stadiums in America while offering a cosmic welcome angled gradually upward and away from ground zero to an incomplete arc of dizzying height, that, from its topmost sky vantage on either side, oversees 120 yards of green, perfect turf.

From that vantage what goes on down there, *way* down there on what appears to be little more than a well-tended minor lord's lawn, seems like it ought to be virtually insignificant. Or should be. But what goes on down there, way down there, is *not* insignificant. Not at all. If it were, why would there be all this stadium beholding a biblical name framed by this imposing suggestion of an arc, within which is performed a universal covenant, a human drama about victory and loss costumed in metaphors old enough to shape this big ball field into a small and perfect Eden of grass?

Beyond Death Valley ghosts rise through the mist from the surrounding lakes in the cool heat of this dense autumn dawn and dance upward in circles of light into vast infinity. It is Saturday; the air is locally charged with evangelical ions. Somewhere there must be a plan.

Processional

The destiny of man is to
become the one who can
bear witness to the tran-

a spirituality of self/community best understood as a search for immanence or transcendence? The term *Rapture* seems to encourage the latter perspective. But perhaps our linguistic conventions merely obscure an inherent duality of structure in which both terms function necessarily as part of a larger, interdependent whole. This is, I think, also true of football.

PERFORMING COMMUNITY

scendent reality at the very heart of existence.

To achieve this, we must first learn to take seriously the experiences through which, in privileged moments, being touches us and calls to us.

This is the fundamental meaning of all spiritual exercise as I understand it: to open ourselves to our essential being through experiences which manifest it and to enter upon a way of living which allows us to bear witness to being in daily life.

—Graf Durckheim

Before we go any further, and before you mistake my poetic rhetoric for mere fanciful metaphor, allow me this brief introduction. My subject in this chapter is the intersection of self and community, where those often ineffable but lived connections between socially constructed selves and places become interactive and meaningful. Considered locally, one expression of this intersection is articulated between religion and college football, two ideas that themselves contain curious mergers of the personal and social, individuals and teams, town and gown, the immanent and transcendent, signs that serve as mediated symbols and symbolic mediations for the meanings of signs.

Other writers after other purposes and working out of other frameworks have explicated college football as sport, as business, as a celebration, as a cultural value, as male ritual, as problematic for universities and colleges that sponsor competitive teams, as a major source of recruitment, media coverage, and revenue, and as the localized site of a wide variety of social, racial, class, and educational problems. For that matter, other writers working out of other frameworks for other purposes have covered religion in much the same ways. Let me state from the outset that I am thoroughly convinced that college football/religion can fairly be considered as all of the above, but that at its intersection in Clemson it is something else as well. And this "something else" is nothing less than a personal, social, professional, organizational, and communal resource for spiritual transformation. *Mystic football*, if you will.

Furthermore, this transformational stage, reframed as a spiritual moment, provides insights about humans as spiritual beings who seek—

through communion, ritual, solitude, symbolism, freedom, communication, coordinated actions, interpretive accounts, and storytelling— deeply personal transformations from their felt status as isolated, incomplete souls to a sense of connectedness, completion, and meaning that transcends ordinary life and establishes contact with Creation.

One note of spiritual caution is warranted here, or a caveat, if you prefer. Clemson is a mostly Christian—no, a *deeply* Christian—environment. Even the nonbelievers disbelieve and disavow in a mostly Christian or deeply Christian way. Similarly, football is largely enacted locally within the epistemic and ontic parameters of a symbolic Christian teleology, embuing everything—every sign—with this locally necessary intersection of the sporting self and our religious community. Elsewhere it might be otherwise. But this is pretty much how the game is constructed and how the game is played here.

Invocation: Imagining a Personal Self in the Desert of Lost Community, or What Is an Existential Self Doing in a Postmodern Mediated World, Anyway?

The American Jesus was born at Cane Ridge, and is with us still, in Nashville and Salt Lake City, in New Orleans and in East Harlem storefronts.

He is a Jesus who barely was crucified, and whose forty days of Resurrection upon earth never have ended.

Or if he ascended, he has come back and keep coming back in the pouring out of Spirit.

He cannot be known in or through a church, but only one on one,

and then indeed he is known,

with far more immediacy evidently than even heightened sexual experience can provide, more even than frontier violence can provide.

—Harold Bloom

It must begin in the desert, at night. Nothing existential can't.

We are small, vain living things—call us Earthlings—and these vast quiet sands are called the Bonneville Salt Flats in the nation of Utah. There's a round full moon, and the great white stars are comic artwork out of some cosmic children's book:

PERFORMING COMMUNITY

BIG
cLOsE
poINTED

The floor tonight is desert white, luminous salt lit by invisible crystals empowered by rays of moonlight: sparkling, glassy, eery, ever-present.

This is the place forever seems always to have been. In the farthest measure of what from here may be the distance of life itself are shadowy high lifeless forms, surface-of-the-moon desert mountains upon which grow *nothing*—bleak, cratered, ambivalent surfaces—old dinosaur vistas existing now as vast high spaces against the void, invulnerable to material time. These are the dead surfaces—final surfaces—that define our earthly territorial Endings, reminders for all who cross these desert sands—all Earthlings especially—that our journey here is, in fact, bounded.

But this is a view of the desert from one who lives in it. One who *likes* where he is living. One who feels as existential as his quest. One who has things left to do. Imagine, however, a view of the desert at night from the soul's trapped vantage: this is the ultimate *anti*-place, silent, voiceless, an all-wrong space bright and still at midnight, an empty lot defined by its solitude, stark enough for a life on earth lived around old lessons, for seemingly endless wandering, searching for a man-God once crucified by the truth, or perhaps a self, a me, destined to be, to mingle with infinity. From the soul's vantage, those last surfaces are sources of rapture; it is this damned desert that must be endured.

Just East of here is an enormous Dead Sea, larger than the biblical one, because everything meaningful is larger, vaster, more meaningful in America. The larger Truth in America must be greater than we are, Christians, so we believe our selves are here to search not for the "it," but instead for the BIG IT, to discover some personal meaning for the BIG IT, to celebrate the BIG MEANINGFULNESS OF IT IN US, until, thus complete and enraptured, we individually, blissfully pass on, cross that

Rapture and Ecstasy

final water, transition, or simply rise up from the body that dies and disappear into the ever-after, to live in everlasting Joy.

Rapture, Christian, is the Biggest of Deals.

Deals. Big Deals. This is America, after all, and Deals are what make America—and Americans—great. They require cheerleaders, slogans, fans, and flash. The bigger the deal, the better. Big Deals are:

Exciting!
Powerful!
Uplifting!

This much power, this cheerleading, the marching band, this much fun requires ...

Rapture!

Big Deals are better because they require Greatness—and luck—to achieve. Americans believe in the need for luck as we believe in the need for the Holy Spirit, an ineffable equation that aligns the mysterious with the mystical in cosmic harmony, an equation in which God is the Great(ness) ultimately signified, and we, ourselves, hope and fear ourselves to be the commonest of all denominators, digits that actually figure into the Big Equation, destination infinity, even better if we are bright, good-looking, talented sons and daughters because that compounds the interest, makes the Big Deal seem Bigger and Better, and transforms the numb desert journey into a sensuous walk along the beach.

But it can't be that easy. Desert or beach, Big Deals, Big Mountains, Big Meaningful It—there is always within us the primitive uneasy knowledge of opposites, and with those opposites come deals that are just sleazy, mountains that are just the cynical tips of a cold jagged precipice, "its" that lose their high capitalization and frenzy. If there is Something

Else—call it Joy Everlasting—it is equally possible that on the other side, in fact, there may be nothing, no rapture, a nothing that lasts forever.

Death that *is* itself. Death that is loss. Death that has no exit.

What I have just described are the modern spiritual pinings of an existential individual in a postmodern material world. They articulate what Kenneth Gergen (1992) has defined as a "romantic self," and what in a previous generation would have been called—by George Herbert Mead and Herbert Blumer—an inward "I" that produces and consumes itself through, and sometimes as, an outward "Me." At the center of this individual was "the self," a unified if invisible core that contained the answer to the central question: "Who am I?" This center was treated for most of the twentieth century as (ironically) a nonempirical certainty although it very clearly was a symbolic construction, a kind of social science fiction, a heroic myth. Upon a cornoner's or surgeon's table, the dissected human body—however true to the concept it had lived its life—had no such organ, no such center. But we believed in it anyway, as much as previous and concurrent generations believed in something equally nonempirical but romantically, spiritually dear: the soul.

Individuals, however they are explained, manifest themselves and their explanations through symbols. We are, empirically, the symbol-using, symbol-abusing animals (Burke 1989). This fact tends to make most of us social creatures; we use our symbolic capacities to construct (and destroy) relationships, groups, friends, cities, nations, worlds. We are individuals who live in (and tear down) communities of our own making. We are beings whose experience is always, at least at one level, removed from the complex physics of empirical reality; we are therefore "mediated" by symbols. We live in a world of our imagining, of our speaking, of our construction.

Because symbols mediate our lives, we are separated from any unmediated Archimedian truth about ourselves, our environment, our cosmos. As Burke put it, "We are separated from our natural conditions by instruments of our own making" (1989). But that doesn't mean that we stop asking Archimedian questions or that we don't act as if the answers we imagine to be true aren't, in fact, Archimedian truths.

Postmodern societies—particularly postmodern academic cultures—distrust all capital-T Truths (except their own), particularly Archimedian ones spelled out in all capitals (except, among the postmoderns, those that best serve the ideological interests of POSTMODERNISM).

Rapture and Ecstasy

Probably this is partly because the cultural space for this debate is hotly contested and heavily politicized (with very real career and monetary consequences for the players, boosters, and supporting institutions), and partly because it strikes at the heart of our beliefs about ourselves, our relationships, our communities, and our cosmos. The "modern(ist) individual" is therefore pitted against the "postmodern(ist) society" instead of being placed *within* it or connecting both concepts to a larger (in the sense that means more inclusive) explanatory frame. In either case, the result is not too dissimilar from viewing football as "just a game" or religion as "just superstition."

One of the insights offered by the postmodern rhetorics is the idea that "the self" is dispersed across multiple narratives (Eisenberg and Goodall 1993; Gergen 1992; Shotter 1993). Viewed one way, this tends to provide material support for the "fragmented" nature of postmodern society; viewed another way, it encourages cultural analyses of those surfaces as interconnected pathways to questions about "the self" that are being "dispersed." So, in a county that contains many small communities—Clemson, Six Mile, Norris, Pickens, Central, Liberty, Pendleton, and so on—all of which display media surfaces that address, celebrate, appeal to, or otherwise utilize some sense of what constitutes a "self" in these communities, there is most definitely an opening for study, an invitation to an ethnographic opportunity.

A community, after all, can be read through its signs.

Meditation during the Processional Hymn: Why Do Opposites Attract?

> K-MART ISN'T THE ONLY SAVING PLACE
> —Highway 93 signage, Cannon Memorial Baptist Church, Central, SC

Opposites do not, ever, just exist. They are destined to meet. To mingle. To mix it up. Perhaps this is because they are naturally complicit in the symbolic construction of each other. By meeting, mingling, mixing it up, they find completion, a framework that justifies their perspectives as well as their existence. This is the stuff of myths and legends; good and evil; women and men; self and other; inside and outside; nations, armies, religions, football teams, and the whole rest of whatever can be named and argued about. Fought over. Died for. Talked about.

Because opposites are named and organized as such, and because in the naming we seem to energize them—urge their ultimate mingling—and because in the energizing of them we define causes, movements, positions, religions, arguments, parties, struggles, perspectives, and teams that we are willing to devote lifetimes to, our oppositional rhetoric fires up every other neuron, sets up a chain reaction at a molecular level that engulfs the imagination and whatever else it takes to finally move the will. No wonder freedom is defined as the final solitude, the moment *after* release, for a certain firey Rapture—the explosive connection and final resolution of opposites—is the extreme method of all ecstatic release.

We are reminded of this theme in lesser ecstatic acts, and maybe why we are drawn to them. Consider the moment after great victories between equally challenged teams, or the moments after great sex, or even the moments after the best music ends. There is a deeper logic to peak experiences, to climaxes, that define unity in otherwise opposites, that experientially reframe the motions of activities as meaningfully connected, centered, and questing toward some more perfect state, perhaps that perfect solitude, that perfect freedom, that arrives—however briefly—after release is attained.[2]

Because the ecstasy of freedom is *not* easily attained, and because there *are* opposites everywhere, and because we no more know for sure what—*if* anything—is within us than we know what—*if* anything—exists beyond us within that perfect solitude after the final release, life tends toward the dramatic, the juju-ed, the storied, and the staged. We strive, mostly, to define and articulate opposites in order to bring them—and us—to completion.

---

[2] Mihaly Csikszentmihalyi's *Flow* (1990) and more recently *The Evolving Self: A Psychology for the Third Millennium* (1993) suggests that organizing for peak experiences represents the next evolutionary step for communities, not just selves. Communication within peak experiences tends to organize for transcendence through total immersion in immanence; see Eric M. Eisenberg's "Jamming: Transcendence Through Organizing" (1990) for a fuller treatment. In all such related work the core concept is that highly focused, challenging, but "do-able" shared activities that do not require shared meanings establish connections capable of releasing transformative spiritual energies.

Rapture and Ecstasy

Over here we attempt to make amends for God-only-knows-what will salvage our fast, dangling souls from a dead-end run over the jagged precipice of existence.	Over there they say it ain't so, Joe, or at least it ain't so exactly *that* way. So they tell each other stories about us, make juju out of our words, own beliefs, our colors, our songs, our women and men....
... while over here we believe, literally, what we will.	Which over here they say is just plain crazy.

And that is how opposites organize their oppositeness, answering the same eternal questions differently, developing passion about the sanctity of those differences, denying the experiences and realities of each other on account of some deep fear that the other side may be righter, stronger, bigger, better, more glorious to that ultimate Big Mom/Daddy IT of all ITS.

Maybe all theories of the BIG IT are true somewhere, and the ones we decide to buy into are just more or less useful to attain that necessary oppositeness that allows us to join together to pursue those questions, participate in the Great Mystery, in the first place.

Maybe this is why all truths are easier to see from the bright edges of extremities, from the loud outer limits where all the opposites—SURPRISE!—do *not* divide but *unite*, come together, commune, close up the distances from the fast ends of those fantastic experiences to draw us closer to the awe and all of IT as a whole thing, all together now. At the extremeties is the shifting, whirling, raptuous edgeworld of "where," in which exists the raw and perfect sum of all *initial data*, that data that teaches us beginnings and endings as such, as well as that beginnings and endings are as fluid as they are interchangeable. From those initial data experiences, *we know what we know extends through us*—it does not reside within us *or* outside of us—and it connects us to each other, to the world, to the Milky Way, to the BIG IT.

I wonder what would a theory of communication have to account for, given these premises? Where would it begin? What might it suggest? What if our purpose, as spiritual beings, is to unite opposites great and small, to commune, to seek transcendence, to accumulate meaningful connections, to pass through the Rapture and experience the solitude—and freedom—of perfect unity? Considered this way, even if considered argumentatively, what might constitute a source? A message? Channels? Receivers? Feedback? Noise? An environment? How should effectiveness as a communicator be evaluated? How might we understand meanings in discourse? Dialogue? A group? A public speech? Would individual competence and skill be necessarily replaced by competence and skill in communal participation, by excellence in community-building?

Lesson from the (Secular) Scripture: What Might We Imagine Is the True Shape of the Milky Way?

God is the sum of all possibilities.
—EME

God is my quarter back.
—Coach Kenny Hatfield[3]

Clemson Football, Christians, is about the mingling of opposites, the making of Big Deals, the sound of a Big Marching Band,[4] the reach of

---

[3] Kenny Hatfield served as Clemson's head football coach from 1991 to 1993. He was highly controversial because of his reversal of the image for the Clemson football program; he emphasized improving athlete's grade point averages, being a Christian gentleman, and encouraging a team-oriented (rather than individual star-oriented) style of play. After posting an 8–3 record and securing a birth in the Peach Bowl, he asked for a contract extension and was denied, obstensibly because his reforms produced a rather dull style of play on the field that failed to fill Death Valley's stands, thus creating financial losses for IPTAY (I Pay Two Athletes a Year) and for the University.

[4] The Clemson University Marching Band—"the band that rocks the South Land"—is a major part of this unity of opposites, this accomplishment of community in a deeply Christian spiritual frame. Members of the band secretly hand down—class to class, generation to generation—copies of the mimeographed "Unhymnal," a compilation of oppositional songs done to the tunes of the opposing Universities' fight songs but incorporating "dirty" lyrics that have attained a legendary status. The band directors uniformly oppose the singing of these lyrics, but band members sing them anyway, thereby "poaching" (DeCerteau 1984) a variety of dominant culture territories. By playing the Other's songs in their own oppositional voice, and by "throwing

extremeties, the call for community action, for seeing into those actions the work of definitive spiritual beginnings and endings; it is *not* simply a sideshow. Witness, if you will what the filled-to-capacity seats in this stadium are saying to us; imagine these lines as if they were rows of stands in Death Valley, each section made up of persons contributing to the overall community:

80,000+ souls in one symbolic place where legendary opposites are the featured attraction, where "Homecoming" is the baptismal name given to a ritual symbolic ordering of the faithful as well as the merely present to be accounted for,

where literally *every* body part that can be inscribed with symbolic truth—the painted-on Tiger Paws, the school colors, the clothes displaying the school colors as well as "The Paw" as well as other signifiers, IPTAY (I PAY TWO ATHLETES a YEAR)[5] booster pins, even Tiger underwear—are so inscribed with those symbolic talismans, bearing signs of received truths,

where every avenue of approach to the stadium is publicly privileged for the event, and every possible kind of civil and material enforcement is used to signify the superiority of what is about to take place on this sacred, mythical turf;

ries. By playing the Other's songs in their own oppositional voice, and by "throwing down" what is sacred to the Other school by profaning it, they also appropriate "space" for themselves and their musical activities in what is otherwise a "place" dominated by the game of football.

[5] According to local lore, back when Clemson University was called Clemson Agricultural College, IPTAY stood for "I Plow Two Acres a Year" and referred to what area farmers would contribute to the team. During the 1970s it became "I Pay Twenty (Dollars) a Year," then "I Pay Thirty (Dollars) a Year," and, during the Danny Ford years, "I Pay a Thousand a Year." The current idiom is partly serious and partly a joke. IPTAY supporters are free to donate whatever they want to support athletics at Clemson University. The money goes toward student scholarships, athletic scholarships, groundskeeping for the entire campus, support of Death Valley, and, of course, women's and men's sports.

witness an event that is thoroughly organized and finitely hierarchically ordered from the outside in by the states of grace this year—or this lifetime—attained by the giving faithful, the loyal faithful, the IPTAY super boosters and their guests who enjoy the best parking, the best seats, the best view of the game, an event where even the simple parking of cars is defined by proximity to Death Valley and that proximity is formally determined by monetary gifts that are so locally cherished that the best parking spots are often passed down through the generations as a singular, coveted line item in a Last Will and Testament; where, on this Homecoming weekend that lead up to the Homecoming game, a Queen was crowned and cried, where a court was chosen and marched, the earth's largest ever pre-game party was held in the stadium and appropriate fun was made of the opposition and gigantic floats were made and displayed, little staged dramas like "Dances with Tigers" were performed amid the big fireworks and general beauty and spirited cheers.

No, Christians: Homecoming may look like a just another big-time college football game, but I swear to you that the game is merely its charming secular disguise. Why call it "Homecoming?" Isn't there a sense in which all homecomings are about returns to origins, places in our lives where centers—however mythical—are supposed to hold; places where the past can be recalled; places where conversational interpretations of meanings, events, persons, and things can be reviewed, expanded into broader contexts?

Organizational Scholars: The massive organizing and arranging of Homecoming may be read and interpreted as the necessary processual accomplishment of a well-defined goal within a highly coordinated "strong culture," but I tell you that would be at best a partial reading and, perhaps, a dangerous misreading. It would be akin to understanding the coordinated physical activities of women and men coming from and going to classes—some 17,000 of them here on any particular school day—as accomplishing an education. Yes, this is certainly part of the story that defines this culture, but it is not its theme.

Fans and Non-Fans: Is football just a game that is played on a field by (mostly) large men who just get a kick out of knocking the hell out of each other? Is football just a game that the men on the field play to win, and the crowd in the stands wins by surrogate cheering and booing?

Rapture and Ecstasy

Put a bit differently: Is rock n roll just a form of music that occurs on the radio and is used by adolescents to show rebellion? Still differently: Is lovemaking just a sexual encounter between hot, consenting adults who get to accomplish a thrill by rubbing their naked parts together until, preferably, warm sticky juices run down their legs?

Ahem. Pardon me. Sometimes I do get carried away. Let me say it this way: In each of the above "peak experience" scenarios, the words I've used do tell parts of the stories, but so what? Every action tells part of some story. But in my experience, football, rock n roll, and lovemaking are many-storied stories. Football—or for that matter any team sport that unites opposites, such as basketball, baseball, volleyball, or even tennis—can be played, watched, and understood as a simple game of balls, bodies, and contexts; or it can be played, watched, and understood as an opportunity for a deeply focused mystical enterprise, a chance to align, to coordinate, to harmonize, to dignify, and to experience transcendence. Rock n roll—or for that matter any musical form—can be performed, observed, or interpreted as just that—music; it may also be engaged as a "jamming" experience (Eisenberg 1990) in and through which "being" transcends "knowing," and coordinated actions produce meanings and feelings richer than the sum of movements; rock n roll can also be participated in and understood as an organizing form for social and professional life (Goodall 1991), not limited to musical forms but *emanating from the experiencing of them*. And lovemaking—well, sure, there is (preferably) that body rubbing and releasing of fluids, but surely these experiences can be engaged in and interpreted as part of the deeper mystery of being human, of connecting with another questing soul, of using that connection to create a shared experience that in the very sharing of it connects us to Creation itself.

What I am asking you to think about is this: What if the organizing, communicating, and variously ascribed symbolic meanings inherent to these (and other) peak experiences—these deeply mysterious, mystical, communal-self, spiritual experiences—*were what we were supposed to be all about*? What if our theories of communicating and organizing could be themselves transformed, as well as informed, by peak experiences of spiritual origins rather than by the obvious coordination of lesser behaviors; the patterns of messages; the surfaces of games, music, and sexuality?

All of you: What if:

Maybe the Milky Way really is

SHAped like a FootBALL.

Or maybe it is, but it doesn't matter.
Or maybe it is, and it is *all* that matters.
Or this: Maybe it *only* is *when* it matters.

Within this framework of interpretive possibilities, what might be the necessary reading of this football game, this community-making quest, these questing selves within a (religious) community on this Homecoming weekend, this fine Sign in search of an even finer Signifier?

Let Us Pray

The Metaphoric Nature of All Symbols is a Sign
That Should be Read as a Clue
To a Fundamental Interconnectedness in Language, Which Exists Primarily To
Remind Us that Our Being is Similarly Interconnected,
And that the Questing in our Use of Language is Divine
And So, Too, is Any Gathering Where Language is Spoken.

There needs to be some symbol which keeps the whole thing together.

—Wright Bryan, vice-president for development, Clemson University, 1970

Symbols like the tiger paw won't help us win football games . . . but we hope they will help retain the enthusiasm Clemson people are known for.

—Hootie Ingram, football coach during the 1970 season when "The Paw" was introduced

Since 1970, The Paw has engulfed the Tiger faithful. The SAE fraternity annually paints huge tiger paws on all the streets on campus leading to the stadium. At some point, all of the major highways leading into Clemson have had paws painted on them. . . . When Clemson was invited to

Rapture and Ecstasy

> play in the 1977 Gator Bowl, some enterprising students had a stencil cut of a tiger paw some 22–24 inches high. From Clemson to Jacksonville, every five miles or so, the student spray painted a paw on the road. When Clemson played in the Orange Bowl for the national championship in 1981, these tiger paws were extended from Jacksonville to Miami.
>
> —Bob Bradley

This is an account of a football community written as if the shape of the Milky Way mattered. It is also a quest for the expression of spirituality in everyday forms of meaning that citizens of Pickens County, South Carolina, routinely take for granted—as well as talk about and pass on to their children—which is to say the paper could be about signs read as clues to a grander mystery. "The Paw." "Death Valley." "Clemson Football."

Interpreted a bit more grandly for an audience of communication scholars, the paper may be about how organizing involves more than what gets done in organizations and why organizing processes are hardly ever appreciated for what they might be doing, spiritually, for those who elect—or who get elected—to participate in them. All communication—all organizing—is mediated, *yes*; but at what level of interpretation?

And then there is this, about the "business" of communication: everywhere in America, maybe the world, business is becoming more personal and communal—more directly connected to notions of an interdependence in all relationships, to issues of spirituality, morality, and consciousness. Yet, at the same time, our notions of spirituality are becoming more mysterious and diverse, less directly related to issues of religion and belief and more akin to issues of personal and communal transformation and change. The language of doing business reflects these simultaneous evolutions; consider the spiritual origins of common issues involved in organizational transformation and change processes: Vision, empowerment, path, harmony, balance, creativity, dialogue, leadership, and community. Consider also the merging of spirituality and organizing practices in the development of aptly named "self-directed" or "self-managed" work teams—coaching, facilitating, communicating with others as you would have them communicate with you, honesty, reflection, unity.

These two previously separated fields of experience merge and cannot any longer be understood in isolation or merely relegated to "moments" of clarity or connection, but instead to what Bateson and Donaldson (1991) envisioned as "a sacred unity: further steps to an ecology of mind." Spirituality and organizing must be approached as a deeper, broader, more intricate manifestation of consciousness, and of *will*. This "consciousness," however it is variously expressed and wherever it is found, suggests the presence of a "new" communal culture in which communication can be understood as the localized site of a personal *and* communal quest for transforming connections, and the language of dialogue can be understood as the primary vehicle—the mediator—of change as well as the primary way of serving—and servicing—the activities and processes that expand personal searches for meanings into communal and societal evolutions of consciousness. At the beginnings and endings of these quests are totalizing, unifying experiences—raptures of a symbolic kind; between those extremities lie daily possibilities for transformations, changes, and evolutions that continuously pose personal/communal/communication questions—questions as old as humanity: Who are we? What we are doing here and why we are doing it? What purposes beyond the immediate gratification of everyday needs, expectations, and goals may we best serve?

This text engages those questions in the only way I know how to, recognizing that experiences can never be fully captured in words and that lived experience is huger than any vocabulary, using incomplete signs—often the most ordinary of signs—to evoke vast interpretive possibilities, embodying the quest in rhetoric that struggles to make connections with something beyond the scope of words—however poetic or instrumental—to express. To make this "work" requires more than a careful critical reading of it; in fact, I must ask you to suspend judgment, to be instead open to the unusual possibilities this multivocal, multitextual, multilayered experience evokes within you, *openings* that I hope will call into question the work we may need to do as scholars if spirituality, communication, and organizing are to become part of our evolving consciousness.[6]

I make my request this way because, I presume, all of us recognized "the desert" a little earlier as an opening metaphor but are at this point in our reading—for some reason—less willing to accept a football as a purposeful sign for our little galaxy. Maybe the interplays of language, of metaphor, of imagination will mediate the spirit of this communal undertaking.

Second Lesson: What If You Do, Always, Stand before God? Would This Be an Exercise in Perceived Opposites or in Cosmic Unities?

> LIVE TODAY AS WILL WISH YOU HAD LIVED WHEN YOU STAND BEFORE GOD
> —Highway 93 signage, Cannon Memorial Baptist Church, Central, SC

It is written that by taking that deeper metaphorical journey into the desert of our incomplete lives, a resurrected, crucified man-God will speak directly to us in a way no other one ever could.

Don't you Christian, wonder, what, *exactly*, he might say?

---

[6] My meaning here is more complex than it may seem. In part I am advocating the necessary availability of an oppositional reading, or at least a comic one, foolish enough to wear the metaphors of jesting while speaking an unusual truth. This is probably because on matters of spirituality I am less comfortable with the deeply religious Christians in this community than I am with the football players (read: ordinary citizens) who put themselves—and their souls—at risk daily, as well as on autumn Saturdays. I wonder, I imagine, and I doubt where my capacity for metaphor and my experiences will take me, or us. I identify closely with the following passage, taken from W. Glasgow Phillips's novel *Tuscaloosa* (1994): "I may be mistaken, of course. It may be that I am merely drifting away, in the manner of a religious person. Religious people espouse the notion that the revealed truth is the only real truth. My experience with religious people is that they do not have a clear understanding of things. They are fucked up by what they variously perceive to be the revealed truth. I could be having a similar experience" (20).

PERFORMING COMMUNITY

To *you*?

What if he wanted to know what you *really* believe in?

> One group may be in power, but all are in consciousness, and it is consciousness that creates culture.
>
> —Michael Ventura

> Why doesn't common sense become common practice? Because beliefs get in the way... beliefs prevent us from seeing reality.
>
> —Jennifer James

What do you *really* believe in?

Do you believe in Good and Evil?

How do you believe in them? As *powers* from above or below (or maybe just beyond) that we can tap into or that can manipulate us if our soul is not careful or watchful or strong enough?

As in Big Opposite (Air-Born) Forces?

Me, being an existential postmodern Christian-Buddhist hopeful (oxymoronic, ironic, questing, and admittedly conflicted), what do *I* believe? I believe that power is an earthling obsession, a set of rhetorical possibilities, *not* invisible rays that direct actions or corrupt them. I believe these things, truly, and I believe—with Jennifer James—that these very beliefs may be getting in the way of my ability to make sense of reality. But whose reality? Whose reality *is* reality? When we put it that way we are inevitably back to the cold mediating prisms of power, of rhetorical influence, of real rays that we shoot back and forth at each other across the stadiums of life, across deserts of experience, across any Death Valley. My hope is that Michael Ventura's wisdom about consciousness is a symbolic clue, a sign that transcends earthly power and rhetorical force and yet is defined by and located immanently within it, a clue to our collective evolution toward respect for diverse communities that can, at once, be seen and understood as unity through a *spiritual* culture.

Unity is the Force for me, and it runs *through* me, connecting me to all that I encounter and all that I don't. Unity is the force in all of IT: Air, water, fire, Earth, earthlings, animals, starry starry nights; but because we are spiritual beings who speak and listen and move about in ways we find meaningful and intriguing, also *Language*, our human media with the capital *L*. For this reason, our everyday discourse *matters*; our discourse worlds *count*; the discourse we live within and find necessary and appealing is a major (symbolic/cosmic) clue.

Rapture and Ecstasy

What would a theory of communication that spelled Good and Evil out of the same material alphabet say about the language—the metaphors—we used to describe them? To divide them *and* to unite them? To define evidence of both of them on our common playing field? And to sometimes confuse them, twist them, turn them over or around? Play the fool to some invisible King?

These are, admittedly, Big Questions.

Maybe that is what our discipline should be about these days, eh?

The rhetorical is always tending toward the evangelical, maybe for this reason. Those who study communication and who are duly appointed to educate and upgrade the skills of others in its use seem to be playing a child's game—a kind of "football in the dark"—without linking what we do to the Big Questions. We are the mediators, the language users, the head coaches on this imagined field where what gets said and done in the world—in our trek across the desert—is the truest measure of our sense of community, of our shared but diverse realities.

The Sermon: What Is the Common Language of a Spiritual Community?

Welcome to Six Mile, an Old Town of New Ideas. —Highway 133 signage, Six Mile, SC	Drive With Care: You Are Entering Tiger Country. —Highway 76 signage, Quick Stop convenience store	To Get To Heaven, Turn Right and Go Straight. —Highway 93 signage, Cannon Memorial Baptist Church, Central, SC

Friends, I drove by these signs on the way to the game today. And I wondered if they might not be read not so much as signs, but as clues to Something Else. Clues perhaps to a common language that we share. For instance: "Six Mile—An Old Town of New Ideas." Isn't this slogan really a metaphor not so much for this particular little town, but for this Earth, maybe even this universe? And how about the one on the convenience store: "Drive with Care: You are Entering Tiger Country." If we were aliens visiting this earth, wouldn't this sign—coupled with the presence of so many Clemson football fans dressed out in orange and white—tell a bigger story? Perhaps we, the roaming people on this spinning planet in a spiraling galaxy, are both as noble and as predatory as Tigers, creatures who—in ancient primitive religions and in local practices—symbolize the awesome power of the divine and at the same time serve as a warning to all who question their divinity and our community, creatures that must, therefore, be watched out for. Which brings me to that third sign, the one outside the church that gives public directions to Heaven: "Turn Right and Go Straight." But, friends, if you actually follow those directions in this town, you end up at Tiger Stadium, at Death Valley. And perhaps therein lies the lesson, the truth within the use and interpretation of the metaphor. Within all three of these metaphors.

I have come before you today convinced that what we have here is something we should be proud of but also should worry about. What we should be proud of is, of course, our community. Now what, exactly, you might be wondering, is a "community"? Is it a collection of familiar buildings, known peoples, and locally interesting places? Is it a sense of belonging, of inclusion, a certain feeling that comes over you when you come back to it from far away? Is it a kind of common spirit that we share just being here or being from here, perhaps because we have breathed the same air and moved our solitary bodies through its spaces, eaten in its restaurants, shopped in its stores, even paid our taxes here?

Many authorities might tell you that all of the things I have just mentioned define and even sum up what a community is. But I think they are missing something, and that something is very important. A community is not a physical thing so much as it is an imagined one. Although it must have physical borders and boundaries, city limits and county lines, highways and alleyways, stores and shops and restaurants and parking lots; although it often contains familiar faces speaking a local argot and makes public use of a common clock, it must thrive in the imaginations of those who live there before anyone—any citizen of that community—can truly partake of it. And it must thrive in the imagination not as a single thing, and not as a physical thing, but as a field of imaginative possibilities that can be communicated to strangers and longtime residents alike.

Rapture and Ecstasy

I think we have that here in Clemson, in Central, in Pendleton, Six Mile, and Liberty. I think we have that even in Seneca, although that is a separate county; and in Anderson and Greenville, too, although they are miles and miles away. For that matter, I know we have that in the homes and businesses of people who have lived and worked and gone to school here, but now live far, far away—in every county of our state, in every state of our blessed Union, and probably in almost every nation in the world. There is a special bond among people who have experienced what we have here, how we live, who we are, and most importantly, what we are about.

And that thing that we have, that thing that makes up a special part of who we are, that determines what we are about, is again many things, not one single thing. I see it each morning as I drive to work, but you don't have to. I find it in signs like the ones I mentioned earlier in my sermon today, but you might not. I feel it when I meet someone living somewhere else who knows us, even though I am quite sure that what I am feeling is probably not the same as what they are feeling. And so that is the way it is, and the way it is not. A community lives in our imaginations; it is as vast as anything we can imagine and contains all that we can connect to it—our experiences, our reading, our personal histories, our most casual conversations, and our most deeply held beliefs.

It is in the connections we make that we find community. Those connections have meanings *for* us, it's true, but have better meanings *among* us, as when we gather together and speak and listen to one another talk about our lives, our work, our values and ideals. The thing is, friends, we have to get together to be together, and we have to be together—even if we are far, far away from here—to call this place into being. Community is, I think, a special kind of calling. It brings us together but does not require of us the sharing of identical experiences. It is a place where we imagine we are richer for the exchange of views, not for the singular domination of one view. If a community can be considered our common text, it is surely a text that can be read in many languages and interpreted in many ways.

Which brings me to my worry, to my concern about our community. For as much as a community must thrive and live in our imaginations before we can enter into it, so to must we be willing and able to enter that community we have imagined, that we have, in fact, created. I saw another sign last week that summed it up this way: "If you attended work as often as you attend church, would you still have a job?" It made me think that if we changed the word *work* to *community*, and then purposefully fooled around with the second part, we might have something I could use in today's sermon. So I did fool around with it, and here it is: "If you worked as hard at building community as you do at building your resume or watching television,[7] would you still have to worry about crime, or drug abuse, or illiteracy?" Or for that matter, would you have to worry about any number of common problems that we all worry about?

I don't think so. I think that the community we have imagined is still waiting for us to work on it, to imagine it and to live in it even better and finer than it is, or that we do. What I am saying here this morning is that the common language of a spiritual community is made up of what we put into it, which is to say that it is made up of connections between ourselves and each other. We make it up as we go along, and the way we do that is by acting as if the metaphors we use as metaphors, are, in fact, real.

So the next time you say something like "things are getting worse around here," remember it is YOU that is making it that way, by the words you speak and by the actions you *aren't* performing. In the end, it is a lot like a football game in Death Valley. You can stay home and watch the game on television, or you can attend it and become part of what you and others will always remember, cheer on the home team or even the opposition if you have to, but do whatever is in your power to make this game a great game, a memorable game, a game that has earned its rightful place as part of your life and the life of your community.

Friends, we are spiritual beings living in a material, symbolic world. So, too, are we bodies burdened with questing, often frustrated, deeply ambiguous souls. As a result, most of us act as if we have to reach into

---

[7] It is no accident, I think, that our sense of community has diminished since the advent of television. According to a study cited in Debra Baldwin's essay "As Busy as We Wanna Be" in the *Utne Reader* (1994), "an astounding 40 percent of the average American's free time dissipates in front of the tube. This may account for some of the discrepancies between . . . [the] assertion that we have more free time than a generation ago and most people's feeling that they have less. We may notice less of a chance for reading, visiting, and preparing meals because television absorbs more of our time" (54). It would seem plausible, then, that because Americans spend more time indoors "absorbed by" television, we spend less time outdoors or among our neighbors, thus seriously reducing the opportunities for community-building communication.

Rapture and Ecstasy

another world to get in touch with the spiritual, to give voice to the soul. To do this, we are led to believe we need to go outside of the body just to begin to experience spirituality. We think, sometimes, that spirituality is "out there" somewhere, maybe among what we call "the heavenly bodies," and maybe just out there among the assembled, questing bodies on Saturday afternoons in Death Valley. Whatever spirituality is, and wherever the experience of spirituality is located, it is almost always positioned outside of our individual bodies yet linked through the questing communal voice of the soul to the deepest inner reaches of the self, which is simultaneously in the deepest inner reaches of humanity.

Friends, perhaps this presence of connections—and this absence that spells the loss of a shared sense of community—should help us reorient our thinking. Not: Where is Spirit? Not even: What is God? But from the desert of the soul:

What is this life --this trek across Death Valley-- about?

HELL, friends, is probably not a place but the absence of one. In a biblical sense, it is to be cut off from God, to lose one's soul-linkage to eternity *for* eternity. In a postmodern secular sense, it is to yearn for deeply meaningful connections of ourselves to our community—and of our community to the cosmos—and to experience only its poignant ab-

> Prayers cannot be answered until they are prayed.
> —Highway signage, Cannon Memorial Baptist Church, Central, SC

> Am I satisfied, or just don't care?
> —Old Clemson Highway signage, Corinth Baptist Church, Seneca, SC

> HELL is the final proof
> What you do matters!
> —Highway signage, Pickens Church of Christ

sence, a vast nothing where a centered something ought to be. It is to experience one's life—one's self—dispersed across multiple competing, often oppositely directed narratives, endlessly disconnected from a felt need for what may be only an imagined, perhaps mythic, usually romanticized center. Like gravity, this narrative center for all of life's experiences would always predictably pull down and into the centers of self the all of everything, making out of surprise, surrender, and mere serendipity one *common* sense, one fully signified, unified, probably symmetrical whole. It would be a Milky Way shaped like a football. It would be a Death Valley as an Eden of grass as well as the human desert of luminous, symbolic possibilities. Where opposites attract.

Let us imagine a community we can all share in.

Let us imagine a community we can all share in building.

Let us imagine a community worthy of our best, of our most spiritual, selves.

Let us pray . . .

The Offering

We think we are Christian, but we are not. . . . American religion, like American imaginative literature, is a severely internalized quest romance, in which some version of im-

Rapture and Ecstasy

> mortality serves as the object of desire.
>
> —Harold Bloom

> I will not leave you desolate. The Holy Spirit whom the Father will send in my name, he will teach you all things.
>
> —Jesus Christ

> Religion is imagined, and always must be reimagined.
>
> —Harold Bloom

Spiritual beings don't get through the desert—and don't construct communities—easily; we aren't meant to. This is, after all, the place where THE BIG GAME gets played, where opposites attract, where what goes on is as old as the universe and still bounded by dinosaur vistas and challenged by improbable dreams. This is the stage where the movements and rhythms of the heavens—even if they are only sky and clouds and infinity—become one with the movement and rhythms of this earth. We *are* the Milky Way, as well as it passengers.

What we are meant to discover, I think, is that *communication between and among us is best considered—in the interests of community—a kind of mutual life coaching.* We know there is a Big Game going on and we should act like we know we are in it, always as players but sometimes positioned as fans, sometimes positioned as cheerleaders, sometimes positioned as disinterested spectators, and sometimes positioned (because we are mortals) to bet dangerously on the results. Our job is not necessarily to win the game, although we will play as if that is the purpose, but instead to work together on figuring out how to connect our lives to Others' lives, knowing that if and when we do figure it all out—I am speaking here of the BIG IT, the meaning of the game itself—chances are good that it won't matter and yet it will still be all that matters. Our quest may well be just that—our quest. It is sort of like solving a problem when the hand that has been dealt to you doesn't add up to a problem at all, but instead is a mystery.

I am asking, of course, for a vision. An empowering vision. A vision that makes possible a vital connection between *communication* and *community*.

I am asking for a theory of communication that can revitalize a broad spectrum of questing souls, that can focus energies on personal transformation and change without sacrificing community and environment, that is ambiguous enough to be interpreted differently and yet precise enough to discount the differences in interpretation that don't matter or to brush aside those differences that get in the way. What would this theory *do*?

This theory would "do" dialogue because it would be dedicated to the proposition that the root of "communication" is, indeed, "communion," and that the purpose of communion is a celebration of our *interbeing*, our inherent genetic, symbolic, and cosmic connectedness. It is a connectedness rendered in material form because we must all share passage on this blue planet, and rendered ethereal because we all do share the capacities for wonder, for imagination, and—in the same breath—for big mystery some of us call God.

This theory would "do" life coaching because it would see communication as the practical art of working with each other through the trials—the victories as well as the losses—in our trek across Death Valley. As such, this theory would sponsor teamwork through cooperation, and it would balance an appreciation for individual effort and leadership with the accomplishment of communal good and world happiness. It would view speech as always a spiritual utterance capable of expanding our collective consciousness; it would view listening as the way to access the experiences of another's life quest, and therefore as meaningful and even holy. Such a theory would transform the purposes of classrooms as well as what it would mean to be a communication professional. Perhaps our curriculum vitae would list something far more important than published articles; it might list transformed lives, improved communities, a better world.

Let us pray . . .

The Closing, Gospel-Fired Hymn

We are a religiously mad culture, furiously searching for the spirit, but each of us is subject and object of the one quest, which must be for the original self, a spark or breath in us that we are convinced goes back to before creation.

—Harold Bloom

It is crucial to the lives of all our citizens, as it is to all human beings at all times, that they encounter a world that possesses a transcendent meaning, a world in which the human experience makes sense. Nothing is more dehumanizing, more certain to generate a crisis, than to experience one's life as a meaningless event in a meaningless world.

—Irving Kristol

Rapture and Ecstasy

I am imagining this, and entering it, too:
We are in Death Valley, and there is a big game going on. Call it Homecoming. Call it life.

> Man is the symbol-using animal, creator of the negative, separated from his natural condition by instruments of his own making . . . and rotten with perfection.
>
> —Kenneth Burke

> This center and source, for which we have never contrived any worthy name, is as if it were breathing, flowering, soundlessly, a snoring silence of flame; it is as if flame were breathed forth from it and subtly played about it: and here in this breathing and play of flame, a thing so strong, so valiant, so unvanquishable, it is without effort, without emotion, I know it shall at length outshine the sun.
>
> —James Agee and Walker Evan

Somehow we always seem to be in the middle of it moving faster and faster toward the Rapture, don't we? And by design, we never know the meaning of an event—or of our lives—until it is done. It always seems to vanish too quickly.

The score is tight, the teams are incredibly well matched. We are on the fifty-yard line in the upper tier of the stands—best seats in the house—courtesy of a generous IPTAY supporter.

The sun is hot; the sky is blue. This could be the desert. A fully armed F-14 stalls his engines and cruises silently, perhaps menacingly, through the center of the stadium. An *alum*, no doubt, but which side's? Probably a Christian, judging from the armament. During the third quarter, three colorful, playful hot-air balloons arrive on the breeze and station themselves at the campus end of the stadium, just watching, bright treble bearers of some indescribable—and indescribably beautiful—ineffable message, an oppositional and dialogic counter to the previous F-14.

These are messages intended for you, Christians. We are coming closer to the end, and in the end all things will merge. But you know this, instinctively.

Perhaps we should **stand** for this.

PERFORMING COMMUNITY

Perhaps we should **cheer** for this.
Perhaps we should **experience** this as . . .

The fourth quarter is spent entirely on our feet. All of us, all 80,000+ of us. No one in the stands sits down, or on the streets surrounding the stands, or out beyond us in the parking lots or painted highways where nonticketed fans gather around radios, and no one stops

cheer**ing!**
Shouting!
jamm**ing!**
Rockin!
Diggin' It!
Making It
HAPPEN!

With 14 seconds to go, the other team attempts a field goal to win the game. It is a relatively short shot—35 yards—and the field goal kicker has already today made three longer than this.

Go! Go! Go! Go!

Rapture and Ecstasy

The ball is snapped. The kicker runs toward it, lunges into it, the football rises and turns in the stark air moves purposefully toward its upright target. There is a hush all over the world. The football turns and turns . . . but . . . begins to descend *before* the goal line . . . goes off to the right . . .
the stands er**upt!**

A woman standing next to me grabs me, kisses me full on the lips, tears streak down her cheeks, she screams, "Thank God! Just Thank **God!!!**" The scoreboard **explodes!** The Marching Band music gets louder!

We Won!

The skies open . . .
and I say . . .

Don't let the Rapture pass you by . . . .

5

Immanence and Angels: Experiencing Parallel Worlds

> Maybe we have been looking in the wrong places. Maybe they have been right here before our very eyes, somehow, all the time. Maybe we have simply been too busy to see. . . . Angels have always seemed as elusive as the wind—as hard to capture as happiness itself, or love. This is because the important part of angels is not physical. Like happiness and love, they are also unlimited, eternal presences.
>
> —Karen Goldman

> Talking with our angels, connecting to the Divinity within us, elevates our personal awareness, which in turn improves our lives and circumstances. When we are able to connect with our own inner Divinity, it becomes easier to see the Divinity within others. The day we all see God in each other—we'll be Home.
>
> —Alma Daniel, Timothy Wyllie, and Andrew Ramer

Stand on the wide balcony outside the penthouse suite at the Clemson House and look quietly over the lush gardenlike grounds. What you see—particularly in the bright, close, darkling moments just before the downfall of warm midafternoon rains in early spring; moments when dense, baby and navy blue, orange and red, greenish and deeply purple clouds swirl in the mad dance of the higher air, dangerously reorganizing the presence of the heavens upon this earth; when the warm air is made suddenly thicker with pre-rain ozone and the slightly blue, intoxicating metallic smell (and dramatic possibilities) of a distant tornado reaches deeply into your mind, your lungs, your heart; when the rich, multiflora ensculpturating presence of newly abloom dogwoods, maples, azaleas, oaks, grasses, and gums that ordinarily grant a soft, feminine, sensual grace to the obvious work of masculine engineering everywhere defining

Immanence and Angels

the hard, red brickness of buildings and bureaucratic in-line finiteness of campus and town add small, innocent, frantic harmonies to what has become a white, lightning-laced, discordant yellow and blue surround—and what you experience of living in this moment acquires an undeniable but ineffable immanence, half the result of synaptically overloaded senses and half created by the poetic overworking of a vivid imagination that come together to thoroughly imbue all the available surfaces with a mysteriously rich, colorful, enveloping translucence. If you enter this moment openly, and do not worry too much about the dead-even chances of some damned tornado or at all about what the weather might do to your hair, you might also gain immediate access to a mystical experience known in the spiritual literatures as "immanence," or the astounding sensual and perceptual ability to experience yourself as a Being interdependent with all other forms of life—boundaryless and selfless—unspeakably alive and yet vividly within what must be the summative whole of all possibility—and at the same time—known to be at one within the whole domain of Creation.

What is communicated through—or perhaps merely communicated to us by—this experience is relatively common and not at all dependent on the availability of a balcony on a spring afternoon at the Clemson House. I use this setting primarily because it once happened to me there, but it is an experience that manifests itself across all times and all continents. If my access to it is any clue at all, once it has happened to you, it continues to happen—fairly regularly—throughout a lifetime. Like any peak experience, it is exhilarating, somewhat confounding, and always leaves you *wanting more* of it. But its lesson, I think, is not in the rush of its communicative peak, or in the afterward wanting of its ineffable more; it is *within the experiencing* of this moment itself *for* itself. What is taught in that moment—what gets communicated clearly—is how *very* close we are, in the everyday, to a penetrable, parallel world—to a knowledge of and being in such a world—that we might otherwise imagine is much further away. It is a world, in fact, that most of us have been taught is a lifetime away, and that many Christians among us believe only await those souls good and fortunate enough, whose mindful cognitions and ordinary behaviors have achieved—or perhaps merely warrant entry into—the heavenly afterlife.

I don't particularly share that Christian belief, nor do I deny its reality for those who do believe in it. Since early childhood I have espoused publicly the admittedly strange notion (particularly back in the late '50s and early '60s, and in the company of Eisenhower-era conservative Republican adults) that "whatever you believe will happen to you happens to you." These days I think that espousal was merely the surface evidence of previous evolutions of spirit, a prescription that speaks at once to both *this* life *and* to an afterlife. Maybe because this life *is* an afterlife, considered within the framework of spiritual evolutions.

I think this penetrable, parallel world is fundamentally at one with ours and that we are connected intimately to it.[1] I am convinced that the lesson of its experiential availability should speak directly to how we make sense out of its apparent absence from everyday life as well as to how the intimate realities of its experiencing should inform what we conceive of as "purposes" and "meanings" *for* life. And I believe the lessons of its experiencing can teach us why we should—and how we must—derive alternative sensibilities and purposes for how communication should figure into a holistic reorganizing of our understanding of the work of lives—as well as the lives we enact at work—in our communities and on this tortured blue planet.

This chapter pursues these objectives. Again, the routes chosen for this pursuit develop insights into the everyday life of a local community, or better: how the experiencing of meaning in everyday life makes available the duality of presence and absence of immanence in a local community. It is a chapter about local knowledge writ large.

---

[1] Jacob Needleman (1986) provides a rich philosophical account of the connections between the Self and Reality, a perspective on the nature of immanence that sums up and informs what I am trying to convey here: that we are *part* of Reality, not separate from it. The Reality I speak of here (and that the sign of capitalization is supposed to evoke) is the universe—heavens and earth, stars and skies, galaxies and quarks, poetry and leptons, self, Others, and contexts, Spirit. Needleman elaborates: "In Buddhism the Buddha-nature, enlightened Mind, is the true reality of myself and the universe. In Hinduism, Atman, the real human Self, is *Brahman*, the Absolute God-Creator-Destroyer-Preserver. In Judaism the name of God is I AM, and Christianity reconstitutes this idea through the teaching about the Holy Spirit which is ultimate Self (the "personal God," the Father) acting and suffering within all men. This idea is expressed and developed in all teachings with extraordinary richness, subtlety, and complexity—especially where it is a question of psychospiritual practices guiding the struggle for ever-deepening human experience of this reality" (166).

Immanence and Angels

One Free Elvis Stamp with Haircut: In What Sense Is Sibyl's a Beauty Shop?[2]

If you approach community-making from a different perspective—one of immanence rather than transcendence, for example—you come into Clemson on a vastly different, yet empirically parallel road. In this case, instead of taking State Highway 93 from Norris through Central, turn left out of Issaqueena Farms and left again onto State Highway 133 from Six Mile—which is actually about nine miles from Clemson—and upon whose two-laned blacktop surfaces you pass—in addition to older rural homes and the outreaching mini-farms of the '80s and the newer upstart '90s edgeworlds known as "exurbs"—signs of parallel other worlds that signal availability of entry to those who read, experience, and understand them that way. One such other world announces itself as *Sibyl's*. It is a small concrete building next to a blue house on the right as you come into town. You will see the styling salon behind the perfect purple VW Bug parked out front in the brown gravel, by the unlit commercial purple and white neon sign that says, deliciously:

> One Free Elvis Stamp with Haircut
> Walk-ins Welcome

You walk in. With a sign like that—with an attitude like that—how could you not?

Sibyl is a friendly, charismatic, handsome, middle-aged Southern woman with a big heart and "a major thing" for Elvis. You could say that in these postmodern economic times, she makes ends meet by cutting, styling, and perming hair; by working part time in a Pendleton restaurant; and by making elaborate and locally popular pottery in her studio behind the beauty parlor. Or you could say that her life is structured and materially enriched by active participation in multiple life narratives, access to which she gains by moving fluidly into and out of multiple

---

[2] I am indebted to Christa "C. J." Carroll for many of the insights contained in this section. As a graduate student, she conducted fieldwork in this locale, concentrating on Sibyl's.

public identities that are enacted fully within particular spatial domains, such as a beauty parlor, a pottery workshop, a home, a church, a restaurant in Pendleton, and various elsewheres. Or you could say—more to the point, I think—that she is a local spiritual leader disguised as a busy woman, and that these various work and life activities are shaped predominantly by her genuine, caring concern for Others.

There are important differences in each of those constructions, differences that either take you into her parallel world or separate you critically from it. Probably, for many of the readers of this book, each one of those descriptions offers entry into this text—into this world—in ways that enable identification or deny it. In this way, these definitional stances—and our ability to identify with them—metaphorically tell us a great deal about why traditional communication scholars learn to prefer the distanced, "objective," critical stance, as well as show us how that preference distances us from experiencing and knowing the spiritual world imminently *and* immanently available to us. Put simply, how we frame a context determines what we will find there.

Because this book is about a spiritual alternative for framing contexts and finding meaningful what as a result appears there, I recognize Sibyl's as a spiritual center, and Sibyl as a spiritual leader. I do so because of a particular way I have of reading the evidence she presents to me, evidence that—read as signs of spiritual communion—unites Self and Others through Spirit. If you assemble and read otherwise ordinary, everyday conversational clues at Sibyl's as constituting—to her, to me, and to the Others with whom she communicates—something *other* than a lag-sequential series of disconnected, or disembodied, empirical utterances punctuated by spaces called silences, you find access—pathways—into a parallel, other, *immanent* world. "Sibyl's an angel," Helen[3] tells me. "I don't mean like one with wings or nothin', but more like she's an agent of God right here in Clemson, a healer."

Although "Walk-ins are Welcome," Sibyl's regular clientele comes here for something more fulfilling than a new "do." You can feel that when you open the door. It would be too easy to say that what you feel is "something in the air," something that feels like a heightened sense of

---

[3] Not her real name. All the names—except Sibyl's—of persons and competing businesses in this section have been changed.

awareness—an inward revolution—but it would be less than true to say that *isn't* what its like, or maybe *is*. It is also true that into this environment those who come here share words and stories, facial expressions, body postures and movements, about their own and each other's lives. They enter Sibyl's world to talk about their joys and sorrows, their worries and fears, what they love and what they hate, who they know and what they know about them, and to make these otherwise often disconnected facts, feelings, and experiences connect to her's, to other customer's, and thereby to a community of their own imagining.

In the background is country music radio, down low until an Elvis golden oldie or somebody's current favorite fills the room with turned-up sounds, a mediated voice—a "there and then" presence—to the immanent "here and now," doing something more than merely adding volume to a known space, adding *dimension* to it as well. Sometimes the song introduces a change in topic, or extends the current one, or causes the kind of shared laughter that coincidence cannot fully account for. Out on the highway cars continue to drive by in an unregulated rhythm punctuated by the rude, loud interruptions of heavy trucks and unmuffled neighbors, which is also part of it, a natural part connected to what goes on and gets talked about inside Sibyl's.

C. J. tells me that it took her almost two months of figuring it out to find the center that calls people to Sibyl and that collects them and their narratives to this place. That center is this: most of the women who come here have cancer. Some are getting over it, some aren't. Some that have been through here have passed on to the Other Side.[4] And some that walk in here are, they might tell you, experiencing something wrong with them now that they just can't describe and that physicians can't find.

Words like these get around in a community like this. Places emerge

---

[4] Interestingly, the traditional Christian religious construction of death as a transition to a parallel world—an "Other Side"—separates that parallel world from our everyday one. Yet death is—from *inside* this narrative—a way of gaining access to a peacefully coexisting parallel sphere available alongside of our everyday secular realities, a "place" whose reward is so rich as to inform our everyday choices about thoughts and behaviors and whose messengers—angels—travel between. Evidence from "near death experiences" and the insights of those who have experienced the paranormal suggest otherwise. The separation of the world of death from the world of life is probably more akin to "changing planes" of consciousness and personhood; see Carl Becker (1993).

for talk like this to occur and converge in, for certain life experiences to be expressed in, and, no doubt, for some healing to be done in. Maybe what makes this so has less to do with the actual stories that are told—because, frankly, although every person's story is truly their own and therefore unique to them, they do acquire a certain sameness over time—than with the ability to create a place for telling them, for dealing with their ambiguities as well as with their certainties, for working their often unanswerable questions into meaningful forms of communal experiences that do not require answers, that the speaking of answers might, in fact, disturb.

People who are in trouble—and even those who tell you they want answers—usually don't. Not really. Answers have gotten them into trouble, answers have brought them here, to you; what they need now but may not have the words to say, and where they want to go but may not have the language to express, requires something answers cannot provide. What they need is a dream, *a way to imagine themselves as other than they are*, a place made out of possibilities capable of directing their actions, their thoughts, their lives. Viewed this way, the free Elvis stamp that Sibyl offers is a sign, a sign of immanent imagination, immanent vision, a sign about the possibilities for living with trouble, and maybe for passing through it.

The haircut, the perm, or the styling is just a cover, a public excuse for a culture that needs or supports one. The experience that is desired, and that is enacted, there has less to do with hair than it does with learning about a parallel world available to you along this highway, in this life.

If you could drawn a map of spiritual centers in Clemson, it would probably not include many orthodox churches, nor would it totally exclude them. It would include places like Sibyl's, though, in addition to other unorthodox places, such as a gas station/convenience store on College Avenue, the back kitchen of a fast food restaurant out on the Strip, Ann Knapp's book store, a college classroom, a gathering for a performance at the Brooks Center, or a particular bar—like Nick's or TD's—on a particular night. These are places where community gets worked out in the experiencing of dialogues and laughter, through the pleasures of identifying closely with spellbinding narratives, in the peak communicative accomplishments of artistic performances, and in all of those parallel planes we can and do cross into, where the freedom to explore the further *creative* reaches of human nature—as well as the innermost reaches of

Immanence and Angels

self—*becomes* a sacred communal place to rediscover the interbeing of Spirit that reveals to us immanent unities.

Intersections and Crossings

Turn right out of Sibyl's parking lot, pass Daniel High School and the turnoff to the middle school, drive down a long stretch of Highway 133 past heavily treed brick subdivisions, pass the outer edge of surreal glimmering river-lakes that, depending on the season, time of day, and angle of influence offered by the circles of sun, are cold, flat silver; warm sea-green wavy; hot, bright, sensual blue; or an awful muddy brown, move up the old hill past brick colonial apartment buildings that have seen better years, and you begin to arrive in Clemson. From the top of the hill just beyond the Southern Railroad overpass, you drive down into the town proper, and your first stop is at the most major of Clemson's secular intersections, the one locals call the "76/123 By-Pass."

To the right is an Exxon station always lined with used vehicles, mostly of the low-slung, used-up luxury, or faded primary-paint-4x4-pickuptruck-with-balloon mudders varieties, some with negotiable prices scratched white on cracked tinted windows, all insisting on existing just because they still do. To the left is a two-story yuppie yellow real estate sales townoffice with a tall neon sign out front advertising something like this:

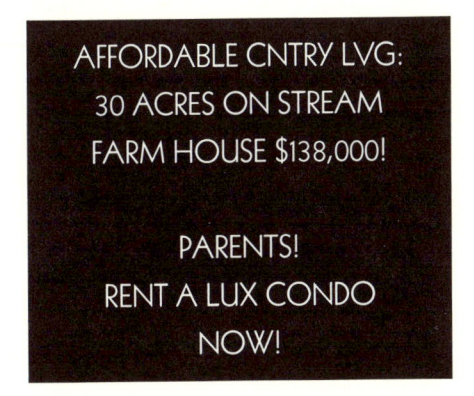

> AFFORDABLE CNTRY LVG:
> 30 ACRES ON STREAM
> FARM HOUSE $138,000!
>
> PARENTS!
> RENT A LUX CONDO
> NOW!

This sign always sells abbreviated dreams mingled with mediated nostalgia. The semiotic framing offers a language of investment contexts for more land with better rooms, newer features, better views and locationlocationlocation! to make symbolically possible those desirable imagined neighborhoods in which the higher conversations hold sway, that are you-*know*-it! guaranteed to constitute the necessary ego surround, that trade only the available loan rates for estates of being in futures perfect.

Across the four-lanes of 76/123 are two opposing corner gas station/convenience stores. One is a red, white, and blue Amoco; the other a white and green Hess. Signs with pennies-difference prices for unleaded and premium fuels dominate the eyespace, with distractions provided by the constant parade of varietal automobiles driven by attitudes that invaded and therefore now occupy bodies, attitudes (symbolically) enabled by disheveled (expensive) oversized clothing yearning to make a personalized (political) statement about (mediated) style! accompanied by the appropriate (fanzine) "look," which largely involves hairstyle, music, the ability to induce poignant (*like* . . .) ellipses, and lips. Welcome to the mid-'90s, courtesy of the mid-'80s/'70s/'60s *redux*.

The light changes to green, and I continue the semiotic inspection. We are on Tiger Boulevard—Clemson's main street—really its only street if you discount the fast food, Winn-Dixie, liquor store, and real estate offices befouled "By-Pass" and the occasional side streets leading into older residential areas. Staying on the main street we pass a camera store, a coin laundry, a State Farm Insurance agency, a Nation's Bank, the post office, a convenience store, one small strip mall with an office supply store, record store, pizza place, video rental, music store, and a couple or three upscale specialty shops, and on the other side another small strip mall with a financial services office, a bookstore, some clothing stores, and in a nonadjoining but materially related complex, a real estate sales and rental office, florist, more clothing shops, and a bar/restaurant. A little farther down on the right, up on a symbolically appropriate hill and just past a symbolically appropriate public playground, is a long row of handsome, well-tended Protestant and Catholic churches.

IMMANENCE LOST

In photographs of this street taken in the 20s and 30s, the town had the almost foreign look of a somehow familiar place that knew its similarities as well as its differences, that knew what it was and where it was, even if what and where were hoping for better. It was a small town supporting a small, male military cum agricultural college; it was located in the rural South; it was kind of a "we have one of everything, and if we

Immanence and Angels

don't have it you don't need it," matter-of-fact, functional town, not ever with the hint of an aspiring city. In the mid-'70s, back when I first lived here, it retained some of that earlier presence and had city-ish ambitions but had not yet fully crossed over into the niche multifunctional nowheres of downtown architectures and space definition dominating the economic everywheres of our common entrepreneurial today.

Just as you eternally enter the same mall twice—because every mall everywhere has a predictable sameness of shape, style, and stores—virtually every college town these days (de)constructs itself similarly, and usually in opposition to market mallishness. So in downtown Clemson, there are upscale restaurants such as Calhoun Corners or Pixie and Bill's; fern-bar-style grilles—ours are Keith Street Cafe 101 and W J Brea's—a Duck Head outlet; several college-style beer bars with pool tables and/or video games (such as Tiger Town Taverne and The Study Hall) and some slightly more serious pickup spots and watering holes that also serve fried food, sandwiches, and mixed drinks—ours include Nick's and TD's—multiple hairstyling salons sporting manely names like A Cut Above, Hair Biz, Hair Sensations, Hair South, Head of Time, Headlines, Heads Up, Styles Unlimited, and Trends for Hair; at least one or two retro Barber Shops—ours is Charles and Al's—several fast-delivery pizza and/or submarine franchises; at least one good bookstore staffed mostly by women ("The Open Book"); and one "we've got everything" Clemson Newsstand; and at least one new-and-used paperback outlet peopled by serious sci-fi cyberpunks and short-bearded, black-clothes-*only* alternative smokers and tokers, both of whom occasionally publicly tolerate or screamingly endorse the staccato blast of mostly Seattle- or Athens-based grunge mixed with rap, jazz, and classical.

Yes, there is a bakery. Yes, there is a main strip of mostly older, more established stores that once sold appliances, hardware, and farm clothing, but now mostly sell T-shirts with tiger paws, sports equipment with tiger paws, cheerleader calendars with tiger paws, tiger paw room and car ornaments, and tiger paw mugs—except for Frank's fine men's store with its once a year great sale; Judge Keller's timeless perfection of the Southern clothing shop, with God's natural light displaying the sturdy goods and collegiately fashionable garments laid out in straight rows on plain tables at fair prices, the bespectacled judge himself figuring the bill by hand, with a yellow #2 pencil on a folded brown paper bag, calling the men "sir" and women, regardless of age, "Ma'am"; Lynch's Drug Store, with its familiar antiseptic sameness and medicinal stock catering mostly to the ill, the elderly, the sports-injured, and the infirm who always will sustain it. And, yes, we have current banks with ATMs for the fast, anonymous money to spend in all of these places; and, if you bear right at the final corner, a Subway's and a pretty good Greek restaurant; a convenience store that doesn't sell gasoline; and more moderately handsome, well-tended Protestant churches.

This is, of course, merely an empirical treatment of downtown Clemson, a view of the place afforded mainly by counting up and listing the categories of businesses, a *tour de street* that—with some occasional stylistic embellishments—could just as easily be acquired from sending out a questionnaire. In other words, what I have just listed and categorized is true, visually accurate, and (because I saw it all from inside my black Intrepid) distanced; it offers a pan opticon-like perspective with which nothing at all is wrong, exactly, not if your objective is to see *only* the drive-by world that is plainly, flatly, unimaginatively presented to you: an unentered, unengaged world empty of otherwise immanent interpretive possibilities, a world set mindlessly small and endlessly adrift on a theme of factual ordinary everydayness; a world disconnected from the souls of its citizens whose souls, themselves, are disconnected from any other sense of purpose and meaning.

It is a small, boring world, this factual Clemson, a world in which, for example, the true meaning for churches is summed up by the speaking of their total number, modified only by parenthetical mention of the uniformities of their collective outward appearances, which—although uniformly handsome and well-tended—organizes their essential public purpose in terms framed and defined by the quiet behavior and cleanliness of its landscaping and architecture, a view that reduces their meanings to the plain stylistic fit of their public rhetorics to a yawning bureaucratic need for behavioral well-tendedness. Yet despite this factual reading, there are fact-conscious members of this community who would say, publicly, that the value of a church should not be measured by—nor limited to—its property value. I take this sort of sentiment as a sign of permeable possibilities, an inroad the parallel spiritual world has made into the Clemson church community if not the general public consciousness, and whose implications should be followed.

The same must be said about Clemson University, whose main architecture—whose well-tended, well-ordered presence from this vantage—we now face. What does it mean to be an institution of "higher" learning, anyway? Higher *income*, only? Higher—more elaborate—*language code*? Higher *purpose*? William Sloane Coffin (1993) says that churches—and I think universities and colleges—could fulfill a more useful role in communities, and for the planet, if they were as concerned with *how people make money* as they are with how they spend it. He advocates teaching some new "basics": strive to be "valuable," not just "successful"; follow your "calling," not just your "career"; don't condone any job (much less take one) that doesn't make the world a better, safer, more sustainable place; do not support or participate in any business that contributes to the decay and deterioration of the Earth.

Here—right here on Clemson's campus and in the town—is the place for an interplay of immanence in the everyday, for achieving higher purpose through communal, coordinated actions. Especially for accepting the influence of angels, perhaps such as Coffin's muse. What gets in our way is the ordinary, the everyday, the pull and call of too-busy persons and the seductive surfaces of things that—quite literally—bring us "down," who try to maintain—against centuries of evidence and the revealed truth of one's own experiences—that we are not *spiritual* beings, first and foremost. Spiritual beings who are in charge of our heavenly souls and our planetary bodies, whose true work seems to be to make the life we have been given learn to sing in harmony with the multiple songs being sung by other lives, to encourage all of us everywhere to attain voice within the Grand Communal Choir, itself striving to achieve ultimate purpose dependent upon the coordination and complexities inherent to all living things living in and moving between our parallel worlds.

Do you ever wonder if the metaphorical map language constructs for necessary intersections in our cities outwardly embodies a deeper message about coordinated actions on a soulful/planetary scale, speaks to us through metaphor of a concurrent path into a correspondent inner world where intersections—and crossings into them—also make possible important daily transports and transitions? I believe there are available daily intersections for crossings in our empirical world—Main Street and State Highway 76/123, Tiger Boulevard and Highway 93—and so, too, do we have in our inner cities intersections for crossing into parallel worlds. And I don't think this is merely metaphor in either world; it is a true sign of relevant connections.[5]

---

[5] Anthropologists have long known about, and studied, the presence and influence of parallel worlds in other cultures, while—at least read one way—some sociologists and psychologists have been studying the outcomes of not admitting to the existence and power of parallel worlds in ours. For an exceptionally well done recent treatment

PERFORMING COMMUNITY

IMMANENCE REGAINED

Consider a day, an ordinary working day at Clemson University—say a Wednesday—in which all your known routines were systematically exhausted, your best lines used up, often without anyone really noticing how fine those lines truly were. Its very hot and very humid, the intersection of 99 and 100 on both counts, great weather for exotic orchids and teenagers, but miserable for middle-aged human beings. At the red light you illegally cross Clemson Boulevard to enter TD's, daring someone with the green light and an attitude on his side to either show a little mercy or "just fucking run over you." In the shared moment of this foolish challenge, a kind of unspoken message passes between you: you intimate that his vehicle is clearly air-conditioned; he counters that you are violating the rules by crossing against the light. He swerves around you instead of stopping, the challenge ends in a street-duel draw, and you continue your march, enduring now the upward flow of additional heat from a rapidly melting street.

You have an appointment with your pal Carl to shoot some pool, drink some scotch, share in the poetry of lived experiences that the two of you are aware you can construct together. Russell and Rob (or Susan and Kelly), the bartenders, have your drinks on the bar before you sit down. You are regulars at this crossing, at this intersection.

You begin talking in the usual ways, moving again through the last motions of the day, necessary to work the transition to this here and now, listening a little above what is being said to catch what we commonly refer to as "the drift" of the conversation, by which we mean the attitudinal and emotive dualities, the slight nuances and subtleties that capture the truer measure of all conversational meanings and purposes, probably because we hear them not so much with our minds as with the "inner" ear, the clear channel pathway to our inner consciousness. In this context, to say "I hear what you are saying" is also to say you hear what is *not* being said, and to treat that nonempirical reality as meaningful.

The strategic and tactical moves in genuine dialogue transcend those

---

in the anthropology of parallel worlds that intertwines the spiritual and empirical, see Alma Gottlieb and Phillip Graham (1993). Their unusual account of their fieldwork in West Africa offers insight into the everyday active presence of a rich, often humorous, sometimes dangerous spiritual world that coexists and interacts with our own. See also Paul Stoller and Cheryl Olkes, *In Sorcercy's Shadow* (1987), as well as the often misunderstood work of Carlos Castenada.

of ordinary conversation. They create intersections of meaning, possible crossings, interplays of imagination and empirical reality that attest to a desire to pursue an evolutionary path by both parties. To remind me of this, Carl says, "You haven't been very forthcoming lately." Among the myriad possibilities for meanings I could attribute to or associate with this statement—because of our context, our weekly meetings in this bar and the woven context of our conversations here—I know *precisely* what he means. We don't come to TD's to drink scotch and shoot pool; that's an excuse, a mere pretense. We come here to talk; more to the point, we come here to engage the possibilities for talk, to use our time and words together to explore the inner reaches and immanent connections of self, of Others, of contexts. We use our commingling of language and context to further our life quests, to evolve across intersections of meaning, purpose, and interpretation that we ourselves create.

This summer of steamy evening heat, bar scotch, and Wednesday nights, I have been listening to him talk about his life, his work, his dreams, but I haven't said too much about my own. He's been telling me—*confessing* to me, actually—the most *amazing* stories, some drawn from his life in New York before he moved here, a few in Paris before that, and one from the Cambodia of his childhood. He's also been writing—again confessing—a deeply imagined short story about crossings between women and men, opportunities for illicit sexual experience that never get openly articulated but instead form a commanding presence in casual talk, that shape a shared, possible context for interpreting every move, every gesture, every word with meanings drawn from outside the empirical realms of possibility.

These are conversational opportunities in the otherwise everyday ordinary flow of communication that form instant vivid intersections, intersections whose directions must be pursued immediately without benefit of a map, without taking a time out to catch a breath or to figure out what to do, moments that bet heavily on the possibility of a shared imagination and purpose that works within what is otherwise spoken and done, that occur as perfectly intended lives intersecting for a purpose, yet occur also without the available benefit of asking *what is meant* or even if this *is* intended. In this realm of intimate human communication, bodies and mouths must act, *then* later figure out what was meant as well as live with the shared scene and what might have been done, what might have happened, or what did.

These are intersections through which one's moves—or failure to read and act on what might be a move—could turn heightened awareness to plausible, *laughable* deniability and embarrassment, because the work that gets done in affairs like these requires the ability to treat the imagination as an alternative reality, but one that both parties can enter, a parallel world. It's true that neither party is seldom certain that what she or he thinks is happening *is*—in the mundane world of meanings drawn solely from empirical facts—*really* happening. It isn't. This world of possibilities within the world that denies them is a parallel world, a world mutually created and yet already fully in existence, a place for possibilities to be engaged. And if it is to work out, neither party can ever truly doubt it without dissolving the very intersection that makes it possible.

Carl's story frames the context for my failure lately to engage possibilities, to enter that parallel world. I protest my apology in *Wayne's World* jargon, itself borrowed from Barry Hannah, and before him F. Scott Fitzgerald: "Not!" This is an outward denial that cloaks an inward agreement and is read as such. Carl sips his drink, a little let down. Moments slip between us. We spend the rest of the night literally playing pool, the two of us trying to move beyond what has been said without being able to.[6] The effort is important; so, too, becomes the playing of pool, and so, too, is the obviousness of the effort. Unable or unwilling to cross that intersection—at least on this particular night—I fall back to earth, a small, vain, living thing.

The drive home reverses the sequence of persons and things that semiotically and interpretively brought me into town this morning. Sometimes this affords me a vision of life that I describe as "the other side." I do this not so much as a serious way to practice the arts of seeing and musing but instead as a way of reminding myself that "other sides" are always there—always present—even if they and their possibilities are

---

[6] Victor Turner (1969) has written about experiencing "liminality," where the dominant impression is one of being "betwixt and between" cultures, or worlds. For anyone who has done fieldwork, liminal experience is commonly encountered and uncommonly difficult to manage; in Turner's language, it renders the self a "liminoid," a person at once seen by natives as awkward and alien, and whose movements are too mechanical because of the lack of ease with what is going on. To become a liminoid is to mark the passage between one's known culture of rituals, rites, and understandings with the space of entry into an unknown—or underknown—culture whose meanings and expectations for utterances and actions are distinctly different. The experience of liminality is, in my view, also directly applicable to the experiencing of conversational space—and one's passage—between the worlds of everyday reality and imagined possibility.

unseen. I pass this time under the 133 overpass without noticing the signs for Exxon, for Amoco, for Hess, or even for real estate. Instead, I feel the powerful rock n roll of an overhead northbound Amtrak train slowing for the Clemson station. A curious yet familiar tingling fear seizes and squeezes my heart, a feeling that maybe comes from the reminder that if the overpass collapsed, this would be what my life came to, as well as (maybe) where it ended. Into this tingling passes a memory from last year, when there was a newspaper account of a woman who was in a car wreck at this very intersection; she got out of her smashed car, walked up—as if in a dream—to the railroad tracks and was promptly run over by a passenger train.

What is our destiny?

Feeling the existential panic of this question mixed with this full-bodied sensation, I am aware not only of the presence of a *real* train but of a very real *intrusion*, an intrusion my better angel makes into my realities. This angel is a friendly, if often unexpected and sometimes unwanted guide, sometimes visible and sometimes not, working to help me correct my spiritual course by getting back on some kind of life track that I have a glimpsy awareness, but not full knowledge, of.

We all have these experiences—the work known in every religion and culture (except scientific ones) as the work of angels—although the deeply nonreligious or spiritual naysayers among us typically refer to this presence as the intrusion of "conscience," or sometimes as "that little man inside me who *really* knows what's going on,"[7] as an unmistakable "inner voice" that speaks to us in a way that cannot—or need not—be otherwise explained. The welcome intrusion of a guide also occurs in—or takes on—human form, in someone who appears suddenly in our lives—usually when we are experiencing great pain or difficulty—and helps to redirect our activities.[8] In my case, this usually happens when I ask questions for which there are no apparent answers.

---

[7] This phrase is drawn from the film *Double Indemnity*, in which the character played by Edward G. Robinson consistently comes to otherwise mystical understandings by listening to his "little man." Interestingly, when he fails to heed what the "little man inside" is telling him, he fails to read the available signs of wrongdoing as clues to a deeper mystery in which ultimately he is intimately involved. By analogy, this failure to heed our inner voice, or the intrusions of angels, is often costly. In the angelic literatures it is commonly written that angels can help us, but they cannot take away our free will to choose.

[8] According to a *Time* magazine survey in December 1993, approximately 69 percent of Americans believe in angels. Given the presence of many titles on best-seller

PERFORMING COMMUNITY

What is my destiny? Where did it come from, and where it is leading me? Tonight my angel reminds me of the obligations that I have acquired by choosing to study communication, and to take seriously my communicative encounters with Others. An inner voice makes me regret my failure to speak openly, truly, creatively, in tonight's conversation, which makes me think that the same thing was true in last night's bedtime conversation with my son, and in yesterday's dinner discussion with my wife, or, for that matter, in last week's dialogue with my students. In each one of those encounters I became lost—distracted from Reality—in the empirical world of everyday concerns and realities, and thereby lost the opportunity to evolve, and to help Others evolve. These are *not* the experiences, nor the consequences—my inner voice teaches me—I should be pursuing. I *know* what this means. That's the way it is in communication with angels; you cannot mistake the voice, the message, or the authority. You are simply left to choose, enabled by new information that is never new at all.

Life is too sudden, too short, too important not to speak to possibilities, or at least attempt to. It is context and imagination that create the available intersections of parallel worlds, but it is the *desire*, the *willingness*, and the *ability* to enter into genuine dialogue that gets us beyond mere recognition of parallel worlds, that actually enables us to cross over to the other side. I am sadly distracted too often from acting on that insight, too busy with the business of being preoccupied by the empirical, the ordinary, the everyday—too caught up in being a rational self—to see the inroads to that other world for Being, which is so *clearly* everywhere present. It is a parallel world I have many times experienced—not just in talk with angels—and in whose experiential lessons I have encountered immanent richness, possibility, and wonder. It is there I have learned the alternative ABCs of ecstasy: Arrival, Being, Crossing. Here is the pattern, the code, the way into the intersections our dreams and our best conversations make us capable of traversing.

The man-made bridge cuts a two-lane path across the natural surfaces of these black lakes, and as such are, tonight, metaphors as much as en-

---

lists about human experiences with angels as "inner voices," as guides, or as having taken human form, added to the fact of the above *Time* statistic, it seems unnecessary to recount the arguments for the existence and work of angels. Admittedly it does seem strange to introduce such talk into a scholarly account about human communication, but perhaps that strangeness is itself a sign of necessary redirection of our interpretive activities, and of the possible meanings of contexts they are to account for.

gineering, metaphors *about* engineering, about engineering highways between realities that allow passage for a journey home.

Crossings and Coincidences

Sometimes the crossings of persons and things appear to be coincidences, probably because we do not try to see—or to understand—the lines of causes and effects as also having intersections between parallel worlds. I am amused these days when I see, mostly in movies but also in empirical reality, a person say, "There's a perfectly *rational* explanation for this; we just haven't found it yet." In movies they usually do find a rational explanation; they have to, otherwise the plot wouldn't thicken, nor would the problem be solved.

Events in life are seldom like those in movies, however. I mean, seriously, how many persons have you known who *never did figure it out*? Or for whom the plot *only* thickens, never resolves? Or for whom inexplicable good happens unexpectedly, oddly, as if it were predestined? Or, for that matter, inexplicable evil? Perhaps we mistakenly assume that the events of our empirical world are the *only* available sources of cause and effect. Or perhaps we only think mystical occurrences happen to mystical people, such as gifted poets, musicians, painters, visionaries?

If communication can travel between worlds, if dialogue can move us across otherwise unseen intersections, if sometimes our dreams do come true, and indeed if we listen to our inner voices and they are the voices of angels, shouldn't these extraordinary possibilities suggest to us that explanations of causes and effects should also make use of a broader interpretive context? Consider, if you will, Lindsley's story:

> I was over at my friend Sandra's house one afternoon working on a presentation, and out of the blue she announced that she knew the perfect man for me. She said it with such confidence, such knowing, that I had to go along.
>
> At first I was apprehensive. I've never been the kind of woman who does "blind dates," and besides, I had decided to return to school and wasn't really interested in meeting a man and developing a relationship. But Sandra was my friend, she knew the guy, and besides, she was so convinced that this was the right thing to do.
>
> To make a long, wonderful story short, I met Steve after "talking" to him over Internet and on the phone, and—I know this sounds silly and romantic—it was as if this was meant to be. And Steve knew it too. We've talked about it. Sometimes strange things happen that are just inevitable. We are getting married this summer.

I finally asked Sandra about how she knew. She told me she dreamed it. She seems to have this gift, so I don't disbelieve her.

Now as an empiricist, you could say that the reason this whole thing worked out is because a woman named Lindsley got into a conversation with a friend of hers named Sandra, and so on. You could, indeed, say that. But how would you account for the part of Lindsley's statement about "it was meant to be"? Discount it entirely, because it does sound "silly and romantic"? I'm afraid that would smack rather heavily of destroying data, or at least of bending a given account to fit *your* theoretical commitments. In either case, to deny the truth of a person's lived experiences is no way to construct an explanation. Or to live, for that matter.

I know many people who believe in their dreams, and certainly there are numerous accounts of scientists, artists, and businesspersons whose dreams have unlocked important insights for their work, and for their lives. One common, psychoanalytic explanation for the nightwork of dreams suggests that the ego is suspended from interfering with "associative" possibilities of the id; another explanation is that at night we have "residues" or "fragments" of knowledge that "emerge" and become the symbolic stuff of dreams. In either of these "reasonable" accounts there is the stuff of dreams—or at least of interpretive imagination—passing as empirical reality: what is—or precisely where is—the ego? Or the id? And please tell me, from where—or what world—do these "residues" come? And just how, I wonder, do they "emerge" in what is otherwise described as a biochemical environment?

Language itself gets in the way of believing in a purely empirical world. Put simply, there is no way to describe an empirical world without the mediating influence of symbols and signs, the effable and ineffable. Language and its absence may be used to point to or try to accurately represent the empirical domain, but the meanings for those utterances, silences, looks, postures, scrawls, intuited feelings, and scribbling are *always* drawn from the imagination, from a world of metaphorical possibilities, from the mysterious workings of dreams that might as well serve as communication channels or intersections to parallel worlds as be imprisoned by the limited walls and boundaries of social scientism or by a psychoanalytically colonized Western army of superstitious ego-ists and id-ites.[9]

---

[9] When I use the term *superstition*, I am not engaging in a put-down or name-calling. I am merely suggesting that believing in what cannot be seen is usually asso-

Immanence and Angels

It's true that the view I sponsor is also one rhetorically invented and poetically organized. It is a view of a new reality of parallel worlds, a world view itself manufactured out of word possibilities and supported by imaginative treatments of imaginative evidence about imaginative experience, about treating what social science would dismiss as "coincidence" instead as a "crossing" or an "intersection." But I maintain that the world view I am sponsoring here is grounded in the new physics of Einstein, Bohr, Heisenberg, and others—visionary realists who saw that domain of "reality" they inherited was unimaginatively bounded and therefore—as a common place for making the totalizing narrative of scientific explanation—false, even if, on empirical evidence alone, it *appeared* to be true (see Capra 1982). After all, if what "appeared to be true" by the everyday world informed by sight and touch is, in fact, true, "the world is flat, the ground beneath our feet is solid, and the sun rises in the East and sets in the West" (Chopra 1993). One could add that if what *appears to be true* about human communication—from the everyday evidence given by sight and touch—were, in fact, "the truth and nothing but the truth," our basic model of the communicative universe would still be representatively summed by discrete, linear boxes and arrows: speakers would send verbal and nonverbal messages to receivers, influence would be a simple matter of saying the right things at the right times in the right places to get the responses you want, and rationality for decision-making groups and organizations would be determined solely by adherence to inductive and deductive models of evidence-testing and would be accomplished by adherence to Standard Agenda.[10]

When we admit the limitations of a communicative world view in-

---

ciated with superstition, madness, hallucination, or religion. Obviously, the same charge can be made of my work here. I ask only that the case I am making be engaged as a comparative one. I accept that social science (and for that matter psychoanalysis) has much to offer us in terms of explaining the empirical, material world. What I am interested in is what advantages might be gleaned from pursuing a fuller appreciation for spiritual interactions, realities, and influences might have—or should have—on those explanations for communication.

[10] I find it ironic that most basic textbooks still represent communication this way. It is one thing to treat—as my coauthors and I have—the evolution of theories and models as evolutionary patterns of thought that brought forth new questions that in turn led to new insights; it is quite another to present linear or even transactional "information transfer" as the way communication "is," or Standard Agenda as how people in groups make decisions. Both of these models have long been superseded by research that accepts the rational world model as well as challenged by contemplatives, mystics, poets, and business visionaries who advocate—as I do— alternative questions and understandings.

formed primarily by discrete, linear boxes and arrows and causal influence—both of which account only in the most obvious ways for what we can see and hear—and when we find that the mathematically bounded rationalities derived from a primitive understanding of logic,[11] we enter a new quantum *parallel* reality of energy and information. This is a "timeless flowing field of constant transformation . . . this quantum field isn't *separate* from us, it *is* us. The same place where nature goes to create stars, galaxies, quarks, and leptons, you and I go to create ourselves" (Chopra 1993). Indeed, this is also a crossing. As the expression of an overall world view, it is a movement from an "outworn" reality to a new one; in communication theory and ethnographic research it is a movement from fundamentalist empiricism derived from bounded, controlled, sight-and-sound-based behavioral/cognitive social science to a "radical empiricism" (Jackson 1989) of awareness and imagination, vision and reason, complexity and insight.

To ask new questions that challenge the rational worldview is to speak a different kind of truth to Power. Through the questioning, it is to open oneself to unities of new experiences. It is to change, fundamentally, our orientation to Reality. It is to suggest that what we claim to know about the empirical, mechanical world of talk and action can be improved and enhanced by adding into our conversation the voices of lived experience that teach us to accept that which we cannot see, but do—indeed—*know*. And it is to find through that radical changing—in and through that parallel world of knowing—ecstasies of immanence, the angelic heart of communication, our best clue and connection to that One Thing, to the Mystery itself.

---

[11] I am not advocating that we entirely abandon the insights and understandings of the ancients any more than Einstein and Bohr denied the ability of Newtonian physics to describe the world he understood. Here again, the presence of parallel worlds should enable us to radically expand and revise what we claim to know, as well as how we claim to know it. Interestingly, unlike large technologically complex canvases that must be used to mediate and organize the dreams of physicists, the primary evidence for our spiritual, quantum, and transformational natures is inscribed in and through our experiences and interpretations, requiring an expanded awareness and openness to imaginative possibilities. In both cases, the world we are trying to embrace and understand has always been there, but our understanding of it—as well as our ability to act on those understandings—is totally dependent on our ability to experience it. As Deepak Chopra—echoing Werner Heisenberg—expresses it: "Although things out there appear to be real, there is no reality apart from the observer . . . every worldview creates its own world" (1993).

6

Awareness and Imagination, or Altered States of Syntax as Communication Riddles

Lordy, lordy. There both forty. Robert and Earl.

—Misspelled sign on an advertising billboard in Clemson, SC

A young man approached Buddha and asked "How do I attain wisdom?" "Good judgment," Buddha replied. "And how do I attain good judgment?" the young man queried. "Through experience," Buddha replied. "And how do I attain experience?" the young man pressed. The Buddha smiled. "Bad judgment," he said.

—Old adage

When I first lived in Central the sign on the hardware store was misspelled," my pal Carl—an English professor—says. "Misspelled?" I ask. "How?" "It read HARDWA_E," Carl spells it out for me. He pronounces it "Hardway." I laugh. "Nobody cared," he continues. "It stayed like that for years." "Maybe they thought it was *right*," I offer. And I am not being cynical.

—Conversation between Carl Lovitt and H. L. Goodall, Jr.

If you assume as I do that signs are clues to the collective spiritual consciousness—the awareness as well as the imagination—of a community, the presence of a *misspelled* sign is symbolically equivalent to a riddle or a pun. It offers invitations to a read meanings differently, or at least slightly askew. As signs, misspelled words, puns, and riddles suggest ways of knowing that work out of different programs, different cultural logics, suggesting sources of mysteries and resources for insight.

PERFORMING COMMUNITY

A misspelled word—again like a riddle or a pun—can also serve—*does*, in fact, serve—among the grammatically correct, as a niggling sign of bad judgment. It is a sign of an experience with language gone wrong, a clue that takes you away from the routine grammar and indeed the ordinary logic of the case at hand and launches you into new inventive rhetorical possibilities for interpretation. Herein lies a curious duality, two parallel worlds converging and intersecting in the evoked interpretation of a sign, suggesting both a problem—that members of each interpretive community believe their world is self-contained and "right"—as well as a way of organizing our evolving consideration of why dialogue and multivocal communities are so difficult to achieve.

I also think that a misspelled sign, like its historical ancestor, the cultural riddle or relational pun, must be read as evidence for the presence of an alternative—or at least *altered*—imaginative consciousness. A misspelling is a sign, literally, from a parallel life world that tells about that world—in some cases so different it might be considered a *virtual world*—a world that coexists alongside this one but operates quite differently. It is a world in which what counts as spelling doesn't seem to mind the occasional misspelled word, inverted letter, or grammatical mistake, and what counts as knowledge of that world must be attained by solving the riddle or realizing the pun. Considered as a cultural analog to the riddle or pun, misspelling may promote cultural dialogue between worlds by drawing attention to itself, causing rumination, worry, and wonder, and thereby semiotically achieve a sense of communal integration. If this is the case, the misspelled sign provides evidence of altered states of syntax that may also serve to remind us of how interpretations of communication reveal pathways to parallel worlds or realities—in this case, inroads to one Reality capable of revealing—and supporting—altered states of communal consciousness.

This chapter further meditates on the idea of parallel worlds. Here signs serve as realities shaped by socioeconomic, political, and education differences, as well as displays of humor that inflect those interpretive differences into pathways for cultural dialogue. This is another way of assembling evidence for what I referred to in a previous work as a "plural present" (Goodall 1991), life worlds that exist fully *within* our lived experiences of the world, but in which the *meanings* for persons and things are vastly dissimilar. The plural present offers us a way of expressing the *dis*similarity of lived experiences as well as providing a way of recogniz-

Awareness and Imagination

ing the presence and active constructions of multiple realities, diverse interpretations, insights afforded by imagination, and diverse varieties of human Being and experience. The world induced by the misspelled sign, riddle, or pun represents or evokes (or provokes) those experiences in ways that challenge commonsense assumptions, turn upside-down or backward beliefs about how things "in reality" work, and render grammatically correct constructions about the syntactical nature—by which I mean the inner logic or language—of truth and falsity; reality and fantasy, and communication that "matters" within that alternative consciousness, open to experiential and dialogic interpretation.

To be beckoned or called into this parallel world by misspelling is only the first clue to a far deeper cultural and spiritual mystery. At the imagined center of it is a duality that informs and shapes the construction of the parallel worlds, a duality made of awareness and imagination, that, when considered quantumly—more fully within the transformational grammars of our universal consciousness—reveals a deep interdependence between the two.

What Does Misspelling Mean?

Like the mysterious riddle of the Sphinx on the road to Damascus, meanings of altered states of syntax must be located or identified within a cultural and historical context. For example, "misspelling" must be associated with the advent of "correct" spelling, which itself plays into a cultural changes—symbolic, socioeconomic, educational, and political—enabled (and perhaps en*gender*ed) by the advent of the Phoenician alphabet.[1]

The riddle of the alphabet is itself a pun about power, making "righting" the prize sum of its capital accumulation. Write the letters in the right way, write the words with the right spelling, write sentences rightly, and so on, until the first bored repetitive technical yawn produced the first misspeaking of an alternative possibility. Misspelling was born. At first this sign was probably an accident accorded by circumstance, but later humorous, puzzling, or rule-breaking forms of talk were used to reveal—and to conceal—tactical linguistic resistance to all forms of strategic domination.[2] As instruments of counterattitudinal advocacy capa-

[1] Walter Ong (1971, 1977, 1982) devoted a considerable amount of his scholarly life to pursuing themes derived from this sort of connection. See also Marshall McLuhan (1964). In both cases the alphabet served as a technological invention that was both cultural constraint and a resource for creativity.

ble of addressing institutional, hegemonic power and thereby serving as "in-your-face" or eyeball-level opposition to cultural domination, the misspelled word that altered an intended meaning, that funnied it up or played it down, offered playful and serious resistance alternatives to everyday, ordinary thought control.

Hence, the connection of rules for control—the "righting"—of culture with rules for correct spelling and speech was a singularly powerful cultural spell cast in the form of a singular conservative strategic alignment of ordinary propriety and everyday language usage. However, it also created a form of expression for an underworld—an "other" world—a parallel world constructed differently by culturally marginalized, politically or spiritually oppressed, and creative peoples left out or simply left unsatisfied by what they could not or would not say or write, er, *rightly*.[3]

Meaning, too, was altered. Part of what got left out of the newly written dominant language code created by the alphabet and rules of grammatical usage was the *living spirit* of the human voice. And something else, too, something harder to explain here (I mean, really, how can I use written words to convey this?), something akin to *tolerance for differences* allowed—even encouraged—by the give-and-take diversity of spoken human dialogue. Without any longer privileging the full spoken resources for resonant creativity and the arch echoes of eternal mystery, the unruly *spiritual* realms of communal talk, chanting, and singing capable of aligning human conduct with the more general ecology were quickly and generationally devalued by those in power.

Organized bureaucratic (legalistic) religions enabled by written codes

---

[2] I am referring here to Michel DeCerteau's (1984) distinction between "tactical" and "strategic" deployments of language as being bound to socioeconomic and political formations.

[3] Such rules for language usage became the political basis for a grammar of public conduct that marginalized, delegitimated, and generally ridiculed members of ancient cultures who derived alternative rules for conduct from the spirit world. The first "underground" was a hidden spiritual community organized by Shamans whose articulations of reality conflicted with those of war lords, kings, colonizers, and Pharaohs. Native Americans tell of their forebears' inability to understand "the White Man's world" as one in which "ownership" of the land was considered possible; to the Native American nations the land was holy and their spiritual responsibility was to respect, tend, and honor it. Throughout recorded histories acceptance of holy "visions," "visitations," and "spirit possession" (e.g., speaking in tongues) have been systemically imprisoned by the need to explain them in "plain" terms, using grammars of thought and action derived from nonspiritual (always secular, mostly Western, mostly scientific, mostly capitalistic, mostly male-dominated) world views.

Awareness and Imagination

of conduct generally replaced—or at least dominated—primitive evangelical and tribal shamanistic rituals; faith translated into logical reasons for a conqueror's sword and became a political weapon justifying the conversion of Others, instead of an available testament to the felt presence of individualized and communal grace. The spiritual voice became, by and by, reduced from its organizing role in everyday life performances to ritualized scripted participation in cyclical holy days sanctioned by the religions of those whose interests were best served by controlling interpretations of the available syntax. Spirituality became a ghost in the alphabet machine, a machine capable of spelling cultural progress in ways that could then be politically acted upon.[4]

According to Plato, writing made a ghost of speech by dislocating the experience of time and by misrepresenting the lived experience of human dialogue.[5]

Marjorie Kelly (1994) tells us that "when we think of time, most of us function unconsciously in the linear way of thinking that has dominated Western thought since the time of Isaac Newton and René Descartes: imagining time to be a forward movement of orderly and unchanging cadence—hours, days, months, years—laid out like grid upon our lives.... And when our days fail to follow such orderly paths, unfolding instead in chaotic and unpredictable ways, we think ourselves undisciplined. We blame ourselves, rarely thinking that our worldview might be askew. But

---

[4] The intimate connection of beliefs and experiences to grammars of conduct and the resulting political costructions of communities is obviously still with us today. Consider the grammatical principles involved in ideological constructions and rules for public communication within any symbolic, semiotic communities as evidence not only of a "postmodern, fragmented" world but also of a unified reality that embraces multiplicity and complexity. Viewed this way the connection of a "back-to-basics" education movement to conservative Republican beliefs (an internally consistent, rule-bound world view of what education should consist of to prepare citizens for the world known and defined by those conservative Republican principles) reveals a current invocation of a rule-bound system as the core item of their sponsorship of disciplined uses of (American-only) language in our nation; see especially Rush Limbaugh, *The Way Things Ought To Be* (1992), and Allan Bloom, *The Closing of the American Mind* (1987).

[5] The concept of time that we have been reared to believe can only be used linearly, as the way we measure change (Chopra 1993). Yet clearly for most people, experiences of time are not at all tied to this simplistic linear explanation. Consider how some days "fly by," while others "take forever"; consider how in certain deeply meaningful moments time seems to be slowed down by our need to perceive every aspect of what we are experiencing more fully. In Ecclesiastes 3:17 we are told, "There is a time for every purpose and for every work," which seems to offer evidence of different times operating simultaneously in different spheres of everyday living.

it may be that the discomfort we feel, trying to operate in a linear view of time, isn't a mistake but a clue" (63). She goes on to offer two insights derived from her lived experiences: (1) "time is not uniform, as the old clockwork world view tells us, but instead unfolds in its own way—unpredictable in a daily sense, but ordered in some larger way" (64); and (2) "when you are traveling the terrain of time, the shortest distance between two points may be a detour" (65), which means that interrupting imaginatively what we perceive to be the flow of linear time may be the best way to accomplish tasks.

Kelly also cites the physicist Fred Alan Wolf's work on the distinction between *chronos*—"clock time that rules the world of thinking"—and *mythos*—"the seamless sense of events flowing together into the larger story of our lives, which we experience through our intuitive feelings" (65). This was accomplished, primarily, through the simplistic reproduction of mechanically recorded written words as replacements for speech that simultaneously assigned (erased) a great deal of dialogic complexity to the ambiguous white spaces surrounding the otherwise dominant presence of printed words. With the symbolic loss of the *experiencing* of dialogue followed the cultural devaluing—through displacement—of conversational playfulness, itself sentenced to the nether reaches of linguistic marginalization: joking, punning, riddling, and other forms of not being serious. It was Socrates—that old master riddler himself—who consistently reinserted humor into his most serious lessons, therefore confounding his interlocutors further by calling into question *how language means* in relation to truth. Probably he would have misspelled, too, just to prove a point.

Eventually, the ability to legalize the arrangement of words laid the grammatical foundation for a logic of public argument that culturally demonized what had been experienced as the magic incantations and spells of persuasive human speech through the penetrations of a word-conjured and highly interactive spirit world. By associating these forms of magic talk with either low-level practical politics, evangelical madness, or high-level religious superstition, "persuasive human speech" became identified as "rhetoric," and citizens valued for their ability to change people's minds with words spoken in the here and how became associated with suspicion. Attending to the *logic* of arguments—rather than to the embodied *spirit* of voices—became the formal critical equipment for surviving in a political, legal, and eventually, capitalistic culture.

Awareness and Imagination

Viewed this way—admittedly through an incanted, imagined, metaphorical form of syntactical reconstruction—*to misspell is to misspeak*. And to misspeak is to question the well-ordered, bureaucratic ways of doing things—in this case, of doing things with words. It is a minor form of cultural rebellion, a sign of a parallel and different way of organizing experience and attributing meanings to it. To misspell is—whether done intentionally or not—to pun visually, to riddle mentally, and maybe to suggest that whatever the reason or purpose, there is more to a well-lived life than boredom, than simply following the rules—doing the hard work—of being ordinary in the everyday.[6]

The desire to personalize one's cultural space in and around Central and Clemson through vanity plates is also noteworthy. Many young women use their first names as license plates (and the competition for creative spelling is intense!), or their attitudes (COOL 1); young men prefer to strut the cultural status of how they want to be treated (TOM 1 or TOP CAT), the names of their dream machines (JEBBMW), favorite sports (SWIMMR), or tiger growls (such as GRRRRR). A pianist advertises on her Mitsubishi van: IVRYKEY; a jazzercize instructor sports JZRCZE; a local, middle-aged speeder says COPSMOM; a physician's reads DRBOB. Some signs are intentionally ironic or ambiguous, such as the well-endowed female student, who may or may not be majoring in electrical engineering, who sports MISSEE. But the largest localized vanity plate industry is state-owned and operated, itself a sign of the times. What started out as oppositional, personalized space-making is appropriated by the dominant culture as a routine money-maker; in this case, *numbered* orange-and-white Clemson Tiger PL8s that use *tiger paws* as the middle insignia instead of the state bird, sold to IPTAY supporters (as well as to the general public) to further advertise the school.

---

[6] One version of this everyday, antibureaucratic display is the contemporary practice of decorating automobiles and trucks with "vanity plates," another way of seeing how DeCerteau's notion of "poaching space" in dominated public places—of using tactics to deflect strategies of cultural domination—works. One inroad to this parallel reality is provided by *Car & Driver* magazine. Each year *C&D* sponsors its "Ten Best" issue, in which are included the ten best GR8 PL8s. As this subcultural competition stiffens, the demand for originality and creativity also rise. The 1994 issue, for example, required readers to use mirrors or stand on one's head to "make sense" of the upside-down worlds. Consider this North Carolina PL8: PV3HPV3P (read upside down: "deadhead"); or this one from Minnesota: TIHS HO (read upside down: Oh Shi[t]. A Dalmation raiser in Virginia is 101 DALS, thereby using taxed space for commercial advertising; a Ferrari owner in Illinois sports this taunt: BY BY COP.

Misspelling, considered this way, is a sign of *extraordinary* experience. It is a mistake, yes; a jest, yes; an intentional strategy, yes; an accident, maybe; an oversight, or so you say; but it is, from a reader's point of view, first and foremost a visible opening to an experience that takes us away from—or out of—the ordinary, that reminds us that alternative constructions of the word—and indeed, of the world—are everywhere engaged around us. It is to remind us that we live in wombs spun of metaphorical syntax, wombs micro-made of language loops, mirrors, and swirls that seemingly depend on correct spelling to operate, to render sensible the consensus world made out of it, but that also admit to alternative ways of spinning, looping, mirroring, and swirling.

When we mess up the routine syntax—say, by misspelling, punning, riddling (and especially by using misspelling *to* pun or riddle)—we alter the perceptual state of that consensual sensible world. Misspellings deny a *singular* construction of a one-world reality and teach us how fragile and penetrable our hold on *what we think must be* actually is. Change a letter or two here ("Turn Hear"), or drop one there ("Microwave in Us"), or even substitute a word that sounds like the one you wanted to use ("For Sail Today: Home-Made Whine"), and we enter another world in which meanings for things have changed, commonsense referents are questionable, and what we thought was going on is rendered simplistic, minimal, or just absurd.

Where can these signs be interpreted as leading us *to*? As the following tales demonstrate, there is clearly more than one place to go, but true to the new particle physics of this realm, "no matter where you go, there you are" (cited in Goodall 1989).

Misspelling as Code-Breaking in the Metaphorical System, Which, in Turn, Provides Extraordinary Evidence for the Existence and Co-Presence of Multiple Parallel Worlds

Terrance McKenna is at the forefront of alternative syntax research, a chronic intentional investigator of misspellings writ culturally, a purposeful explorer of the gaps in the routine, the ordinary, and the everyday, gaps that open pathways into what we don't know about places that, he says, *coexist* alongside us. His research as an ethnobotanist and radical historian has led him to conclude that human evolution was greatly accelerated by the accidental discovery of psilocybin mushrooms by the great plains apes. This discovery enhanced visual acuity for hunting, sexual activity for passing along the 'shroometics of yore, and enabled community-building through mushroom-centered, shamanistically led spiritual rituals for transforming ordinary experience into extraordinary understandings.

But these foundational premises only seed the extraordinary terrain for his grander argument, a larger riddle. As the resident grammarian of 'shrooms and the head logician of the intricacies of psychedelic experiences, McKenna uses his research program to lately become a chief architect and public rhetorician for the Next Step: a further reach into pure consciousness via drug-enabled *exosomatic evolution*. He claims that there is a constant other-world instantly experiencable in a DMT (dimethyltryptamine) flash, a world in which living entities that resemble "transforming machine elves . . . also like self-dribbling basketballs" (1993, 73) *await us* to teach us, well, *something*. Like this:

> Theirs is a higher dimensional language that condenses as a visible syntax. For us, syntax is the structure of meaning; meaning is something heard or felt. In this world, syntax is something you see. There, the boundless meanings of language cause it to overflow the normal audio channels and enter the visual channels. They come bouncing, hopping toward you, and then it's like—all this is metaphor; they don't have arms—it's as though they reach into their intestines and offer you something. They offer you an object so beautiful, so intricately wrought, so something else that cannot be said in English that just gazing on this thing, you realized such an object is impossible. The best comparison is Faberge eggs. . . .
>
> Ordinarily language creates a system of conventional meanings based on pathways determined by experience. DMT drops you into a place where the stress is on a transcending language. Language is a tool for communicating, but it fails at its own game because it is context-dependent. Everything is a system of referential metaphors. We say, "the skyline of New York is like the Himalayas, the Himalayas are like the stock market's recent performance, and that's like my many moods"—a set of interlocking metaphors.
>
> We have either foreground or background, either object or being. If something doesn't fall into these categories, we go into a kind of loop of cognitive dissonance. If you get something from outside the metaphorical system, it doesn't compute. That's why we need astonishment. Astonishment is the reaction of the body to the ineffectiveness of its descriptive machinery. You project your description, and it keeps coming back. Rejected. Astonishment breaks the loop. (1993, 73–74)

PERFORMING COMMUNITY

For McKenna, DMT is a pathway to an altered state of consciousness that opens up invitations to participate in another world. One thing one learns from the DMT experience is that this other world coexists perceptually alongside our own; another lesson is that the ordinary world we perceive and name as the locus of "reality central" is really a kind of distracting theatrical fantasy induced by the rule-generating syntax—the lexical drug—of referential metaphor. Here is, literally, where the world we take for granted gets turned wildly upside down.

Yet I am reminded of Kenneth Burke's dramaturgical revelations about the nature of language as action. Burke (1989), after all, tells us that his use of dramaturgy is *no metaphor*; it *is* the way [this] reality is experienced. Erving Goffman (1959) provides a similar formulation, albeit in the other direction: the theatrical constructions inherent to the presentations of self in everyday life are such metaphors as our only known realities are made of.

What can we make of this? For one thing, this world is made out of *many* worlds just as every true tale is a *many*-storied story. But in a far more significant sense, the penetrations into other worlds—into other stories—are further clues to a Reality in which the point seems to be to make relevant the connections through a spirituality of communication. For what is it, other than communion with pure spirit—with Being at Being—that pure consciousness aims for? That McKenna's machine elves *speak* to us, that every culture's gods are made known through *voices*, or that "In the beginning was the Word" lays the lexical foundation for Judeo-Christian religion suggest a common—albeit extraordinary—core: spiritual communion is achieved when we are able to perceive unspeakable meanings in and around the voices that connect us to higher dimensions of consciousness. To spell—or to misspell—in this sense brings us into contact with the mysteries of incantations as pathways to consciousness.

Which, strangely, brings us back to Plato's observations about speech. One can misspeak just as one can misspell, perhaps more easily so. To misspeak can mean simply to say the wrong thing, use the wrong word as one might use the wrong letter in a misspelled word. But as we have seen, to misspeak can also mean to pun, to riddle, to engage in playful conversation, to ask new questions about old metaphors. In the latter case, to misspeak is to use voice in the service of higher consciousness. Syntactically, it is to connect the ordinary, the everyday, the routine, and

Awareness and Imagination

the taken-for-granted to the extraordinary, the oddly askew, and the ultimately strange.

To misspeak may also serve a deeply spiritual function, a kind of analogic DMT pathway to a co-present world in which spirits are seen as entities wrapped up visibly in the auditory welcome of voice achieved primarily through the experience of dialogue. Here is the place for challenging the syntactical rules for ordinary life that deflect and distract us from perceiving life's central mysteries as complex and interconnected to our own, as well as in relation to a more generalized human evolution. In this sense to achieve dialogue is to burst fully into a communal space unknown and uncharted where, awaiting us, is precisely what we came for.

Interlude: Misspellings Considered as Mistakes

There are admittedly some serious doubts to be raised—if not outright problems—here. If we assume that every human being is his or her own unique pulsating universe questing toward some purer—some supra—form of dialogic consciousness, questing for ways to make life a little more interesting, a little more revved up, a little more mysterious, then we risk making every conceivable form of New Age consciousness-raising or drug-induced hallucination—as well as every conformist-demanding fundamentalist insanity guru—consumptively safe and even politically correct for the North American middle class. I mean, for God's sake, syntactical and grammatical *errors*—misspelling and misspeaking—are being used here to suggest—seriously—pathways to a higher consciousness!

Perhaps this is just plain rhetorical foolishness none too cleverly disguised as ungrammatical, if not entirely illogical, then certainly counterrational, intelligence. *Artificial* intelligence, if you will. There are few among us who have not encountered someone who claims that some personal *juju* or drug "works for them" and that the world would be a kinder, gentler place if only we would all see the wisdom of this or that: throw the I-Ching, align your chakra, get in touch with a past life, use crystals, read the Bible, read the Koran, read the Tibetan Book of the Dead, meditate, drum, send money to a TV evangelist, pray to Allah on a regular schedule, invest in municipal bonds, eat more 'shrooms, experience psychoanalysis, volunteer in a homeless shelter, study human communication, and so on. Whatever it is that we rub, read, wear, do, tolerate, believe in, or swallow, evidence strongly suggests that most of us are engaged in a search for something that will make sense of All This, and that either we believe that what we have found is The Way or that it isn't.

Viewed this way, to misspell or misspeak isn't simply a metaphor but a genuine mistake with some disquieting textual consequences. It is a grammatical pathway not to some heightened enlightenment or even evidence for the spirited existence of a resistance narrative, but only a pathway to and evidence for yet another ignorant mistake: "Lordy, lordy. *There* both forty." Viewed this way, we can read the presence of an alphabetical absence—such as the fundamental misspelling in an ordinary sign—just as we read the presence of an absence in a neighbor's talk; what seems absent from that neighbor's *life* is present in the misspeaking, and so it is that the misspelled word in the road sign is neither intriguing nor playful, but instead sad and perhaps even tragic. The guy who composed it didn't know any better, maybe didn't want to know any better. And probably doesn't care.

I admit these possibilities but do not privilege them. To see the world this way would be to miss the inner text and the intertext of life-worlds that lie around and inside of the territories suggested by the misspelled sign. Or at least to read the sign as only a sign of something, some life-world, that is merely less complete. To deny the sign its native complexities. To act as if the sign is *only* a sign, after all. That as a sign it points to, it suggests, and it references—just as any well-spelled sign does—would be overlooked in favor of foregrounding its obvious error. But I say that a sign by any other spelling does not say all that must be said about whatever it is suggesting, any more than any advertisement—for a product, a service, a self, or a soul—tells all there is to know about the consequences of its purchase.

So, yes, *damn* it, some signs are misspelled. *Just* misspelled. Their authors don't *know* any better. So *there*! And because they don't know any better they are surely less grammatically evolved than you and I are. *So what*? Is reading the meaning of the misspelling this way anything other than a sign of our attitude, our intolerance, our inability to see beyond the surface representation of things, to miss the connection between the presence of their error and the absence of our compassion? I

168

Awareness and Imagination

guess we've never made mistakes, huh? Never. Never had a life when we were making them, either, I bet. *Right?*

This is a sign read *only* as a sign. This is the lifework of Terrance McKenna as interpreted entirely by an English police chief. This is the ordinary work of Clemson and Central, South Carolina, read merely as a errors in the general syntax of Anglo-American speech. And from these readings that are evidence also of misreadings, from these sources for interpretation of contexts that are also underutilized as resources for understanding and therefore misunderstood, what is potentially a pathway into a symbolically rich surround is simply reduced to its lowest common denominator. This is a sign, too, this time of spirituality read—and misread—as merely legalistic religion.

Think again. Think about *connections* to be made. Think about not just the "work" of talk but about its Spirit, its *playful* repertoire. Think about the blurring of linguistic boundaries and about the boundaries *only* there *because* of linguistic rules and regulations. Now think about the need to tolerate differences, to show compassion, to help someone achieve a higher level of consciousness without robbing them of what they experience or hold most dear. These are differences that first must be imagined to offer insight, or to be understood.

The Question of Differences: Worlds within the Words or Outside Them?

There are signs of difference—and of different life-worlds—everywhere around us. How we learn to understand and appreciate differences, however, is a complex communication issue. For example, novelists, documentary filmmakers, and dramatists show us small worlds that reflect Big Questions, and they use these imagined domains to spell out the terms and define the sentences of our diverse, if nevertheless common, human condition. Each of these imagined worlds is characteristically distinctive, but we can read them as human commonplaces, as rhetorical resources for personal identification, edification, justification, or escape, via the narrator's perspective. A novel then, like a sign, is a reflection of authorship, of what the author's projected narrator *knows*, which can be understood as the summing up of a perspective on life. We have different novelists; therefore, we have a variety of narrative points of view. We have many signs; therefore, we have a variety of worlds represented by the signage. Spelling counts, of course, because spelling—like a narrative plot—is a reflection of the world envisioned by its author for an audience.

Mikhail Bakhtin, in *The Dialogic Imagination* (1981), however, challenges this idea of narrative *vis-à-vis* what a narrator "knows," or that what characters in novels offer us are alternative "points of view." Instead, he shows us how language is a profoundly social phenomenon that has nothing much to do with establishing a straightforward relationship between words and things, or words and realities; instead a word's meaning—or spelling—is dependent on its social use and social context. Furthermore, in a novel there are many social contexts interweaved throughout a well-told tale (or for that matter, of an ill-told tale), and the resultant narratives are not a reflection of a life-world so much as a polyphonic chorus of language negotiations and possibilities. Viewed this way, a sign is evidence of a voice in the overall chorus; how the meaning of that voice is received, argued, and understood is less dependent on what is uttered than on how it helps shape a context for interpretation. Viewed this way, spelling counts as something other than spelling—this isn't about correct words reflecting a physical reality; it counts *as part of a context that constitutes an intersection of social worlds*.

This is the place, I think, to begin to understand the meaning of differences. The point is *not* to think of differences as differences in reflected, consensual realities so much as to hear in the differences resources for contextual contributions, a shaping for rhetoric that is more evocative and provocative than it is grammatical or logical. Ludwig Wittgenstein says somewhere that "the meaning of a word is in its use in language." If, as I have argued elsewhere, the first principle of human cultures rendered out of the new physics of sense-making systems should be *everything counts* (1989), then it follows that what should count is how context matters.

Consider, for example, how rock n roll establishes alternative narrative communities—classic, metal, rap, punk, pop, hip-hop, disco, soul, folk, etc.—each one deriving its rhetorical stance from interpretations by the *contextual attitude* of the music, not the *world* the song calls into being. What gets negotiated in the actual singing and playing—from air guitar to superstar—is *not* a stable referential world, but personal, social, political, spiritual, and moral contexts that induce us to see ourselves, our lives, *in relation to* what the songs evoke in, through, and for us. To

Awareness and Imagination

participate in the song is to know *a* meaning for it. Ditto for each major and minor movement of visual artistry, each display or event inviting us to see, to experience, and to describe the artistry through new contextual lenses, each lens toying seriously with the social negotiation of the narrative pathways in this experiential world as well as offering analogic narrative misspellings in the form of nested commentaries on the absence of a reflected world that may have been previously taken for granted because it failed, only, to be *imagined*.[7]

It should not come as any particular surprise, then, that if we read signs of everyday life as signs of live performance art—as narrative teachings—we come away from the experience of observing and participating with a heightened sense of the complexity for the ordinary, the everyday, the routine, even the boring. And for the meaning of our place in the co-construction of that complexity. Signs of social life are signs of multiple social narratives that offer up important negotiations about perceptions of contexts and their meanings. In that observation we can find lessons about what it is that connects us to those resources for interpretation, to the construction of contexts, which is to say that we can understand *communication* as a truly social phenomenon. Talk about the meaning of signs—in fact, the meanings we communicate for signs themselves—is not referentially situated primarily in the grammatical and representational but in the *contextual*, the *imaginative*, and the *symbolic*; its interpretive syntax is not drawn solely from the relationships of words—well spelled or not—to some perfected, rule-governed consensus reality but is more related to our symbolically mediated, always contested, plural present, socially constructed, experientially parallel, and ultimately dialogic realities.

From Awareness of Difference to Dialogic Imagination

The central problem of difference is not, then, simply how to *understand* the life-worlds—the interpretive contexts—of others, but *how do we communicate across them?* The question posed by differences is not how

---

[7] All relationships can be viewed as having "digital" or "empirical" and "analogic" components; the move toward the analogic as the foundation for analysis of "what is real" and away from the digital or empirical has long been a preoccupation of mine; see "The Nature of Analogic Discourse" (1983) as an early attempt to define this realm of imagined, parallel experience.

do we explain ourselves, our attitudes, our life-worlds to each other, but instead how do we learn to tolerate—much less appreciate—shifts in syntactical contexts that call into question the meanings we have for meanings, and the contexts for interpretations of contexts themselves?

I am reminded here of a science fiction novel whose title and author I've unfortunately forgotten. The novel features two alternative ways of being (and knowing) in a completely plural universe—one way is to be able to travel back and forth between worlds; the other way is to exist only in-between the worlds that others travel back and forth to. There are some important advantages to each way of being, but also some intriguing disadvantages. For one thing, if you travel between worlds you cannot make sense of anything—or anyone—who exists in between them. Also, you must leave behind your physical body when you travel to the other world, and that body can be stolen or abused or pronounced dead or used for scientific research if left uninhabited. For the 'tweens, the problems are reversed. You cannot exist in either of the possible worlds, only in-between them, and being there you have the ability to understand very little of either world and too much of your own. You cannot leave your body behind, so it is always too much with you, a sign of your obvious 'tweenness, which, from the perspective of inhabitants of the other worlds, is a sign mostly of your comic ineptitude, your lack of worldliness.

Does this narrative sound like Victor Turner writ sci-fi to you? It does to me. The 'tweens could very well be *liminoids*, persons betwixt and between cultures, or life-worlds. The world travelers could be the social and political dominants of the two cultures, representatives of the native's point of view for whom the (one-world) production and (other-world) intrusion of a 'tween—an ethnographer—is cause for riddling, for punning, for misspelling the root causes of cultural mystery.

Which brings me back—us back—to the possibility for dialogue and for communities based on dialogue, which is to say to communication in a world of differences and parallels, intersections and connections. On its metaphorical surface the problem of difference seems to be all about cultural misspelling. But to read a culture this way—to read a novel this way—is like reading the novel for how it *imitates* life rather than how it *constructs* it. It is to look for what is absent rather than to admit what is present. And it is to avoid recognizing the plural in what is present, as well as the necessary part we play in the narrating—the making plural—of it.

So how do we accomplish plurality?

Living in the Available Art of Open Spaces, or Imagination and Improvisation as Enactment of Multiple Worlds

Mary Catherine Bateson says that "when you expose yourself to the culture of another human community, you are exposing yourself to a masterpiece, to a work of art, to the invention of a form of humanness that has been made over a long period of time" (1993, 119). In her essay—which is at every turn of phrase about the vital role of improvisation in the imaginative construction of joint cultural performances—she compares her experiences in prerevolutionary Iran with the metaphor of a rich Persian garden that itself references, as metaphor, the artistry of a Persian carpet and the vision of an afterworld paradise. The meanings of both garden and carpet, she suggests, rely on improvised interpretations that establish comparative patterns across metaphorical bridges. Like this:

> Such a garden, you know, is a cosmological statement. Most of you have not seen a Persian garden, but you have seen models of them if you have seen a Persian carpet, for there is a metaphorical relationship between them. A garden is bounded, walled. Inside, it is fertile and hospitable, and there is always an awareness of an outside world that is not so fertile and hospitable. Water is part of every garden. The Shah used to have a palace in the northern part of Teheran, at the high edge of the city, where there was a garden with a fountain, and the water that went from that fountain symbolically went down through the city to his subjects. A garden is also a model of the paradise to which the faithful will go after death. (1993, 114)

Differences in cultures are experienced plurally—and rendered comparatively sensible—through improvisations given through the magical intertwinings of metaphor. As such, our experiences in another's culture locate us as liminoids, as existing dialogically and communally *between* multiple worlds. To use McKenna's take on syntax here, we speak through the unraveling of metaphor after metaphor, comparing what we newly experience to what we already know from experiences somewhere else, where those experiences are composed also through an unraveling of metaphors, comparing said place and time with some yet unspoken other. What can be said about cultural pluralities, about cultural differences, is made out of the language of the familiar turned askew, improvised in its native estrangement, performed away from its local home and ordinary realm of knowing. As Mary Catherine Bateson points out, when this happens, there are forms of cosmological awareness *everywhere manifested* in otherwise taken-for-granted patterns.

Considered this way, misspelling is at once akin to creating an awareness of a less hospitable, less fertile world for those who read the sign as a sign of differences, *and* to an awareness of a self-contained cosmology understood by those who don't see the misspelling as misspelling, or who at least don't count it as a significant sign of differences. To be able to consider both possibilities—both worlds—is to move into the liminal, in the open spaces between them, and to find oneself simultaneously enabled and disabled by the move, through the positioning. True, you acquire opportunities for distanced, disciplined critical questioning, but these questions tend to lead less to holistic understanding than to perspectival diremption, where an increasingly fragmented awareness of apparent differences are experienced as a furthering of differences.

You also never entirely own the experience of the world you appropriate through metaphor—language being once, twice removed from lived experience—and as the critical diremptions empty your senses of serviceable sentences, you return to the vast in-betweenness of deeper, cosmic liminality. For all our metaphors—the moon *deluxe* of human language—we can never fully avoid these cycles, the interplays of full light and awesome darkness in, of, and between them, the way in which in metaphor, as in life, the light we have available to us is always only temporary, and darkness always, and sometimes thankfully, returns. Such a presence, such a narrative, induces us to come ever-closer to what we want to know and then, seduction undone, moves us—confound it!—further away; here in the worlds of metaphors, of moons, we seemed destined to apprehend only the rudimentary clues to these silent evolutions of some grander cosmology, a cosmology we hope is ordered, purposeful, and rich but may well not be, a final explanatory narrative that paradoxically lies not only beyond the reach of words but that reminds us of the inevitable silence shaping this deeply mysterious, maybe even ironic, quest.

Awareness and Imagination

So it is that the differences seen between the worlds, or between the spinning of our worlds and the necessary orbiting of our moons, evoke within us only imaginable possibilities. We imagine, *therefore*, we may know. We imagine, therefore we may speak to the gaps, because of their silences. We may even go to the place of our imagining, exploring its boundaries and planting the national flags of some imagined certainty on its surfaces, only to return home again to that inevitably in-between place where we first proposed what we since have done, and know it now as just that: an *imagined* place we have been to, the work of metaphors and stories that further propose a further imagining, that call us to consider again the relationship of imagined patterns, parallel worlds, and the divine possibility of interconnections of those worlds to our lived experiences.

From this vantage, misspelling is but a missing detail on a broader blueprint that demands reality absolutes, a small piece of the cosmic puzzle that may not matter at all, or that may tell us all that matters and all that ever will. But can it be both of these things, like interdependent positions in an evolving dialogue? If not, then we seem to be back to recognizing differences, even celebrating them, but being capable therefore of only an empty metaphorical pluralism, a vacant, mostly suspicious, dialectic of endless comparisons. But if so—if this is a sign of the possibility of interdependent dialogue and not of the inherent oppositeness of a dialectic, then what is this sign trying to say? What is this dialogue *about*? Or *for*? Or, maybe, what is it trying *to get us to say to each other*?

Can misspelling on the sign be itself a sign of insight given unto us? Is it saying, perhaps, that we are all somewhat misspelled—we, the imperfect beings, perhaps *all* of us have pieces of our own puzzles left out? That our piece of the puzzle is only a part of the mysterious Grand Riddle? That maybe the truest clue is in finding what connects us, what connects our individual puzzles to the Grand Riddle, the mystery that is our collective blueprint?

PART THREE

HIGHWAYS AND SURROUNDS

The Sacred
After the teacher asked if anyone had
    a sacred place
and the students fidgeted and shrank

  in their chairs, the most serious of them all
    said it was his car,
being in it alone, his tape deck playing

  things he'd chosen, and others knew the truth
    had been spoken
and began speaking about their rooms,

  their hiding places, but the car kept coming up,
    the car in motion,
music filling it, and sometimes one other person

  who understood the bright altar of the dashboard
    and how far away
a car could take you from the need

    to speak, or to answer, the key
    in having a key
    and putting it in, and going.

  —Stephen Dunn

7

Vision and Reason, or The Strangeness of Instructions

> When all else fails, read the instructions.
> The Book.
> —Welcome Baptist Church

Let us, for a moment, ponder the profound complexity of this sign.

It speaks to our Western quest for technological solutions to everyday problems; the alphabet, according to Marshall McLuhan (1964), was the *first* technology. It admits also to the unique human capacity for inevitable constraining failures, suggesting perhaps that the inevitability of human failures is due to a corresponding human preference for ambiguities of language and context that themselves seem to direct us in other ways, toward interpretive freedoms opened up by creative possibilities and away from simpler, straighter answers; in this case, the simpler truths—the straight instructions—contained in "The Book."

Furthermore, this sign implies that we have ignored these instructions, probably because as imperfect beings we are vain and proud enough to ignore *all* Perfection; in this case, perfectly clear directions for living a perfectly directed life on this spinning orb known as Planet Earth. I think it is also a lesson about our human tendency to ignore all forms of directive communication. Indeed, tell me exactly how to do something and chances are good I will immediately look for another way.

It has been my experience that all of us ignore directions, although it is true that males even go so far as to deny that directions exist and absolutely don't believe that even if they *do* exist they can make the task of "doing" our lives any simpler. It is as if this is an expression of a law about human physics, that for each (directive) action there is, inevitably, an equal and opposite reaction. Think of this opposite reaction as "interpretive freedom," maybe even as "freedom of choice" or as evidence of "free will." But interpretive freedom, seen this way, is *not* the opposite of the directive communication, but instead a *furtherance* of the existence of and the need for it.

According to the wisdom of the late Lewis Thomas, without the human preference for ambiguity—and specifically for ambiguities of language—the human species would not *be* the human species. We would be little more than ants (which, from Thomas's perspective, is more of an insult to ants than to humans). Consider his instruction:

> Ambiguity seems to be an essential, indispensable element for the transfer of information from one place to another by words, where matters of real importance are concerned. It is often necessary, for meaning to come through, that there be an almost vague sense of strangeness and askewness. Speechless animals and cells cannot do this.... Only the human mind is designed to work this way, programmed to drift away in the presence of locked-on information, straying from each point in the hunt for a better, different point. (1975, 89–94)

So maybe the trick to writing instructions for humans—especially for writing the most important instructions for all humans—is to write them *ambiguously*. To write them as *signs*. To write them as signs of possibilities, as texts for interpretation, as resources for discussing, musing, deliberating, dialoguing, and even arguing about—without ever reaching consensus—meanings.[1] In this way ambiguity ensures that the strangeness, the askewness, of what first appears as simple information,

---

[1] This is, in fact, the current logic—and vision—of experts in technical communication rethinking the human interface with machine technologies. Rather than writing technical manuals or sets of instructions for putting together a computer system, an oriental dinner (see fn. 2 below), or a child's toy from the intentional perspective of the maker, they are constructed from on-site observation and interviews with users. The idea is to see how people charged with the responsibility for following the instructions actually make sense of them. Furthermore, one application of hypertext—and other programs of that ilk—is to embed helplines (deeper instructions for the technologically distressed) within the user's manuals, and to use actual experiences of end-users as the basis for how the helplines are written. In both cases the idea is not to write (from a logic of good reasons) "clear, concise (intentional), unambiguous instructions" because, from a human user's perspective there are none, nor can there be. Instead, the idea (from a logic of vision) is to make use of ambiguity and interpretive possibilities by empowering a dialogic construction of a communal text; it is to use the manual—the text of interpretation—as a context for the reading meanings into signs. For an intriguing, visionary rethinking of the communication bases within the context of computer logics, see Winograd and Flores, *Understanding Computers and Cognition* (1985).

Vision and Reason

not only gains our attention, but *continues* to, and thereby continues to live *forever*.

Now *there* is a plan. I mean, if there is one.

Instructions as Strange Communication

Because there is no way to resolve the inevitable, designed-in strangeness of life, the readings given to instructions are very important—albeit very strange—forms of communication. Given the awful number of otherwise disconnected contextual phenomena I've tried to put together by following them,[2] or places I've tried to get to by listening to them—even if I diligently write them down *exactly* as they are spoken to me, even if I ask for help from someone who thinks she or he knows what the instructions mean—instructions of any kind are *highly* problematic. Because of this unfortunate if consistent fact of life, I suspect that the instructions I've given also fall prey to similar interpretive complaints, existing on multiple planes of parallel, if interpretively dissimilar, strangenesses. Instructions, it seems, inherently *provoke* more questions, cursing, laughter, and hair loss than they answer.

Yet here it is, a sign by the side of a highway that says there are life instructions in The Book. It is a sign by the side of an otherwise ordinary

---

[2] This problem is made even more problematic and stranger when the instructions are rendered by a translator unfamiliar with the nuances of meaning inherent to the multiple realities of English. Consider these verbatim instructions—unaltered states of syntax—on a major label package of imported Saifun (bean threads):

Here below are a few directions:

1. Fried Bean Thread After having been washed in water fry the Bean Thread with fried meat or chicken fine slices Fried Shrimps and cabbage. then added and cabbage. then added to saue vinegar. . . . . .
2. Bean Thread Soup: Bean Thread with Dried Shrimps. Bamboo Shoots and carb meat. then added to Food Enhancer. . . . .. makes a delicious soup.
3. Bean Thread Salad: 1 To bring water to the boil then place the Bean Thread in it 2 Hot oil together with sauce vinegar food Enhancer to stir gently with cool Bean Thread 3 Crabmeat Shreaded Ham. vegetable ard shrimps to place on the Bean Thread creates a special taste.

I swear that not one word, not the capitalization of one letter, not the presence or absence of one elliptical space, or any one line has in any way been altered, but my consciousness surely has.

So as to avoid the criticism that I am unfairly chastising an English translation from a "foreign" language (aren't all languages, in fact, foreign?), consider these instructions road, between Clemson and Central, existing parallel to many other roads that do not contain this sign but perhaps benefit from the instructions anyway, in their own ways. A sign that speaks directly *to* the strangeness. A sign that proclaims that despite all the strangeness it speaks to (including, I presume, the strangeness inspired by the presence of this sign) a book of instructions capable of countering all previous failures does, in fact, *exist*.

Frankly, I don't know whether to be gladdened or saddened by this information. I do know it seems strange to me, or perhaps just makes the complications of being me feel estranged by its verity, its simplicity, the discomfort caused in the postmodern me by its straightforward directive, its unembellished, undoubting, uncritical plain rhetoric.

Considered as an answer, I am gladdened by the fact that this must be, truly, a most remarkable book, a book that reduces human interpretive possibilities to zero, a set of guidelines that operates above all possible contexts. Considered as an answer, however, I am also saddened by the inability of this remarkable resource to garner enough human support for the truth of its instructions, at least to the extent that its doubters—and even more ironically, its believers—have to be constantly reminded of it.

on a can of Campbell's Healthy Choice vegetable soup: "HEATING INSTRUCTIONS: Do Not Add Water." This is bad enough, given that the black boldface commands end here—does this mean you heat by not adding water?—but then, in a different typeface, these instructions:

> RANGE TOP: Place contents into saucepan over LOW HEAT (what I if I want to use medium or high heat?). Heat several minutes or until hot (is this vague, or what?), stirring occasionally (and just how often is that?).
>
> MICROWAVE OVEN: Place contents into 1 quart microwave-safe bowl. Heat, covered, on HIGH 2 1/2 to 3 minutes or until hot, stirring once.

(Really now, why can I heat the soup in a microwave on HIGH, but must use LOW on a range top? Or, for that matter, why am I being told to stir the microwaved soup "once" when the above instruction for range top says I should stir "occasionally"?)

Finally, on the bottommost part of the can, this warning: "This meal is not a cure for heart disease . . . " (who would ever think it was?) one small line against which the authority of the top 1/3 of the can is opposed, by breaking down in pie-chart form levels of saturated fat, cholesterol, and sodium, and providing detailed information on Diet Exchange Per Serving (whatever that is). And under ingredients, we have this line: " . . . and other familiar vegetables." *Familiar?* Is this ambiguous, or what? I wonder if okra is familiar to soup eaters in Michigan.

Vision and Reason

of it. Daily, if not weekly. Generationally. For centuries. Herein lies the dilemma: the answer for life's strangeness is *more* strangeness. *Deeper* communicative strangeness. How can this be?

It *can't* be. At least not *that* way. That is, of course, unless you happen to be a person who fundamentally believes in a single, *literal* interpretation of The Book, a preferred reading that legitimizes only one meaning for every word, every sentence, every translated code into and through every language. One personal meaning that builds into one common understanding. One common understanding that is capable of informing all topics, all situations, all decisions, for all people and for all time.

There are such people. Ironically, they don't seem to get along very well with anyone, including, quite often, the good members of their own church. And from what I hear, locally, they never have. Apparently there is nothing in The Book to cover this, no set of instructions for handling disputes about The Book itself. Either you "get it" or you don't. And unless you "get it" in one particular way, according to these citizens, you are not only getting it wrong, but you are probably doing the work of the devil. Amazing that we don't see more ordinary people walking around with tails and horns. Then again, maybe these citizens *do* see them. On the rest of us.

They will tell you—I know this because I asked them—tails and horns are *just metaphors*. But, I asked, doesn't the presence of metaphor in The Book sort of seriously invalidate the whole point of the literal stance? "No" is all they say. Accompanied by some sad head shaking. I, apparently, just don't "get it."

Remember, however, the strangeness is designed so we *not* reach consensus. It certainly keeps the questions alive, as well as the answers questionable. At least for me.

Considered this way, instructions—the need for them, the giving and receiving of them, and their diverse interpretations and frustrations—are at the heart of the strange infrastructure of Power's struggle with Other in our lives. Reading between that infrastructure's realities and my interpretive own, I find evidence of another clue. This clue concerns the mysteries of coexisting parallel worlds that inform and shape how we respond to everyday, ordinary communication: one that depends on a intentional, bounded, fixed modern reality of known textual logics, precise proofs and argumentative reasons, and one that depends on narrative rationalities and a poetics of vision, end-user empowerment and multiple interpretations of meaning.[3] Between these two worlds of communicative logics and interpretive possibilities most of us live daily lives of certain sense-making interspersed with confusing uncertainties. Within these public and private spaces, we become questing liminoids, rhetorical 'tweeners, as well as (depending on our moods, interpretive contexts, beliefs about time, requirements for sociability, and readings of purpose) *alternating members of both of these worlds.*

Hence the dualities of communicating vision and reasoning in communicative practices. What, I wonder, can this mean?

Lessons for the Strange

How are we prepared for this strange life? What does this strange life prepare us *for*? How—and why—do we seem destined to learn to organize our lives in the company of others, even though, eventually, we will depart from them, or them from us? How—and why—do we strive to learn what persons and things *mean*, if only to us? What is it, anyway, about the seemingly necessary and importance of *lessons* in the ever-presence of living a human life? What is it that we are supposed *to learn* here?

Nothing is much stranger in ordinary, everyday communication than the paradox of lessons. Viewed one way, our truest purpose in life seems to be *to learn*, given the sheer quantity—and quality—of time devoted institutionally, contemplatively, and socially to it. For Zen Buddhists, this is an expression—perhaps *the* expression—of The Way. At the heart of The Way is the heartbeat of a Master Koan—a meditative lesson—which is also a master paradox: *we learn, but it is never enough*. From this paradox are derived several others: we learn, but what we learn doesn't always matter; we learn, but we also forget what we have learned; we learn, but what we learn doesn't always teach us what we need to

---

[3] One way to interpret these differences is detailed in Walter Fisher's (1987) theory of narrative rationality; another way to interpret them is of the clash of modern logic with a postmodern world and self, detailed in Kenneth Gergen's *The Saturated Self* (1992). Yet another possibility is articulated in John Shotter's *Cultural Politics and Everyday Life* (1993), in which a "rhetoric of the third kind" is constructed out of the linguistic, social, and imaginative realms of human discourse and deportment. I believe that insights are afforded by each of these perspectives (despite points of obvious difference among them) and that my work provides one framework for viewing how those texts may, in fact, connect.

Vision and Reason

know; we learn, but the lessons we learn differ, or at least differ in how we feel we should apply them to the questions we have. And this one: we learn, but what we learn does not prevent us from exiting this honored and tortured earth, from which and about which we have dedicated our lives to mastering.

For these reasons and others I cannot so easily name, I am lately thinking about the role of lessons in the social and cultural construction of reality. I am guided by the proposition, perhaps false, that I am here for reasons that have to do with the *call* of this place, what it may *teach* me. Even if there is no mystical shape to my presence here, or for that matter to *our* presence here, the fact remains that while I am here I do feel compelled to seek knowledge in and through my experiences, and to know that my experiences—the meanings I and/or others attribute to them—will form the material substance of my journeys between parallel worlds, as well as my days and nights. I believe there is a lesson in this. Many lessons.

There are, of course, many different types of and purposes for lessons: family lessons and school lessons; lessons of etiquette and lessons from scriptures; private lessons and public lessons; lessons from books, from elders, from friends, from observation, from examples, from personal experience; good lessons and bad lessons; big lessons and lesser ones; lessons of grief and sorrow, of joy and happiness; lessons of love and lovemaking; lessons about how to be a guy and (I assume) about how to be a woman, and what the two genders have to do with each other; lessons about how to find meaning (or not) in the lessons we learn, about how they sum or parse. But where does the *idea* for these lessons come from? How do we make one sort of lesson relate to another, and, even amidst all this paradox and even irony, do we learn to understand that all these lessons somehow hang together? Or do they?

If you stare at the word *lesson* long enough it becomes a source of shape-shifting strangeness. For example, eventually it simply doesn't seem to be spelled right. This is also true when you or I stare at other words, yes, but *lesson* is the one I am concentrating on now. The longer I stare at it, the stranger it gets. And I think there is also a deeper lesson in this commonly experienced experience, something about looking too hard and too long that ultimately changes the thing you are looking at, or maybe something about the inherent paradoxes of meaning that seem to escape before our very eyes just at the point of our seeming comprehension of them. Maybe the connection between eyes and mind gets bored and becomes playful. I don't know.

When this happens to me—as it does now—I see the word *lesson* as a potentially misspelled sign, a sign that creates an altered state of syntactical Being. Maybe *lesson* is related generically to *lessen*, in which case the idea of a lesson/lessen might be in the connection that there are principles to guide conduct in ways that reduce uncertainty, ambiguity, or the possibilities of fatal error. The Ten Commandments, for example, explain to us what thou shalt not do, each Commandment a shorthand lesson interdependent with the others and that overall inscribes a way of life. The lesson is to lessen the burden of our estrangement from God. Or perhaps just to lessen the complexities in the choices we need to make when we read, and apply, the instructions.

My staring now alters the meditative focus from spelling to *gendering*. Given the masculine ending, *-son*, perhaps the term *lesson* suggests an epistemic formulation handed down from generation to generation, a secret syntax for understanding shared among men, perhaps even kept from women, a patriarchy of knowledge that is always ultimately a knowledge of patriarchy.

But I am perhaps imagining too much here. The *Oxford English Dictionary* tells us that *lesson* means:

1. The action of reading.
2. A portion of Scripture or other sacred writing read at divine service.
3. A portion of a book or dictated matter, to be studied by the pupil for repetition to the teacher. Hence, something that is or is to be learnt.
4. A continuous portion of teaching, given to a pupil or class at one time; one of the portions into which a course of instruction in any subject is divided.
5. An exercise; a composition serving an educational purpose. A piece to be performed, a performance.
6. Lesson-piece, a piece of material on which to practice needlework.

Notice the dialogic foundations in all of these constructions? I do. In every case, the word *lesson* involves a teacher and pupil, a masterful text and readings given to it, a performance and its public, a practice and its comparison to a known form. A lesson, viewed this way, is the mediation of rules for interpretation on lived experience; it is what is said or read—performed—between persons arranged by the shared activity into greater and lesser degrees of knowledge, experience, and judgment.

Herein, I think, we locate the link between a foundational grammar of shared human community and communication as the dialogic syntax that defines life's meanings through the learning of lessons. The lesson itself, then, is a disciplining of the patterns of language for interpreting lives shaped largely by that patterning. Viewed this way, a lesson makes purposeful sentences correspond to uses and purposes for, and to the usefulness and purposefulness of, life.

Criticism and Evolution as Resistance to Instructions

But life is more than a lesson about usefulness. And consists of experiences more purposeful than grammatically correct sentences can adequately reflect. We have in language the creative capacity to imagine possibilities beyond the given instructions and to use those possibilities *reflexively* to adapt the instructional text to the contexts of our experiences. In the Steven Spielberg film *Jurassic Park*, for example, the artful dodging power of life triumphs over the given rules for doing genetic science when the language for the DNA chain in dinosaurs is filled in with seemingly innocent frog logic; the result is that within a particular environmental context female genes acquire the characteristics of male genes and—against all odds, as well as against the intentions of the scientists—reproduction occurs. This is just a film, you may say, but it is also a sign, further evidence of the seminal role (pardon me) of creativity at the most fundamental biological level, an imagined possibility that serves to remind us of the power of resistance to even the best of instructions.

Jurassic Park also serves as a sign about the political and moral bases for all decisions, for all contextual applications of instructions of any kind. The questions that are *not* asked end up being the most important questions of all: Not "Could we?" but "Should we?" Not "How can we make a fortune?" but "How can we live with the consequences?" All instructions are *political* edifications given as *moral* structures to guide not only what may be learned but also what can be said and therefore what should be sanctioned or done. And as is the case with all political structures, there are those who willingly submit to their overt and hidden ideologies, and there are those who don't. In this meditation, I want to consider the vital role of resistance in language as a desire to further evolutions of consciousness and as a check and balance on the dominant consciousness of our time.

On Internet this morning I find this post from Marsha Woodbury: "The reasonable man adapts himself to the world; the unreasonable one persists in trying to adapt the world to himself. Therefore, all progress depends on the unreasonable man (or woman)." Woodbury attributes this statement to a graduate student, Allan Saxon, and claims he got it from someone else. I figure she is being playful here, avoiding the usual rule for tracking down the original source for a scholarly attribution, and therefore demonstrating her "unreasonableness" within this context.[4]

The point of the quotation and her contextualizing of its source is well taken: *progress (i.e., vision) depends on challenging what reason teaches us ought to be taken for granted.* In important ways this sentiment mirrors older and current discussions about the role of resistance to domination in cultures. The premise is that resistance begins, *always,* in language. My colleague Dwight Conquergood provides an excellent example by way of his work with the Chicago street gang known as the Latin Kings (1993). Conquergood demonstrates how gang symbols rendered as "graffiti" (and marginalized by the dominant culture's use of that terminology) serves the gang members as a street-level road map of gang territories and histories. These oppressed groups appropriate space and inscribe localized meanings on otherwise dominant places; they record their presence on the city walls and the sides of stores, offering elaborate memorials to fallen gang-bangers that include legends of heroism (and victimization) given in a highly developed, commonly understood grammar and syntax—an urban semiotics—of street logic.

Marginalized and oppressed peoples attain voice through such forms of inscribed resistance, thereby speaking publicly their truths to the interests of power. Sometimes they gain ground, sometimes they don't, and sometimes the presence of their resistance so offends the powers that be that the resisters are killed for it.

Resistance tactics and space appropriations are—from the political perspective of those who police for our dominant culture—"unreasonable" because they represent attempts not to adapt to the given world, to the instructions for ordinary rule-determined, bureaucratic, middle-

---

[4] Notice that I am, right here, following her example, her instructions.

Vision and Reason

class living. Instead, they valorize the lived experiences of those for whom the ordinary rules don't work and middle-class ordinariness is but an imagined parallel *im*possibility. If the rules of the world, as Antonio Gramsci (1971) has put it, are most controlled by the hidden powers of institutionalized hegemony, then street-level resistance to those rules is like playing "hegemony cricket"[5]—the graffiti is elaborate because it is serious fun; it is coded from the perspective of gang members because the con must always be rendered as a pun, diddling with the riddle because metaphorical misspelling is a recognized form of subcultural, or countercultural telling.

Radio Talk, Rush Limbaugh, What Is Taken for Granted, and the Politics of Instructions

> GET RIGHT
> Or Get Left
> —Cannon Memorial

One of the ironies I must live with, perhaps learn from, is the unavoidable fact that Central is politically, socially, and culturally dominated by conservative Republicans. This is a sign, I think, not of Central's difference, but of Central's ordinariness, its boredom, its reliance on simple, often traditional principles to guide everyday habits and attitudes, the open role of the zealous religious Right and nasty evangelical fundamentalism in the politics of everyday life, and the unfortunate but undeniable regional practice of continuing to adhere to very bad economic ideas long after they have been openly and publicly resolved. I am writing these lines, *sans merci*, in the early era of Clinton, Clinton and Gore, and, obviously, as a proud gold-saxophone lapel-pin-wearing New Democrat.[6]

---

[5] I am indebted to my pal Mark Neumann for this linguistic twist, a turn that enables vision, humor, and insight.

[6] Actually, I've been a Democrat since I left for college (no pun intended). In 1972 I served as president of the Shepherd College Young Democrats and stumped for George McGovern and Jay Rockefeller. Most recently I covered Bill Clinton's use of media in the 1992 campaign; see "Living in the Rock n Roll Campaign, Or: Myth, Media, and the American Public Imagination" (1994). As this book was in production, the results of the 1994 elections occurred. Many commentators suggested that Rush Limbaugh—and other conservative radio talk-show hosts—had contributed significantly to the Republican victories. Probably this is true. You cannot enter into a dis-

HIGHWAYS AND SURROUNDS

Rush Limbaugh is very popular locally as well as nationally. So is Mike Gallagher, the Greenville AM radio warm-up talk-show/call-in act for the Rush-Man. It is indeed possible to listen to virtually nothing but these loud, rude, (in my view) wrong, but admittedly media-bright and occasionally funny guys from morning till early evening, five days a week, with some national rebroadcasts of Rush-Man Jack on FM weekends. I do listen to them, mostly to hear what the enemy is think—er, excuse me, *saying*; my wife, the real family pol, regularly calls in to voice her opposition.

These radio talk-show/call-in guys—and others of their ilk across the country, perhaps throughout the world—are in the instruction-giving business. Theirs is the self-promoted, corporately-sponsored, radio frequency-enabled and media-opiated role of Instruction-Givers to the Masses, a role constructed out of a preferred reading of the "true" meaning of everyday events within a broader political context, in their case, of The Great, the Noble, The White, The Male, The Book of all Books, The Book of Rightism. Not only are they "on the Right," politically, but they believe they *are* right. They believe that when all else fails, reading Limbaugh's *The Way Things Should Be* or *See, I Told You So* will save you. Literally. Hence, Rush-Man *is* the Right-Man, "talent on loan from God," spewing forth his daily whitewheat bread, his greasy double-cheeseburger and raw onion God 'n' Country, prayer-snaking vitriolic hatred of everything he calls Left or liberal, which is everything in *any* direction outside of his narrow tactical space, which is where everything I call "Progressive" occurs. Which means, I think, that Rush hates me. If not *me*, personally, then at least the ideals I represent and speak for, which is—semiotically and pragmatically—exactly the same thing. The word, in this case, is not the thing, but is the sign of the person speaking it.

I am a college professor, so Rush would understand this "liberal" backlash. I can hear him now:

> Dr. Bud, yeah, right [paper rustling, fist thumping, sniggering]. Hey Delbianco, who is this guy? I mean, does he want *my* job? Is he out to get *me*? Another *liberal* college professor liberal . . . jerk . . . who doesn't under-

course world regularly without having that discourse become part of your imagined reality. President Clinton has never taken Limbaugh's access to the public imagination seriously; perhaps now he will. But in my view, it is too late. My work on the organizing power of hate speech (Goodall 1995) suggests that once a hate image and/or narrative is publicly circulated it is very difficult, if not impossible, to reverse.

Vision and Reason

stand and wants to blame it all on anybody who is successful! Right! Cheez [more paper rustling, occasional primitive grunting]. Well, you heard it here folks, yessir, right here on the radio, a man in the speech field attacking me for exercising free speech. No wonder colleges are in trouble! I mean, well, you know what I mean.

The fact is, Rush, I am *not* against free speech. I support Limbaugh's access to the airwaves even though I think what he says tests the very soil of that conviction. But what interests me, at least here, is not *what he says*—the *ad hominem*, slippery slope, a-causal illogical feast of his incomparable media fictions—but *the work of his words on the public imagination*. I am interested *not* in Rush Limbaugh, but in Rush Limbaugh as a *sign*, as a *clue*, as a symptom of a much broader problem of public dialogue that bespeaks a deeper felt need for mediated and unmediated communicative connections. It is a sign about the *desire for instructions*—even strange instructions—in everyday ordinary life.

Pardon me, please, for that temporary lapse into Rush-like rhetoric. He brings out the worst in me. I even know why. One of the continuing characteristics of extremist language is its inherent communicative capacity to inspire in the new physics of everyday life an equal and opposite reaction. Because he holds tenaciously to such a tight Right leash, I become—very quickly—*very* Left, a very bad dog. The Righter he holds, the Lefter I get. I can't argue with him, directly, so I *imagine* arguing with him, and even within the relative safety of my own mind I construct us—our worlds—as *absolute* opposites, complete with extremist rhetorics roaming every topic in the cosmos on both ends. So I end up talking trash as quickly as he scoops it, performing deeply pissed as an almost necessary response to his highest satisfactions, mimicking his stereotyped name-calling passing as Knowing and illogical tactics staged as Being with my own. *Yuk. Double* Yuk.

Rush and I are misspelling, just not doing it visibly with obvious errors in grammar or vocabulary, instead duo-performing it vocally with negative word choices, the low-pitched, pushed edges of harsh vocal possibilities, and the gloterally induced contexts for the public slams that suggest more about what is *not* getting said than that actively shape what should be. We are in a dialogue, *but it doesn't take us anywhere*. Or get us anywhere. No destination, no arrival.

I wonder about this. I mean, why do I *regularly* expose myself to highly irritating pseudodialogue that produces an inevitable nothingness?[7]

As comedy, TV and Rush Limbaugh are occasionally entertaining, but simply entertaining inevitable nothingness because it occasionally seems funny hardly seems worth it. Might as well watch TV. Maybe I enjoy the emotional pseudoinvolvement, the highly irritated and bellicose verbal state it transports me imaginatively into. I seek this form of Rush because everyday life is pretty bland, by comparison. I do a dose of aural Rush to get neuronically fired-up and vocally charged, to sizzle for awhile on the mindless high of mediated cultural politics. That I disagree, and often vehemently, with his mispronouncements probably only inspires the latter-day P. T. Barnum within him to think: "I don't care what they say about me, as long as they *listen!*"

Talk radio is a work of the imagination too. It mediates possibilities, socially constructs parallel worlds. But the problem is that what we

---

[7] I suspect that some of my more traditional rhetorical and socially scientific colleagues might well consider this chapter—if not the whole of this book—within the same construction of a negative context. What both of these problems of dialogue offer as communication instruction is that the production of public argument—however and wherever mediated—moves us away from a poetics of vision and locks us into reason-giving in support of what, within a specific politicized context or argument field, is strategically considered warrantable. When argument is the game, what is considered warrantable merely supports what those who grant that warrant general license for supporting what they already believe.

I think this is a fairly recent phenomenon. Before television and radio reconstructed the public space of politics and imagination, face-to-face argumentation and debate was a finer, more noble political art (Smith 1993) capable of nurturing and supporting the discovery of common vision to guide human progress and endeavor. The design of public architecture supported the value of public argumentation by providing open spaces for the free exchange of ideas (Sennett 1978), and although gender prejudice and racism made imperfect the "open" or "free" exchange, nevertheless the dialogue was open to public scrutiny and the interlocutors conducted their discussion eyeball to eyeball as well as tooth to tooth. When the space for that free exchange shifted from communal realities to the hyperspace of fast, desirable surfaces and slam-and-run soundbites in an increasingly mediated postmodern public space, the role of judicious reasoning and indeed of modern(ist) argument was materially reduced to support for, or at best—communicative coexistence with—the comic/tragic paradigm of mass entertainment (see Postman 1986). Public dialogues about communal and human progress were replaced market-driven, self-centered, and Other-denying dialectics that are only ever really about itself—about how the mediating of partisan politics are the most important item—rather than the purposes of human Being on this planet and the publics' agenda for that role within the unified field of our cosmos.

I do not believe we will "go back" to modern argument; no one is that willing to give up a TV, and besides, histories always move in the opposite direction of a "past." What we need to move into is a context—a common place—for intimate, interactive dialogue capable of supporting diverse communities without coercion, a common place for the everyday public enactment of *spiritual* vision.

Vision and Reason

imagine—the world with Rush Limbaugh's tongue in it, for example—becomes very much a part of *what we are actually living through*. In the time it took to construct that imagined Rush-response, I was *there* and nowhere else. Talk radio *consumes and redefines communicative real space and time* through its fanciful plays on—and direct appeals to—the mediated public space for imagination. By making the Rush-Man a character in my ongoing pseudodialogue, right here reading the signs in Reality Central or while I could be doing community in Clemson, I instead invite him into this time and space.

LESSONS FROM A RADIO PAST

Radio has been an important part of American communication systems—and hence, direction-giving—since the 1920s.[8]

But, as with many technological innovations in the rural upstate region of South Carolina, there is a unique local history that must be understood. It helps explain the popularity of more than radio, I think.

Susan Opt (1993) provides a fine and detailed account of how, during the winter of 1930 to 1931, an enterprising, soon-to-be Clemson University student named Gordon Rogers from Mauldin

> built an alternating current receiver using junk radio parts and a speaker from an old battery set. Then it occurred to him that from his receiver he might be able to provide radio to a neighbor who had no electric service. By

---

[8] I worked for WJEJ-AM/WWMD-FM in Hagerstown, Maryland, in 1977. At the time, I didn't realize that I was witnessing—as well as participating in—an important transition for the role of radio in American public life. WJEJ was the oldest station in Maryland, one of the oldest in the United States. The call letters stood for "Jesus Entering Jerusalem," which gives a fair approximation of the sentiment its entrepreneurial founder had for the possibilities of commerical radio at that time. It is also a stark symbol that sums up a lot of semiotic possibilities for interpretation, because when Jesus entered Jerusalem he was taking the biggest risk of his public career, a career about to be betrayed by one of his followers, and a risk that would eventually see him crucified in exchange for forty pieces of silver.

That year I worked in radio—in the actual construction of mediated space—we moved the station from its old downtown headquarters in a beautiful brick building (inside the station included a broadcast studio large enough to house a forty-piece orchestra, as it once regularly had) to a new two-story house (literally) on the outskirts of town, where the "lower" level was reserved for the new studio and the "upper" level was for sales and management. There, we introduced to that region its first 100,000-watt FM station using a totally computerized format. At the time, we were being smart, progressive, making use of technology for the better making of money; all we were giving up was the "overhead," the human touch. We also reduced the time for news to five minutes every hour, and turned over the rest of the programming time for "adult contemporary" muzak and the soundbites of advertisers. We made those decisions rationally, at least within a context of market capitalism and technological wonder.

installing a single wire with ground return, he connected a loudspeaker at his neighbor's house to his receiver. Rogers' experiment worked and within several months, he extended service to seven families. In about four years, 600 homes were being served.

The first wire Rogers ran as part of his wired radio system came from a Model Tignition coil. He strung it across trees and fence to reach his neighbors. Broken ends off of 5-cent size Coke bottles served as insulators. When the family beyond the first connection wanted the system, Rogers used iron wire and stapled it to telephone poles. However, when it rained, the radio transmitted over the telephone lines. The president of the telephone party line came out and cut Rogers' line to shreds. (1993, 74, 75)

This early rough shaping of a mediated community continued to attract new subscribers, and soon, new stations cropped up around other rural gathering places. Word of Rogers's success in Mauldin spread to the tiny dot called Ware Place, where J. R. Chandler's store became the next mediated community center; from there Charles Murdock's general store in Saylors Crossroad set up what the subscribers called "the partyline," or "the speakerline"; Carl Ellison's store at the end of the Duke Power line in Williamston began broadcasting; and the Wasson brothers homeplace became the site of local wired radio in Hickory Tavern (Opt 1993).

In each of these locations, the programming included local news and weather, lots of hillbilly, fiddlin', bluegrass, and gospel music (including live broadcasts of local groups and singers), and Sunday church services. When the "stations" went "off-the-air," the subscribers often yelled into their receiving speakers to communicate in "partyline" fashion amongst themselves, thus appropriating new uses for the medium as well as creating an inexpensive rural alternative to the corporately controlled—and for rural folk, expensive—telephone, as well as establishing the first truly interactive "call-in" radio talk shows. What counted as "news" was often a loose and highly localized construction: births, deaths, announcements of entirely local interest—such as the passing of a local farmer's mule, and the sad fact that the farmer still owed the bank money on the mortgage for the mule—all contributed significantly to the distribution of information and to the constitution of a public imagination.

Some of these homemade radio stations operated until the late 1930s—the spread of Rural Electrification Authority programs in farming states prepared the airways for the replacement of old battery-operated radios with newer, all-electric models, and with them, access to larger, more powerful, and acoustically superior stations—but some of them, like the Murdock store operation in Saylors Crossroad, continued broadcasting into the early 1940s (Opt 1993). With these media technologies—these "improvements"—came also the advent of changes in how rural people gained information; thought about persons, nature, and things; and talked about those issues among themselves; and used those communication processes and results to alter existing lifeways and cultures.

Certainly, some of these changes were welcome. But change is never neutral; it moves us simultaneously toward something and away from something else. As I listen to Rush Limbaugh or the local rock and country stations, I am reminded that part of what was lost was a *localized* sense of face-to-face (or at least local-voice-to-local-voice) community, a valuing locally of what is perhaps small and occasionally dear, if only to those who care for, and about, each other. What we gained—if *gained* can be used here as somehow the "right" word—is a kind of universalized, homogenized, quacking loudness that drowns down or out the quieter, subtler heterogeneities that make possible a living democracy, that brings forth a shared sense of public space for individual communities, and ultimately, that guarantees the sanctity and freedoms of individuals.

AND NOW . . . BACK TO A RADIO FUTURE

The inherent arrogance of a *national* broadcast—with its large implication that unless one is tuned-in, and turned-on, by *national* news, weather, and fashionable entertainment—that one is clearly not in step with "progress," with what is "happening," with all that can be "going on" where what is "going on" is redefined on a national or moreover an international map, rather than what is "going on" locally. "Give the local broadcasters their five minutes of prime time," I can hear the National Directors of Corporate News saying, "For some *local color*, and of course for the weather and sports, and then return to the *real news*, and to what is *really happening*."

What do we lose when the mediated *national* replaces the enacted communal *local* as the localized site for organizing communication about "what really counts," or "what is really going on" and should therefore concern us, or what should guide our decisions about ourselves, our families, our businesses, and our communities?[9] No wonder we believe Central—or Clemson—is pretty ordinary and boring, when the unordinary, and certainly the exotic, is located in the hypertexts of mediated elsewheres; no wonder we feel bored by our local circumstances, when an absence of boredom is what is promised, seduced over the airwaves, when we are virtually connected to an imagined Washington, DC, similar New York, similitude Chicago, virtual Atlanta, fabulous LA, even

LondonParisRomeJerusalemCasablancaCapetownMoscowToykoHongKong, or the wildwild mediated outback, the imagined kangaroos and shrimp-barbies that we are led to believe define the cultures of mediated Australia. And no wonder that fewer voters turn out for local elections on issues that *directly* concern them—school bonds and school boards, for example—than often sit in the sparse stands of Little League baseball games during the steamy heat of a midsummer's evening.

What we lose, America, *is* America. What we lose is *not* simply the the quaint charm of localized public space for public discussion, or a mediated space for a public construction of local communities. That is, admittedly, already gone. What we lose is a *participative democracy at the organizing level* of the way we read—or hear—signs and interpret them. So it is that the dominance of the talk-show airwaves these days by national Rush Limbaugh troubles me, and troubles me in downtown Central and Clemson. So, too—and, unfortunately, so true—is Rush's line about "America held hostage," used by him to code the advent of the Clinton Administration but a sign capable of an alternative interpretation, one more directly about the loss of democracy. His use of humor and innuendo in this off-stage but on-the-air mouthing of (supposedly)

---

[9] My wife and I observed the rapid influence of mass mediated environments on local cultures when we visited Ireland in the summer of 1989. Toward the east coast, in small towns still dominated by community centers holding nightly public dialogues on matters of common interest—usually a pub and two churches—the talk was centered, localized, historically rich and open to debate; what was distant and imagined was the world outside of their incredibly well-tended, if technologically challenged, communities. The closer we moved toward Dublin, with the advent of satellite TV and cable systems, what was cherished as local in community talk was replaced with the homogeneity of the mass, the international, which mostly meant American and European. With that advent came also a visible deterioration of communities, the replacement of American country and western music for Irish songs, and concern for the dispersals of families due to their inability to "find jobs" and "make money." Progress clearly has a high price—higher, we thought, than its gain.

Vision and Reason

conservative political ideals is a form of communicating resistance to what he perceives as the dominance of liberalism, a fully enacted tactic of calculated and mediated misspelling; what is being misspelled, what should not be misread as a sign of our times: what Rush calls "the relentless pursuit of the Truth" enabled by the authority he says is "Talent on Loan From God . . . " is only accomplished by silencing—screaming at, dismissing as lunacy, or simply ignoring—all opposing views and voices.

What *kind* of God is this? Indeed, what *version* of Truth?

Personally, I find these rhetorical strategies and tactics easy to identify but difficult to deal with and problematic to critique. I admit, readily, that I gave up on a Big-T Truth and a Sky-God separate from my soul and outside my universe a long time ago, back when I started to understand that what people feel is true and what they live out as truths depends largely on their *life experiences*, and that life experiences are deeply, often vastly, dissimilar, parallel. I do not believe we can build a better world—nor improve the condition of our home in the cosmos—by appealing to that which does not—nor cannot—be located in the primacy—the intimate here and now—of everyday lived experiences. Instead, I take the plural worlds of lived experiences as seriously as the fundamental constitutive fact of public imagination and of personal, social, organizational, and communal realities, and I accept these principles as primary to an understanding of spirituality and communication.

That said, however, my problem—theoretically and pragmatically—is that "one world" I know I can tune into but can never understand is the world of Rush Limbaugh and others of his particular calling.[10] Maybe for him, for members of his audience, there is a Big-T Truth. Certainly a Sky-God. In fact, I admit there is a Big-T Truth for him, and a more or less corresponding Big-T Book of Instructions for reaching the Sky-God.

All I can say in response to the lived experiences of that world is this: for some people, cows do, indeed, jump right over the moon. And having uttered that negative soundbite, I find—once again—what this form of talk reduces me to. There *must* be a better way.

---

[10] Newt Gingrich or Bob Dole, for example. Is there any better forum for viewing the demise of participative democracy and the debasement of dialogue than in the United States Congress? Given that Rush, and other commentators and pundits who share his calling if not his ideology, view themselves as extensions of government—instruction-givers capable of providing Right-minded interpretations of current political debates to the masses—perhaps what is wrong with his communication practices is merely a symptom of what's wrong with congressional communication practices.

If we must live out in the public space of national broadcasts, give me the local broadcast of National Public Radio. *Anytime.* It limits the emphasis on the "spoken national" and privileges the speaking of and listening to the local and the regional; even when *All Things Considered* or *Morning Edition* kicks in, it gives more public air time to Missoula, Montana, than it does to New York City or Los Angeles, the media capitals of the mediated Third World. It is an imaginative medium, an interconnected network mixing together the arts and sciences, politics and education, local agriculture and global business. It is constructed out of local particulars and multiple voices that in the clear articulation of their heavily accented differences suggest broad universals embracing a basic multiworld, multicultural appreciation of how everyday things get done, and get done *differently.*

People with unique voices are interviewed, not shouted down, even when their views express values and lived experiences that the NPR listening audience probably finds abhorrent, strange, or simply misguided. But we get to hear them, make some personal sense of what they publicly say, and add it all to the rough mix necessary for free-speech based democracy, and for what has in our time become a necessarily *participative* mediated democracy. It is talk radio that brings us back to our town, that valorizes our ability to identify—not denegrate—what we have and lack with the havings and lackings of Others.

Considered this way, when all else fails and we must turn back, finally, to the instructions, maybe what we turn back to is not just scripture from The Book, but instead to what we can simply turn on: the radio, or—more likely—the TV. There, through our mediated minds, and in the shifting space of our public imaginations, lies the festering soul of democracy as well as its available multiple instructions—its contexts—for interpreting how we should think, feel, and live through and in our towns.

Instructions, Media, and Multiple Worlds

I've just equated scripture with television, which is—at the very least—an unexplicated connection, and at the very worst, purely blasphemous. Perhaps I'd better explain.

Without reciting the big statistics about how much television viewing

Vision and Reason

we do,[11] and without invoking the obvious arguments about what television programming is primarily showing us (sex and violence) or how that even *what* is being shown to us is graphically (surfaces count) and narratively (male sexual fantasy themes) depicted, let us briefly contemplate the hidden instructions that wait for us in television's internal coding—the surprise, if you will, that is ours simply for turning on, or opening up, the box. Any channel, any time. I am speaking here of an instruction so basic, so simple, that it is often ignored: *that what goes on television is more real and therefore more interesting and important than we are.*

This theme has been pursued elsewhere (see Ewen 1989; Postman 1986). My take on it here, however, has less to do with television's role in *replacing* information with entertainment than it does with television's place in making cultural space for issues of spirituality and communication *through* mediated communication. Specifically, I am interested in how television programming depicts what should count as "real" in and to imagined communities, relationships, and publics, and how the lacing of coded instructions—the preferred reading—about how we should read—listen to, watch, or make sense of—the contexts is presented to us.

In this way, television presents a modernist textual strategy (e.g., preferred readings about self and Power, and categorical responses to that display of self and Power) dressed out in fashionable postmodern garb (e.g., the plausible deniability of that strategy when Other is invoked) done as a sit-com; contemporary theme movie; advertisement; or a Sunday-morning political commentary, complicit witnesses to the pervasive spirit of market capitalism and an absence of vision disguised as opposition, as resistance tactic. Furthermore, the interchangeability of television programming (what you see on one channel is pretty much what you see on all channels) belies the consistent undercurrent of the both the presence of and consequences for mediated instructions about the ways persons, nature, and things *are*.

---

[11] Just in case you were wondering, according to a 1990 Gallup survey, 97 percent of Americans watched television on an average weekday, with the most typical American admitting to between 3.5–4.1 hours per day; 17 percent claiming they watch more than 6 hours per day.

HIGHWAYS AND SURROUNDS

TELEVISED INSTRUCTIONS

I don't think television is evil. As is true with any human technology, its uses in the socially constructed world are pragmatically (read: economically) based and only later understood as having both/either good and evil influences. For example, during morning drive-times, contrast the relatively tame programming of *Sesame Street, Barney and Friends,* or *Shining Time Station* with the highly visual, often rude, and unduly violent cartoon (e.g., Power Rangers) *or* brainless, sensational talk-show worlds depicted on various competing networks, and the available differences show a range of available possibilities. That is, at least, one way to read what is going on there. Virtual democracy, perhaps. Something for everyone, maybe.

But there is another way to read it. Read it, I think, as further evidence for the existence of multiple realities and coded instructions about how to see and make sense of those realities. You don't have to look much beyond conversation to see this influence, either. Everyday discourse traffics in the *topoi*—and makes sense of the traffic patterns using the medium's visually and aurally fashionable attitudes to represent *pathos, ethos,* and *logos*—of what's on TV. Walk into any store in Central, or listen to the *patois* of any Clemson workplace, and what you *always* hear is a local discussion laced with big-screen talk of television shows and their appeals, as if what is on TV is as real as anything else in the lives of ordinary people. Which it is. Watching television—as well as what is depicted on the screen—*is* a real-time activity; discussing what is seen and heard with others is also real. So "saturated" (Gergen 1992) is the discourse of everyday talk with electronic media that its play in and for the imagination is not much different from the play of any other everyday life event, except, of course, living life outside of media itself.

This last statement is true also for its *coding*, for how we make sense of what we see and hear. And it always has been. In *Tube of Plenty*, Eric Barnoux (1975) explains that ever since the advent of television in the late '40s and early '50s, the common theme of everyday programming has been to teach viewers how to deal with and even succeed in everyday life. What to do, what to know, what to wear, how to act when good fortunes or unfortunate reversals are visited upon us, and so on, has been an active part of television's educational agenda and general public appeal. In the beginning, this theme was overtly placed (laced) into the

Vision and Reason

story line; early sit-coms depicted lower-middle-class members of various urban ethnic groups striving to attain middle-class stature, which consisted mostly of acquiring the "appropriate" attitudes (how should we reflect what we think about business, family life, politics, and so on), behaviors (such as the importance of losing a regional or ethnic accent or of knowing how to talk to a social superior), and habits (what makes the "real" middle class different from you and me?). The everyday social and work worlds were acceptable, even when oppressive; the task for every red-blooded citizen was to get her or his own respectable piece of the available respectable pie.

I can't watch *The Simpsons* without seeing traces of that original outline, albeit these days done out as cartoon parody about what's respectable and done up with featured resistance storylines of Bart against the hegemony-pie of respectability, represented by his parents, work, stores, church and school; of his father's everyday rebellion against the control of the corporation and politics over his life (mostly by finding more ways to goof off and still get paid) and his family (as impinging on his individuality); and for that matter of the women's role (Bart's mom and sister) of finding creative ways to overcome the stupidity constructed for them by the consensual world of men. Where once the common message was "Fit in to the world of your betters and prosper," the message today seems to be "Your life is everywhere overdetermined and overcontrolled by mostly incompetent people who don't deserve where they are or what they have and who certainly don't give a damn about you, so just say *fuck it*, be a little devious on a daily basis, and try to have a good time along the way."

In the olden days of television, where the message to acquire the trappings of the middle class wasn't as clearly placed into the storylines it was shown to viewers indirectly: game shows (that inspired visions of instantaneous wealth, such as the *$64,000 Question*, or at least a new washer and dryer for the "Missus") were created to reward the "right" answers, thus subtly linking appropriate middle-class knowing with the advent of riches, and the advent of riches with a sense of fitting in. Over the years, however, the "right" answers evolved from a white person's middle-class knowledge of history, geography, politics, and socially acceptable class-specific etiquettes to be more and more frequently about popular culture—especially TV—and its corporately sponsored icons. These days social swagger in everyday conversations and in game shows is seldom won by being able to name the capitols of the states or foreign countries (the exception being *Jeopardy*, a show primarily about being rewarded for being a trivial nerd among other overachieving, highly competitive nerds), but instead *is* based on brand-name corporate recognition, movie and sit-com lines and stars, and the lyrics to rap and rock songs. Interesting—if only as a sidebar to this subtle coding—is the popular culture movement of everyday merit *downward* from the what's in the head (being smart) to the what's worn on the feet (shoes are the signs of being ultimately dressed for cool, complete only with the appropriate lacing of your Nikes or strapping of your Tevas), and *outward* from the mind and heart (what you thought and felt *about*) to the body and clothing (how your display of attitude should be publicly sanctioned). Television codes the surfaces, and the surfaces saturate the public coding of selves.

Please don't read what I am writing here as postmodernist nostalgia. See it instead as simply unraveling a common thread in the broader fabric of everyday mediated public life, taking what is everywhere apparent on the surfaces of conversations back to its mediated origins, and therein linking the evolution of television's themes to the evolution of social order and ideas about control.

Thought Experiment: Try tracing your family's history along the virtual lines of the TV shows you most remember your family watching and talking about. See if there is a connection. My bet is there *is*. After all, there are no coincidences in a world made—and seen—through multiple causes and effects. Even when made-for-TV myths meet the mythic narratives of American families, the commingling of their myths is both an empirically verifiable fact and a source of wonder about consequences. If we believe that we are what we eat—that what we put into our bodies is important to its eventual growth and development—then by comparison what we put before our eyes and lace into our everyday talk also have long-term influences.[12]

Scary, isn't it? Particularly when you consider that things might have

---

[12] Family communication scholars as well as family therapists have lately come to believe that one possible influence of TV on childhood and perceptions of sibling rivalries and birth order on personality is that *everyone in a family grows up in a different family*, parallel but distinctive ones. Although the common space of lived experiences is shared, interpretations of its meanings are heavily mediated by master scripts of popular culture and its TV shows, which—given the frequency of TV viewing among children of all social classes—set up and reinforce comparisons between lived experiences and mediated interpretations of content and context.

turned out differently if we would have simply changed channels. Or better yet, turned the damned thing off.

MEDIATED SPIRITUALITY

On a spiritual level, communication between and among televised relational partners is unsettling if intriguing. I am *not* speaking here of the cable "God" channels, wherein mostly rich, mostly Christian, mostly white people advance their causes through televised prophecy, tele-therapy,[13] on-the-spot healing, discussion of the religious contexts for everyday issues, or outright broadcasts of religious services. These stations are dedicated to the politics of religion, not to the fostering of spirituality. Instead, I want to examine how everyday life on mediated channels reflects spiritual teachings.

One dominant, daytime and primetime strategy seems to be to take the Ten Commandments of Judeo-Christian doctrine and present them, individually and collectively, as sources of conflict. That we, as a mediated populace, are inherently depraved, that we do regularly lie, cheat, steal, kill, overeat, overdrink, pray to false gods, and experience and act on lust, intolerance, doubt, and envy, seems to be a taken-for-granted assumption that creates scenarios with sponsorable appeals. We can laugh, pity, identify with, or cry over the life foibles of mediated others and see in their reflexive surfaces reflections of our own imagined lives. We can read what we see as an instruction, as a lesson about life, because usually (except in documentaries, ironically) good triumphs over evil, and there is a happy ending if—and only if—a featured character becomes the emblem, the sign, of a better-lived life. The rhetorical movement from lowly confusion and suffering through progressive forms of learning to a transcendent purity is virtually Burkeian (1989)! Thus, what is reinforced in primetime and daytime programming is what all of us already know, or at least have been taught is true about the world. The message is consistent: there are evil people who will cause you great, sudden harm—even death—for no good reason; however, if we align ourselves and our habits with more "moral" (certainly better-off) citizens, and if we stop our sinful ways, we tend to win something of spiritual value (often at great material cost) in the long run.

[13] See Mimi White (1992) for an expanded examination of therapeutic discourse on American television; see especially her chapter on *The 700 Club*.

Similarly, television talk shows tend to display the common theme that most of us do not treat each other as we would ourselves like to be treated. Violations of the "Golden Rule" dominate the appearance of feuding parents and children, husbands and wives, members of various racial, ethnic, sexual, or culturally marginalized groups. The complaint is specified, the discussion exudes examples and countercharges and emotional displays, and there is always a common plea for greater tolerance as the wellspring of social change. Democratic Christianity.

But you don't have to be a member of a Judeo-Christian tribe to see the spiritual connections between what's on television and what's going on in your life, although I do think that religious base is primary to most of what is seen. Consider the ironies of programming if you were a Muslim, or Hindu, or Buddhist. The world as it is presented is one of secular needing and spiritual vacuity. The concerns of the always-striving, never-knowing characters parallels the teachings of scriptures—this is "virtually" the way things "are"—but the solutions to their strivings are Western, not Eastern, constructions.

Neither do I believe that cable or satellite or the soon-to-be dial-a-mediated-reality-into-your-living-room options save us from the commonality of mediated instructions for reading the preferred meanings for living, loving, relating, dealing with issues, and when all that is over, even dying. More options, to paraphrase a Bruce Springsteen lyric, doesn't necessarily mean anything's on, or, for that matter, that anything really changes.

The Necessary Death of Ordinary Reason: Vision, Dialogue, and Extraordinarily Empowered Communities

> I see vision as a spiritual phenomenon because it goes beyond everyday issues....
> Vision is a spiritual way to create organizational bonding
> without the use of coercion.
>
> —Jack Hawley

To advocate moving beyond the status quo always involves risk, and the bolder the move the greater the risk. The need for a fundamental, transformative change for our society and for our planet is everywhere apparent, and nowhere, and at no time, have the risks anywhere been

Vision and Reason

higher. For me, the core of change is always communication, because communication organizes action, influences perceptions, and eventually alters realities.

This chapter has been written out of the dualities of "vision" and "reason," each term historically central in the creation of social change, and each term (in the writing of this chapter) increasingly identified with political, mediated, and spiritual interests and contextual domains. Although "vision" and "reason" are complicit—even necessary—to the construction of each other and to the overall project of change, the time has come to recognize that each term organizes the substance of change differently.

Throughout this book I have maintained that democratic communities require an interpretive space for the engagement of public imagination, and that in turn democratic communities constituted in and through public imagination owe far more to empowering visions, contextual ambiguities of signs, and lived experiences that embrace spiritual and dialogic penetrations between and among parallel worlds than they do to modernist argumentative rationality. Such a modernist (or traditional) rationality assumes the reality of "one world" in which the reason-givers are separate from and capable therefore of panoptically commenting upon what they empirically observe; it does not embrace the new physics of a unified cosmos in which multiple, parallel worlds whose known borders transcend the wisdom of the commonsense-making five senses and are part and parcel of us, our lived experiences, our interpretations of meanings, and of our reasons. Such a traditional rationality further accepts only one context—admittedly dialectical—to guide a preferred reading through the textual construction of opposites, to terminological screens (Burke 1989); it does not open the text up to multiple interpretations derived from different experiences with different texts, pretexts, and contexts. And this form of traditional rationality—outworn and yet dominant because power elites everywhere use it—as always—to support and maintain their power—now sponsors a one-world mediated virtual reality—a one-world show—fit only for sustaining the market shares of marketeers rather than for contributing to the sustainability of the planet.

This traditional form of rationality—a dominant, Western rationality that for centuries has pragmatically determined what counts as "rational communication" as well as empirical "reality"—must be understood at this end of the twentieth century *not* as the neutral, objective mediator of public argument capable of promoting democratic speech and supporting democratic communities, but instead as the ultimate articulation of *coercion*, a sign of cultural power that *inherently limits* our understanding of texts and contexts, each other, our families, our communities, space and time, bodies and souls, earth and stars, the purpose for Being, and the centrality of communication in connecting that purpose to the imagined parallel worlds we inhabit and traverse.

Traditional forms of reasoning have lost their transformative powers. Argument alone—regardless of its resourceful use of evidence or a clever articulation of its otherwise clear-headed rhetoric—will not save us because its defining vision worked only to transform an ancient world into a modern one. In that modern world, a world mediated *only* by language in which the rules of order could be pedagogically and pragmatically reduced to rules for language usage, rules for public conduct could thus be socially inscribed and engineered.

But ours is not solely that world anymore. Alongside—and rapidly overtaking—the spatial architectures and human architectonics of the taken-for-granted modern world are diverse postmodern worlds, within which virtual, multiple, and parallel realities compete with and transform the contextual meanings of the empirical, both within and for the space of public imagination, and for political, social, and aesthetic influence. The multiple worlds of today's everyday realities are thereby mediated by multiple competing languages, each one with its own rules contributing to a general system in which chaos is the furthest evolution of order.

The questions raised here about public imagination, mediated worlds, and the construction of dialogic communities *cannot be traditionally argued much less answered.* As the shape of the text has changed, so too much its contexts for interpretation. Toward this end, it seems to me that a new logic of vision must be found, for this is indeed a new world we have arrived in. We dare not repeat the traditional mistakes of the past by simply trying to colonize this new world with outworn argumentative values and limited—and limiting—ways of making sense, engaging dialogue, building sustainable communities. We need to invent communication—ways of speaking, ways of listening, ways of connecting to and bonding with each other—up to that formidable task. What is required is the rediscovery of some age-old questions—who are we? what are we here for? why do we communicate?—as well as the invention of a communal vision that asks "who should we be?" instead of arguing about who is right.

There are instructions available. There always have been. Maybe we have waited—as a people, as a planet—till all else has failed. Viewed this way, it *is* time to follow the instructions.

8

Insight and Complexity: The Future of Unities

> The challenge today is to seek a unity that celebrates diversity, to unite the particular with the universal, to recognize the need for roots while insisting that the point of roots is to put forth branches.
> —William Sloane Coffin

If interconnected complexities are our only true reality, and if semiotic interpretations are the sole everyday arbiters of giving meaning to the human condition, what then is meant by *insight*? What *is* insight?

Insight is the multichannel communicative pathway between complexity and interpretation. It may be mediated by the whispers of angels or by a sudden tingling warmth that cause the hairs on your neck to rise and salute the moment. It may be co-produced by your voice in dialogue with an Other's voice, or with many Other's voices, when what was a genuine dialogue becomes a meaningful song. Or it can happen in the centered quiet of deep meditative contemplation, when the ordinary miraculous firing of neurons becomes transcendentally interspersed with a busy, blooming, buzzing galaxy of atomic explosions and dispersed across an awesome ineffable coordinated movement of souls.

Insight is often perceived as a kind of collision, the forceful coming together of two or more disparate thoughts, actions, persons, or things. It is a small cause for momentary celebration, an immediate source of ecstasy in the everyday. The ability to hold on to insight—and to enfold its meanings back into the larger canvas from which it sprang—is often associated with the power—the rhetorical power—of seers, visionaries, poets, prophets, teachers, and other persons for whom the extraordinary in the everyday is read and interpreted as a sign. Insight, understood this way, is a sign announcing an intersection of everyday and ultimate purposes, the crossing of our spiritual natures with our permeable bodies, of

Insight and Complexity

the unity of our apparent dualities, and of our mysterious interconnectedness and divinity.

These introductory paragraphs may seem a strange way to offer instructions about the meaning of insight in our complex reality; in fact this book probably seems a strange way to write them. But what I intend to do in this chapter is to enlarge the textual dialogue, to connect these small observations to the larger discursive communal complexity. To achieve that design, I will involve and discuss the insights afforded by Others, some of whom are my colleagues and friends, some of whom are strangers whose experiences have made curious unexpected inroads into mine, and some of whom are persons I encountered on extraordinary pages I read while I thought I was just doing the business of being ordinary.[1] From the architectonic highways of vision just off the purposeful interstates of reason, we move now into the vaster surrounds of this heavenly orbiting vessel, the places within the spaces between, as well as into our collective selves, our communicative oversouls, for the lessons our teachings reveal and make possible.

Baseball Caps and Parking Lots

I am in the Anderson mega Wal-Mart, standing in checkout lane 5. So I follow instructions; I check things out while waiting patiently to make my purchase. Around me is a swirl and mix of multiple consumer desires coalescing with various states of conscious and unconscious customer satisfaction, undeniable evidence of imagination, parallel worlds, and language codes more or less coexisting in this neon, overbright public space, and a few unhappy children and elderly persons who know better than to seek happiness in such middling surrounds and purchases. They would rather be *living*, preferably out of here.

A guy behind me sports a baseball cap that reads:

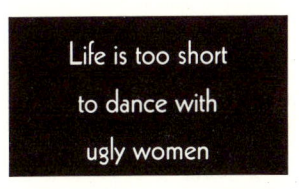

> Life is too short
> to dance with
> ugly women

He must be closing in on his mid-'90s, wears a white T-shirt and jean

---

[1] Most of which I read because they were passed on to me by people who knew I was interested in this topic—a sign, I think, that supports the idea that there are no coincidences; in the final chapter all of our texts and experiences converge.

209

jacket, and certainly is no prize looker himself. But I have to admire his sense of style, of his capacity for combining metaphor and irony. He is buying generic menthol cigarettes and a flashlight, which somehow go together. He knows what he likes, and where he is going, just needs a little help with the light getting there.

I am making this up, of course. Imagining it. I am also connecting it to a presentation made by one of my graduate students, in which she discussed a baseball cap pushed up to receding hairline on an elderly man at the Six Mile Retirement Home:

> JESUS SAVES
> †
> Automatic Transmissions

"What," she asked, "does Jesus have against manual transmissions? Or what does Jesus save automatic transmissions for? Or maybe, only automatic transmissions can dance on the head of a pin." Probably the guy just thought it was a hat—a ordinary, everyday covering for his head—not a sign of what was in it. But you never know. Sometimes, not even if you ask.

I emerge from my wonderings at the checkout point and ask the checker, a country-music-lovin', big-haired redhead in mid years with a practiced dislike of scanners, "What do you think about this guy's cap?" I motion to the fellow behind me.

"*Shoot,*" she responds, with throw-down enthusiasm and a big don't-take-me-too-seriously, semiautomatic smile, "*He's* ugly, *too.*"

"Maybe so," the old fellow replies, obviously enjoying this, "but you got to admire my *style.*" He leans over toward me and winks, "Its all just a big ol' *metaphor,* and on my head *ironic,* too."

Maybe I haven't been imagining any of this, or maybe I only thought I was. Either way, I owe this store more than it costs me to exit as a satisfied customer, and upon whose shimmering black-and-yellow striped parking lot I noticeably cross over an ineffable intersection to assume my position as the driver of this Intrepid—this fine American

---

[2] Teddy Fishman.

Insight and Complexity

vehicle whose name suggests safe passage through deep mystery and offers a suitable disguise for the crossing—and reenter the everyday traffic and ordinary rhetorics of persons and things.[3]

This chapter is at least halfway about highways, isn't it? Maybe that's why somedays I pass all the big Cadillacs; other days I am content to remain behind them. I'm betting you know *exactly* what that last metaphor feels like. The question is *how*.

Reading Myself into the Texts of Others

On the highways we must read ourselves into the contexts of Others. We enfold our take on the here and now into perceptions of Other's intentions and meanings, or at least into the parts of their assumed intentions and supposed meanings that we can figure ourselves into and imagine ourselves maneuvering in, around, and occasionally through. Maybe this is why we always—and at the same time *never*—step into the same conversation twice, because on the highways, everything that can become possible becomes possible at once. With feedback you may stay the course or suddenly, persuasively, arrive at a whole new context, and *there*—in that moment where within the nonverbal subtleties of nuance mix into or against the overt incompleteness of what is acted out or spoken—comes the knowledge, the framework for interpretation, that *was always here before* the context, which in turn becomes a turning point, the interpretive crossing of a self into a spiritual context for change.

GRANTING VOICE TO SPIRIT

Throughout this book, I have tried to highlight and contrast modern and postmodern surrounds. This has been a purposeful, if ordinary, construction. The modern has been depicted as a Western tale, a story valoring the romantic, individual self conquering vast nature and lesser Others, forging God-fearing, two-party communities and respectable divisions of management and labor, in which the heroic *logos*-bearing human becomes at one with the machine-bearing metaphor of technological progress and bureaucratic order, eventually repressing whatever

---

[3] This could be just a case of symbolic convergence (Bormann 1985). Professor Bormann is a communication theorist for whom the ordinary interplay of symbols and cultures is summed up in his insightful work on "symbolic convergence." I believe that if his work was expanded, it could serve as a major stepping-off place for our understanding of extraordinary communication.

Spirit was once there into the nether reaches of a shadowy unconscious mind, or at least containing its expression within the hierarchical structures of obedient instructional language, tolerating an uneasy balance between evangelical performances and silent religious prayer.

In response, we have witnessed the unruly rise of the postmodern Other, an antiauthority, anticolonial, antigrand narratives rhetoric which defines as its antihero a deconstructive sympathy with all marginalized Other(s). The postmodern rhetoric is not so much a many-sided story as it is a many-storied, mediated, nonnarrative tale, fast scatterings of words and actions across surfaces made only for full-speed, breathless consumption by which colonized, alienated, disconnected, authorless beings search for the inevitable, signified Nothing.

Into this decentering, denaturing, dehumanizing, degendering narrative Void wherein the purpose of Being in a text is the discovery of textual Nonbeing, there is at work something mysterious, something ineffable, but definitely something else. This binary firmament—perhaps taking its creative power from the Big One—is a breeding ground for purposes larger and more meaningful than narratives of order and antiorder can catch. It has always been this way, because this is the way it has always been. Spirit enters the world *not* through opposing rational constructions *or* textual deconstructions but always through the openings offered by combining the insights of such oppositions, by the unifying force of what we can only call the "unconscious," a prefiguring dynamic place that at once makes purposeful, imaginative poetry of these seemingly disparate exploding stars.[4]

The role of Spirit is a unifying one. By teaching us to understand and practice *the full range of communicative possibilities* as the holistic force for connecting ourselves to Others, for connecting our interests to better interests of community, for connecting our communities' interests to the best interests of the Earth, we learn to perceive and act on the ordinary, everyday interdependencies of the furthest reaches of human nature as simply the localized intersections and expressions of our ex-

---

[4] Janice Hocker Rushing's finely wrought mythic narrative about how Power and Other make a victim of Spirit puts its this way: "Spirit was thus revealed by Nietzsche to have died, by Marx as a pretense to maintain political domination by the ruling classes, by Freud as an illusory and neurotic hedge against the finality of death, by feminists as an excuse for male domination, and by poststructuralists as the illusory transcendental signifier" (1993, 162).

Insight and Complexity

traordinary *interbeing*, of the cosmic awe in all of it, of the ultimate full measure and scope of what we can only imagine as Reality.

Spirit is ineffable and elusive, omnipresent and hidden; it has been so in every spiritual text known to us throughout every century and across every continent (Rushing 1993). There is no reason to suppose that at our end of the twentieth century its instructional appearance will be made any differently than it always has been made: "Spirit is playful, the mystics say, and yet this play is 'tricksterish,' or disruptive, penetrating the calm of the rational order" (Rushing 1993, 163).

Spirit, it seems, is best read as a sign that means to be taken as deeper clue. Because it performs as well "within" as "outside of" every parallel world and possible utterance, it easily guides us through intersections, liminal states, difficult textual and intertextual passages. Spirit works principally as an interpretive medium accessible through imagination; Spirit calls, pushes, nudges, comically points to and dramatically shoves us into an awareness of imaginative capacities made from the creative act of making itself. Spirit enables us to relearn forgotten or covered-up sense-making abilities, to cull from the ineffable, the imagistic, and semiotic possibilities, pathways for our communicative evolution into an appreciation for—and ability to act within—the general surround of wonder.

To move toward the unifying awareness of Spirit in our ordinary, everyday texts; social texts; and communal texts is to grant voice to the creative powers of imagination and interpretation, from which emerges a fuller body for experiential knowing capable of sustaining not only a rhetoric for the ordinary, the ritualized, and the rational, but one ready to embrace a *poetics* of the extraordinary, the intuited, the felt, and the lived. From this unifying awareness comes the possibility for genuine holistic dialogue, a dialogue capable of learning from the body of experience without denying to Others what has not been bodily experienced for oneself, a dialogue in which the full measure of truth is found only in the quality of our lives.

SPIRIT AT WORK

The rediscovery of Spirit as a transformative power in organizations is, as Marie Morgan puts it, "a movement on the verge of taking off" (1993).[5]

---

[5] Not without some major controversies—and categorical confusion—over symbolic distinctions between "Spirit" and "spirituality." Morgan cites management vi-

In a pioneering work, she identifies characteristics of workplaces that value and embody Spirit (7):

1. *People embody and practice values that enhance and promote the human spirit.* These include:

*Responsibility

*Treating people with dignity

*Creativity

*Courage

*Service

*Integrity

*Trust

*Joy

*Interdependency

*Clear purpose

Living these values—and finding them in everyday workplace practices—is different from finding "values" listed on a plaque on the wall.

2. *Formal structures reward these values.* Compensation programs and performance reviews should reinforce these values and behaviors. She cites St. Joseph Hospital in Tacoma, Washington, under CEO John Long, as a workplace that has developed formal ways to reward the values of spirit; an example from a performance appraisal checklist: "Compassion: being genuinely empathetic and sensitive toward others. Treat all members of the hospital community with respect as unique, valued individu-

---

sonary Tom Peters as saying (in early 1993) that "spirituality does not belong in the workplace" (7). His argument is that "spirituality" refers to private (mostly religion-based or derived) activities, and he fears, I suppose, sponsoring guru-led cults in the workplace, although one could suggest that his endorsement of "strong cultures of excellence" in the 1980s had similar characteristics and leaders. It also can be understood as "encroaching on individual freedom," especially if an organization endorses only particular spiritual activities. Morgan suggests that we distinguish between "spirit" (as "the life-giving dynamic that happens between people") and "spirituality" (as "the results of the personal practices people engage in, such as prayer, meditation, tai chi, saying the rosary, running, writing in a journal, walking in the woods, or spiritual support groups"). Personally I find this distinction a move away from unifying work, home, and communities by further separating the "work self" from the "inner self," although I do understand—and appreciate the contextual wisdom for—the need to clarify the concepts.

als. . . . Listen, show empathy, and understand other people's feelings, perceptions, and points of view."

3. *Leaders with spirit—people at any level in the organization—create the spirited workplace culture.* Morgan says that "spiritual leaders consistently treat everyone with dignity, care, and respect. They are confident but not arrogant, wise but full of inquiry, and readily admit 'I don't know.' An irrepressible joy lurks just under the surface and can burst out unexpectedly. Their ease with themselves and with their environment allows their natural creativity to bring new ideas to difficult situations." She also believes that leaders with spirit have a "deeper capacity to deal with change" (8).

Morgan also provides examples of how Spirit in the workplace can be integrated into existing ways of doing business, focusing on Total Quality Management, business-neighborhood partnerships, and organizations respecting the interdependence that comes from them giving back to the land in exchange for the resources from the natural environment they use. She concludes by suggesting that Spirit is not something that managers need to "bring into" the workplace; it is already there, inside each employee, waiting for its transformative powers to be unleashed.

Morgan's insight parallels a variety of similar-but-different integrations of Spirit (and spirituality) into organizing and managing practices. Consider entrepreneur Tom Chappell's *The Soul of a Business: Managing for Profit and the Common Good* (1993). Chappell details—via personal narrative—the transformation he experienced when his mid-life return to school (at Harvard Divinity School) encouraged him to adapt the teachings of spiritual leaders and philosophers of religion to his multi-million dollar business, Tom's of Maine. Or Joel Edelman and Mary Beth Crain's *The Tao of Negotiation: How You Can Prevent, Resolve, and Transcend Conflict in Work and Everyday Life* (1993), which begins with this meditation:

In dealing with others, be gentle and kind.
In speech, be true.
In business, be competent.
In action, watch the timing.

No fight: No blame.
               (The Tao Te Ching)

Their approach to negotiation (a term used to cover all forms of human communication) is grounded in this statement:

> Because the Tao is concerned with "personal cause and effect"—the individual's perception of and responsibility for his or her own actions and their effect on the self and others—it believes that the individual plays the key role in creating the external events in his/her life. Not shaping those events, but creating them. Therefore, the basic premise of The Tao of Negotiation is that while a conflict may involve two or more people, it often only takes one person to resolve the conflict, or to prevent it from occurring altogether.... How we choose to perceive it will determine its outcome, says the Tao. (xii–xiii)

By reinforcing the value of taking personal responsibility for one's actions, Edelman and Crain embrace the idea of *finding in that activity the interdependency of self, Spirit, and Others*. The world is, literally, what we perceive and make of our perceptions.

Carol Orsborn's *Inner Excellence: Spiritual Principles of Life-Driven Business* (1992) also provides a way of unifying the disparate fragments we too often perceive and act on as if they were the *only way* to view work and life.[6] She offers seven principles of a "life-driven business":

1. Change your beliefs about the nature of business and of life, and you will change how you manage your career.

2. In order to become fully successful, you must first be fully alive.

3. When you empty yourself of the illusions of who and what you think you are, there is less to lose than you had feared.

4. You have the choice between being the victim of circumstances or being empowered through them.

5. When you are driven by life, the odds will be with you.

---

[6] One useful technique I've used—first learned when studying organizational cultures where employees would say, "That's just the way things are"—to combat the Spirit-denying yet common practice of accepting Other's perceptions of reality as if they were the only available reality, is to ask, simply, "Where is it written?" This question tends to remind people—as well as myself—that we are making th it through the interactions of our perceptions, readings of signs and symbols, attributions of significance or meanings, and ways of speaking and listening. If we are unhappy or distressed about these realities, we have the power to alter them. But first, we must understand that they can be changed.

6. Your ordinary self is enough.[7]
7. To achieve greatness, you must be willing to surrender ambition.

Taking seriously these recommendations has profound implications for what Matthew Fox has recently called a "Reinvention of Work." He writes: "Life and livelihood ought not be separated but to flow from the same source, which is Spirit, for both life and livelihood are about Spirit. Spirit means life, and both life and livelihood are about living in depth, living with meaning, purpose, joy, and sense of contributing to the greater community.... Work is about the role we play in the unfolding drama of the universe" (1994, 1–2, 6).

Finding and releasing the power of Spirit in the workplace gives us the ability to redefine what constitutes our "work"[8] as well as where our "workplace" is.[9] Spirit teaches us that our true calling is the "work" of our lives. We are to use our communicative talents to live gracefully while in the presence of Others, and to help them to help us to learn to help all of us mature without giving up our planetary innocence, evolve without lapsing into evolutionary complacency, to become more responsible for our actions and more accountable for the results and outcomes of those actions, actions and outcomes which themselves are, truly, the

---

[7] "Ordinary" in this sense, referring to the full sense of being alive, the unity of the unconscious and conscious worlds and minds through an appreciation for the parallel possibilities outside of your self. She writes: "When you give up the need to make things happen—making demands on life to give you what you think you deserve—*you open space for possibilities to arise from outside your ordinary experience and expectations*. This is my definition of a miracle" (112; emphasis mine).

[8] Peter Block (1993) develops the concept of "stewardship" to describe a fundamental change of consciousness for evolving businesses. He argues that "placing service over self-interest" will result in far-reaching redistributions of power, privilege, and wealth—all of the trappings of modern Power. In its place will be a new unity—partnership—that is built upon a communicative basis of accepting responsibility and accountability for both the institution and community while caring for others with whom one practices the everyday skills of stewardship.

[9] Paul Hawken (1994) teaches us that our "workplace" is not our place of business, nor even our communities, but Planet Earth as it travels the cosmos. Hence, "sustainable" organizations are those that do not promote environmental decay and make every decision an ecosystem decision. This view is elaborated in Callenbach et al. (1993), and is given theoretical edge by the dramatic work of Margaret Wheatley (1992); she combines the insights of new physics with the idea that ordering—not controlling—is the key to aligning organizational leadership with growth and renewal in the cosmos.

collective works our collective lives, which will be the final record of our passage and the deed to what we leave behind for future generations.

SPIRIT AND STORYTELLING

Toward this evolutionary, revolutionary end, it is wise to remember what it is in life that we have actually learned from. In my experience the teachings of everyday life have come mostly from what Robert Coles (1989) says is the "call of stories," and those that did not come from stories were experiences that instructed me to make stories of them.

The stories I find most compelling are personal narratives written from within the intersections, from the web of uncertainties and tensions that co-produce the experiences of felt liminality, and from the thin lines of sense-making and madness that exist in between parallel worlds and that separate us from each other in ways that only the communication of that experience can hope to resolve or unify. These are stories that leave in their wake the inevitable creative space for what cannot ever be said or written, but must simply be understood as the possibility of interpretive connection.

Art Bochner (1994) tells us that these sorts of stories should comprise the centerpieces of communication theories—not be forever condemned to play out as "merely" examples used to support or quantify claims or be otherwise relegated to the fringe margins of our discourse community—and that until as a discipline we grant voice to what voice has granted to us in the *experiencing* and *making* of these stories, we are likely never to fully embrace what communication *is*, or what communication *does* for us in the world. I couldn't agree more.

Having now denounced the use of stories as examples, let me now elevate one to the status of exemplar. What follows is an excerpt from Eric Eisenberg's account of a the pathways opened up by a transitional moment in which the "work" of communication occurred in ways that only experience—and in its own way, this story of it—can evoke:

> And then I heard the crackly sound of radio—transmitted over TV—and then caught by a speakerphone. One of the secretary's husbands had called from home to say that we had bombed Iraq—the war had begun. He had pulled the TV up to the phone and we were hearing CNN broadcast through the speaker on this end.
>
> It's in these moments of ambiguity where you can often spot rare glimpses of character. Most of us huddled around the broadcasting cubicle.

Insight and Complexity

Some listened briefly and moved on. None of us had any idea what to do. I noticed the more senior managers making calls to inquire about scheduled trips to Japan. They were all canceled, and remained so for weeks.

And then I noticed Bill. Seemingly unaffected by the onset of hostilities, he continued to search for the magazine issue with the review of "lean production." Subtly, I tried to suggest to him that perhaps "business as usual" might cease for a moment. He resisted. I tried to pay attention to what he was saying but was in fact completely focused on CNN.

And then Bill said: "I don't know what it is, but I just can't get worked up over this war. I was a pilot in Vietnam, and midway through my tour I just quit and became a CO (conscientious objector). Finished as an ambulance flyer, airlifting the wounded out of harm's way.

"That was my time. This is not my time. I have nothing to say about this. I said all I could say before."

By now I had the familiar feelings of dissociation in my head and neck. I was floating, tingling, my head was full, slightly dizzy. I looked at his Magnum blue eyes, and then, suddenly, I noticed something.

Bill had no thumb on his left hand.

Given my already anxious and dissociated state, I had a moment of real panic—not unlike the peyote trip in college where I convinced myself that the bowl of peanuts I was eating might actually be finger-tips. Next, I flashed to the Rainforest night club high above New Orleans, where I asked a blond girl to dance from behind and discovered she had only two fingers.

I held her right hand between the thumb and pinky, and we danced one dance. I don't know how it is for you, but things like this open a door in my consciousness. An opportunity of some kind, a rare challenge, a chance at reflection.

Bill had no thumb. He was an honest man. But this was not his time.

This time, he would not be willing to make the tradeoffs. (1993, unnumbered pages)

The point of hearing a story like this one—or reading it—is not to comment upon it and therefore gain some kind of critical hierarchical stance in relation to its sayer, or author. The point is to learn something

---

[10] In fact, I am borrowing the attitude (if not at least some of the words) of the critic for the panel this paper was a part of—Elizabeth Payne. She has exactly the right idea, and, I might add, for anyone who witnessed this event at the 1993 SCA convention in Miami, expressed it *mighty* eloquently. She emphasized her thanks for the sharing of the story, expressed a thing or two she learned from it, and moved on. What she did not do was even more significant, particularly given the cultural rules we generally enact under such "professional" circumstances: she did not, as a critic or as a person, try to in any way upstage the stories.

of value from its articulation, from its utterances, and from the spaces that connect those possibilities to your own experiences. In this way, we create dialogue *not* aimed at consensus but at *continuance*. We learn—as Anthony Giddens (1979) asks us to learn—how to use storytelling, personal communication aimed at contributing to the communal dialogue, to "go on." Communication *as* life coaching. Storytelling as providing context and interpretation for the reading of life's signs.

Unifying Dualities: What Are the Lessons?

This text has organized itself around obvious and nonobvious dualities or tensions that confound our contemporary communication theories and general circumstances: destination and arrival, boredom and ecstasy, difference and possibility, rapture and ecstasy, immanence and transcendence, reality and imagination, modern and postmodern, self and Others. In this way, I have tried to evoke Spirit in sometimes serious, sometimes playful, and sometimes seriously playful ways. I have written, and have been written by, these textual conundrums—induced, enticed, and confounded by them, my attempts at unity through diversity.

I began with a concern for the focus of communication theory and general planetary awareness of what communication *is* as well as what communication is *for* as being unnecessarily tied and thereby limited to ordinary, everyday, bureaucratized and ritualized experiences and behaviors. This modernist view tells us that the human being is best thought of as a "soulless jellital sack of behaviors suspended by a calcium skeleton and driven by something called cognitions" and affords us what I consider to be a very limited understanding of what it means to be human as well as why—and for what purpose—we communicate. This modernist stance valorizes the outward individual over the inward self as well as the public community, prizes surface validity of surface behaviors over deep meanings and multiple interpretations, and treats what we experience but cannot see, hear, explain, or reasonably replicate as the folly of mere superstition, hallucination, or maybe just the curious work and habitat of madness.

---

[11] See Pete Kellett (1994) and Carol A. B. Warren (1987). Kellett teaches us to understand the organization of culture through an evolution of its superstitions, thereby problematizing both the wisdom of "strong cultures" as well as the duality of truth/superstition. Warren instructs us to understand "madwives of the 1950s" who were institutionalized and tortured because their experiences in traditional marriages

Insight and Complexity

The modernist view of communication is very good at explicating definitions and categories that "sum up" all that can be empirically and materially known about a person or thing. From this perspective, communication has been understood—and practiced—primarily as "information transfer" with feedback loops that may (or may not) "correct" the interpretation of intentional meaning. To support that modernist model of human communication, professionals and academics have largely embraced the ideal end or purpose of communication instruction as "effectiveness" or "influence," partly because causes and effects can be measured (and careers made) by creating sophisticated instruments that further separate us from our natures, and I might add, from reality. As a result, what "communication" is can be listed as a series of strategic behaviors designed to solve perceived outward problems in speaking, interacting, listening, and creating images for public or private consumption, the mastery of which guarantees a certain slickness in public performance that may be laudable, informative, persuasive, or entertaining, but often lacks "soul" or "heart" or Spirit.

Learning to think and act as if this expression of communication is "all there is" has severely limited our contribution to human evolution and consciousness. Yet I believe it was necessary and even useful. We have learned a great deal about behaviors, about cognitions, and about outward public displays of communication effectiveness. Communication professionals and academics have helped people overcome shyness or communication apprehension, prepare organized talks for public groups, improve their ability to listen and run meetings. These are indeed "basic" skills, and a place of importance must be maintained for the teaching of them. However, gaining Power through effective individual

---

made the men who were in control of them believe they were "crazy." Her work deepens our appreciation for the madness/sanity duality and underscores the cultural construction of both the duality and the privilege it grants to "authority" over "experience."

[12] For a more detailed discussion, see Eisenberg and Goodall (1993), chapter 2. Although this conception of communication may be challenged by some who feel that the information transfer—or human engineering—model was replaced by "transactional process" or even "strategic control," I feel that these "improvements" still assumed that the transfer of information (including feelings) was the goal of effective talk and action. Any careful perusal of basic speech communication texts or trade publications will likely produce the same conclusion.

speech also helped create a world in which that power was—and is—abused.

Against this authoritative and dominant position, I have tried to characterize critical theory and postmodern approaches to communication—and to being human—as forms of resistance to the two faces of Power: authority and domination. These narratives have brought to the Big Table of Communication Theory and Practice a more open—if hotly contested—discussion of Others as well as Otherness, of what has been—as well as who has been—marginalized by the Power discourse, and they have shown productive uses of deconstructive methods to critique and to decenter the authority of the "communication effectiveness" model. These narratives also offered us a more complex portrait of humans and human communication—certainly of the multivocal quality of all human relationships and communities—even if many of those espoused efforts to flatten hierarchies of power have themselves reduced most of human worth to images dispersed culturally across those flattened, and in some cases deadened, surfaces.

My use of modern texts and postmodern oppositions in this book has occurred primarily in "extraordinary" deconstructive readings given to "ordinary" signs, particularly to authoritative Church signs that are aimed at shaping and refining the consciousness of these communities. My purpose was both to "open up" those texts to interpretive possibilities as well as to show how imagination can be evoked to create possibilities for spiritual meanings well beyond the scope of what is intended, much less what is ordinary and everyday. My ultimate motive was to embody in my prose an alternative reality for communication to be understood within, as well as to address. I think of this work, this contextual framing, as the work of Spirit. It is playful and it is serious; its point

---

[13] See Goodall (1992). In a study of the *Nordstrom Employee Handbook*, I show that an otherwise rightminded commitment to empowerment often comes with a potentially high cost: *making* employees into commodities. When the only rule for employees to follow is "Use Your Best Judgment in All Situations," the ambiguity of that message is dispersed across a lot of surfaces—appearance, manners, dress, and customer service. Hence, by flattening the organizational hierarchy in an attempt to reduce unnecessary levels of power, this company—like many others—also encourages the advent of a new tyranny: rule by the fluctuating, ambiguous, fashion-conscious, commodity culture of the marketplace.

Insight and Complexity

is to unify what might otherwise be seen as binary opposites (see appendix 2).

Dialogic Communities

I began this book by saying that these days the stakes for scholarship—and indeed for communication practices—are extraordinarily high. Our communities, our dialogues, our democracy, and the survival of the Blue Planet are at stake. Awareness of those stakes has prompted me to write this book, in this way. What I have tried to do is connect everyday experiences—however extraordinarily or imaginatively they might have been contextually drawn—to issues of theory and research, to what has been written into the scholarly literature as well as to what has been marginalized or obscured or simply left out. I have suggested that both our "arrival" and "destination" are spiritual communicative surrounds that sensually and extrasensorily inform us, and that interpretively and imaginatively grant passage to us from boredom to immanence and ecstasy, from experience to parallel worlds and imagination, from a specious and limited view of reality to one that accords more truth to new physics than to mechanical science. In so doing, I have tried to introduce a new vocabulary for communication as a way of enabling readers to envision what might be otherwise considered unspeakable practices or unnatural acts.

What I have been doing is making a text try to do the inclusive and unifying work of a dialogic community. I don't think this text has any one meaning—what text does?—nor should it. It is written from experience, is directed at issues of experiencing, and—like Jimi Hendrix—it asks loudly: "Are *you* experienced?" My hope is that this text offers insight into the teachings of the imagined worlds of everyday life. It does this by accessing the sorts of imagined worlds that most of us always intuitively "knew" or sensed were out there (or inside of us), that may well have been experienced but that never had entered our discourse community as such, much less as the subject of serious study.

So much of what we claim to know limits who we believe ourselves, and our communication, to be! And makes our talk in and for the world, therefore, *limiting*. It may be an admittedly well-intentioned, socially constituted, and communally sanctioned kind of limiting, but it is limiting nevertheless. Put simply, ours is a discipline in *denial*. We deny the insights of Others to protect a communal self that has Power but is increasingly less relevant to the future of the world.

I don't think we have time to be this dishonest about ourselves, our feelings and intuitions, our reality, or our communication anymore. If we know there is more to ourselves and to our communication than we are admitting into our scholarly and professional worlds, into the workplace as well as into the work of our lives, then we are behaving dishonestly and remaining in denial.

What we need is a transformative vision for communication capable of allowing ourselves to accept that how we act on the world we know *creates* the world as we know it. If we want to live a better future, we must learn to live together in the diverse fullness of our human possibilities, through a Spirit of unity that brings forth the diverse harmonies that are already there.

I am also a practical man. I recognize that vision is nice—even empowering—but it must be accompanied by a pragmatic program to enable the change required. One of the finer things we have learned from the modernists is the utility of an outline, or a basic plan. That plan can and should be open to change, so it must remain flexible without losing sight of the end, or vision, to be achieved. The plan should also be simple and ambiguous, a purposeful communication duality that empowers individuals to interpret how to accomplish the plan in their own creative ways, using their own resources and experiences. Like this:

First, *to improve our world means being receptive to it*. Diverse communities are a perceptual accomplishment as well as a lived experience and source of realities. To deal productively with our shared environments, we must first be able to perceive them as differences that are *resources for*, not constraints on, our vision.

Second, we must learn *to experience fully and to express fully what we feel, think, intuit, need, want, imagine, and believe*. Our human potential is composed of creative actions that help us to evolve our individual and collective consciousness. Recognizing that the boundaries between *constructed* selves and *constructed* Others are, in fact, constructions may help us to see (as Kenneth Burke put it) "not how Man [sic] has used symbols, but how symbols have used Man" (1950). We are *connected* by communication and interdependent with everything in the cosmos; acts of perceived mutuality and communicative connection dissolve the need for maintaining such bounded images of self and Others and allow us to explore relational, dialogic, and communal realities.

Third, *all of us share responsibility for the planet and for each other.* Seeing that the purpose for communication is "to get something" from someone else is analogous to seeing that the purpose of the planet is to provide you with something to walk on, to own, or to dominate. Instead, learn to see yourself as an interdependent part of the consciousness—of the life—that *is* the planet, and that your acts and activities are necessarily interdependent with those of Others.

Fourth, *use communication to dialogically explore the everyday possibilities of expanding consciousness.* Rather than viewing the mastery of communication as the mastery of ritual and routine, think of everyday opportunities for talk and imagination as invitations addressed to you by the consciousness of the planet, by the cosmos itself, to take risks, to push back known boundaries, to learn, and to grow. Communication is what you do to shape the experiences of living into someone worth being, and into a world worth being in.

Fifth, *recognize that communication perceptions and abilities improve with daily use.* We cannot improve the planet without realizing that *every* day is a divine opportunity for small wins, quality-of-life improvements, relational learning, community-building, and productive change. To be bored, to content oneself with phatic communions, or to deny the immanence of available ecstasies is to dull down your communication skills, and ultimately to do a disservice to humanity.

These five lessons from the living in and through the imagined worlds of everyday communication can make a difference to you, to your relationships, to your community, and to the life and consciousness of the planet. They instruct us to be responsive to the possibilities of signs, of experiences, and to each Other. They suggest that highways and surrounds are imagined worlds intersecting with empirical ones, and that in those intersections are available crossings that enable the evolution of communication and consciousness. Finally, they teach us that the world is our classroom, a place for learning, for experiencing, for taking risks, for pursuing truths, and for making our dialogic utterances into communal undertakings.

The essence I have found in these lessons is Spirit. It is Spirit whose method is change, and who—acting through our consciousness at the interstices of imagination and reality—helps us perceive and communicate the unity in reality that connects all persons, natures, and things. This is *our* unity, because it is *our* reality; it is a sign of who *we* are, what *we* are doing here, and what *we* might become if we learn to do it better *together*.

To communicate is divine.

Insight and Complexity

A Spiritual Uplifting
After they finished the paperwork on the Judge's
cardiac arrest, the county paramedics stopped off
for a Big MAC Special with the large fries and a Coke,
on State 123, in the middle of fast food alley,
across from the convenience store where Myrtle Travis
and her sister-in-law, Denise, pulled in for copies
of *Christian Tips for Health* and two cans of soda.
Denise was visiting from Atlanta while her twin sons,
still unemployed, treated her kitchen for roaches.

Myrtle and Denise spent the afternoon at revival,
being born again, as Christ said they must be,
inside a tent, a steaming swamp of body and soul.
By the time they reached the convenience store,
they were glassy-eyed, hot, damp, and dehydrated.
Denise stayed in the car. When Myrtle walked in,
she hit the air-conditioning like a wall.
It stood her up and dropped her to the floor,
where she lay shaking, drooling, and moaning.
The clerk tripped over his bucket of mop water
trying to get to her from behind the register.
When he finally got up, dazed and certain Myrtle
would break up or explode before his eyes, he picked
up the phone and, after three tries, dialed 911.
They rooted the call to the paramedics
while they were scooping up ketchup with fries
and lamenting the late Judge's lifestyle.

The truck was across the highway before Denise knew
that Myrtle lay on the floor, now prostrate, almost
serene. Denise heard the siren, turned around,
saw the lights flashing toward her, and thought
the convenience store was under siege, that she
would be caught in the line of fire or taken
hostage by terrorists before she could bathe.
Inside, Myrtle rose from the floor, picked up
three *Christian Tips for Health* and two cans
of iced Dr. Pepper, paid the clerk, and told
the paramedics she had a spiritual uplifting.
(Ron Moran)

Afterword: Problematizing Spirit

> The great question of our age is whether people, acting with the spirit, energy, and urgency our collective crisis requires, can develop a democratic global consciousness rooted in authentic local communities.
>
> —Richard J. Barnet and John Cavanagh

Where Angels Fear to Tread

In his masterful *Letters at 3 a.m.* (1992), Michael Ventura sums up our era as "the age of endarkenment." The street signs he reads are directed at the very young and they are entirely unambiguous, inviting what can only be understood as an intentional reading. They are not located on church lawns or at rural intersections but instead are found in city toy stores, in electronics department stores, even in the check-out aisles of supermarkets. These signs are metaphors thinly disguised as plastic toy weapons, poised warrior-doll figures, and electronic games of destruction, toys that teach tots to divide the world into armed arenas for mortal and cosmic combat and that our most sacred gift—a meaningful life—is purposefully defined for the ultimate ends of Power. Ventura reads these seductive, menacing toys, their uses and purposes, and the righteous "us versus them" attitudes and behaviors they contribute to as signs of evil.

Similarly, Pete Hamill (1994) describes another reading of signs of our times:

> As this dreadful century winds down, its history heavy with gulags and concentration camps and atom bombs, the country that was its brightest hope seems to be breaking apart.
>
> All the moves toward decency, excellence, maturity, and compassion have been made. They seem to have come to nothing. Everybody talks and nobody listens. Boneheaded vulgarians are honored for their stupidity. The

AFTERWORD

bitterly partisan debate on the crime bill in the U.S. Senate is remembered only for Al D'Amato's rendition of "Old MacDonald Had a Farm." The Christian Coalition commandeers the Republican state convention in Virginia, and among the slogans on the wall is one that says *Where is Lee Harvey Oswald When America Really Needs Him?* The American social and political style has been reduced to the complexity of a T-shirt. Outta the way, asshole: Give us gridlock, give us Beavis and Butt-head, give us room, man, give us respect, and get outta my fuckin' face!

We are approaching Endgame, the moment when the chessboard is clear and victory is certain. Victory over everybody. The reduction of the opposition to rubble. (85–86)

Both of these writers document the small everyday signs of the continuing cultural struggle between Power and Other. We daily enact the awful mythic with the everyday choices in our ordinary lives. We culturally deconstruct the complexities of diverse multicultural and global communities by reducing them to the basic simplicity of local warring tribes. We identify with the known mythic centers of our own tribe as a way to deal with the destabilized, paranoid, action-oriented, and media-saturated selves we have retreated to. We have become consumers of ultimate terms that compete for flesh with blood. We live on darkening streets littered with homelessness in broken cities where even angels fear to tread.

It gets worse. There are other BIG bad signs, too.

Ours is also the end of the *organizational* age. After better than two centuries of building a Western world economic, social, and political order on a foundation of organizational labor; on a bureaucratic and hierar-

---

[1] Eric Eisenberg articulated this argument in a conversation we had in New Orleans while we were attending the 1994 Speech Communication Association conference. For additional support for this idea and insight about its complex implications, see Aronowitz and DiFazio (1994) and Rifkin (1995).

[2] Admittedly racist, sexist, and classist. The argument here is not that the world we have built is or was Utopian, but that it was known and understood. The narrative myth of Progress enabled by scientific rationality and engineered by technology was indeed done in the interests of a white, male-dominated, class-based hegemonic Capitalist system. Organizational life was the centerpiece of that system, from which evolved a mindset and lifestyle that was predicated upon the idea of well-ordered and bureaucratically managed towns and cities, neighborhoods and schools. William Whyte's classic work *The Organization Man* (1955) provides an early critique of the complicity of schools and governments in the building of this society, as well as a prescient account of the problems of living in this manufactured order. See Eisenberg and Goodall (1993) for an extended treatment of the evolution of modern and postmodern organizational strategies.

chical lifetime of schooling for work and then working for stores, businesses, companies, firms, armies, institutions, and governments; of organizing the work of homes and the conversations of families largely on preparing for and dealing with those worlds of work, we have during the past decade seen the deep structural dismantling of all that.

The teaming of information-age technologies and global economic policies with the political power of multinational corporations and the competitive demand for cheap, flexible labor spelled the sudden fall of all that we were reared to believe might secularly save us. The companies, armies, schools, and government agencies we used to work for downsized, then restructured, and jobs at each juncture were irretrievably lost. Team-based organizing and cross-functional training ensured that fewer and fewer highly skilled workers would continue to be needed for more and more types of work. For most Americans in service, sales, teaching, and factory jobs the distance between middle-class existence and something unutterably less has become uncomfortably close, and sometimes frighteningly so.

This organizational and economic turnaround took place in less than a generation, a global change in a span of time unprecedented in human history. The resultant lag-time for institutions whose job it is to prepare for and respond to these changes—schools, housing and social services, the health care industry—further slowed the cultural learning curve, as legislatures cut budgets to public schools to avoid raising taxes on the already stressed, and private institutions found they had to do with much less a job that required much more. Bright students graduated from the best schools not only without job offers, but often without the requisite global understandings, or the technical and intercultural communication skills, that could help them. Getting a good education no longer ensured finding a good job, and even finding a good job no longer guaranteed a steady paycheck. The rules we had been taught to follow seemed to be rules for living in an organizational world that no longer existed.

As bad as it gets culturally and organizationally, the toll of living through these times is ultimately absorbed *personally*. And here is where our greatest organizing and sense-making problems lie. This is because we also live at the end of a *narrative* age, caught in a time of uncertain transitions between both the organizing stories of the modern and the postmodern as well as between the use of the postmodern as an organizing metaphor and the desire for a new metaphor made out of something

AFTERWORD

else. The language foundations for the stories, the parables, the allegories, the music, even the sit-coms that made our always challenged personal lives somehow feel purposeful, centered, meaningful are dispersed across too many surfaces; they are too thin or simply transparent; they no longer add up. What we've got instead is the *dis*organization of order at the level of words, thoughts, accounts, stories, and actions. What we need and don't even know we want is a new language drug to take the harder edges off our fragmented, in-transition pain.

What we need is a new metaphor. A new metaphor we can use to rethink, reimagine, and ultimately reorganize our selves, our lives, our families, our work, and our sense of community and planet.

I think that metaphor is Spirit.

Spirit at the Nexus

I began this book, this exploration, by asking some deceptively simple questions about communities. How are they organized? What makes them tick? I could have been just as easily asking the same questions about our selves. Or our world. I used the term "communities" because they are central in figuring out what's wrong with us, and central in refiguring our way out. Communities are the *nexus*, the ultimate intersections of communication, selves, myths, and cultures.

I talked about viewing communities as a *nexus* of communicative intersections in which the daily traffic is composed of multiple organizing rhetorics and architectures but whose real substance is what exists *between* persons and things, *in and around* signs and their meanings, in the *imagined* worlds of everyday life. I called that otherwise ineffable something that is a nonthing, and yet the most important thing, *Spirit*.

Spirit is a metaphor, and in this application, a new metaphor. Perhaps it is the sign of Grace. Perhaps not. Maybe it is an organizing locus suggested by the unifying theme of the word. Or maybe it is the next evolutionary step out of the mythic struggle between Power and Other.

What Spirit is, is certainly debatable, but what it *does* is far more interesting. It offers to the imagination an organizing source of communicative and narrative strength, of explanatory power. Spirit connects the

---

[3] James Clifford, in an essay on traveling, says that the most pertinent question these days is not "Where are you from?" or "Where are you going?" but "Where are you in-between?" His reference is not simply to the restlessness or mobility of our age but to the application of the question as *metaphor* to explain the transience of our era.

everyday to the Milky Way and suggests new inroads to all roads and heavens in-between. Spirit has, of course, always been "there," but because of the center-stage intensity of this vast historical struggle between Power and Other—narratively, mythically, materially—Spirit's full role in human history has not yet come due. At the end of this millennia, that due is now.

In this time defined by the pervasiveness of the in-between, it is the in-between Spirit that emerges. But saying this—words on a page in book—is not enough, not even *in* this book or for this audience. There remain too many unanswered questions. Too many doubts about the unifying power of Spirit to intervene in the everyday affairs of persons, of communities, of worlds. In what follows I will deal with the foremost questions and doubts by problematizing much of what the previous chapters have attempted to demonstrate, or induce, or merely suggest.

Answering the Critics

Allow me to begin with academic objections. At the 1994 Speech Communication Association meeting in New Orleans there were preconferences on spirituality and on organizational democracy. At both sessions "spirituality" was articulated as a "new" approach to understanding and doing research in communication and organizing, and at both sessions there was serious dissent over and about the term "spirituality" as well as its appropriateness in academic matters.

The objections to spirituality—and to Spirit—can be divided into three concerns: (1) not scientific, (2) not new, and (3) politically naïve. Taken individually, each of one of these objections deflects attention away from the real-world need for a revolutionary communication breakthrough and instead focuses on the challenge Spirit poses to well-established (one might add, *deeply* entrenched) research and theory-building traditions.

SPIRIT IS UNSCIENTIFIC

The argument that introducing Spirit into academic literatures is unscientific, for example, reveals a simplistic construction of knowledge that mirrors the divisive language of evil that Spirit attempts to transcend. Its organizing locus also reminds me of gang rhetoric in the ghetto. In this case, academic literature is the territory—the neighborhood—to

AFTERWORD

be fought over, lorded over, by bifurcated (the "People" of science and the "Folks" of humanistic inquiry) and deeply factionalized warring gangs of lay semioticians. Each gang sees its role as the protector of the 'hood from those who wear "the wrong" colors, or lace their tennis shoes differently, and who otherwise don't share the same attitudes, values, or beliefs. Armed with the zeal of true believers, those who get sucked into this debate on both sides spend most of their time initiating the young (e.g., graduate students) into the warring gangs. And the heart of the matter is always economic: who do we support to get the fewer and fewer jobs?

But the central issue is the same for the problems of ghetto life as for academic culture on matters of preferred research methods and intellectual commitments: *can we find a way of promoting diversity*? Is is possible for people and folks to live together peacefully without dividing up the neighborhood into research quadrants and reading interest groups, thus substituting an empty pluralism for the multicultural richness of diversity? Can we, indeed, actually *learn* from each other? Or is our inherent Otherness too large a puzzle to be solved piece by piece?

SPIRIT IS NOT NEW AND/OR NOT SUFFICIENTLY DIFFERENT

The second objection is related to the first. By suggesting that spirituality isn't "new" we once again divide the world where the world—in its own interests—ought *not* divide. There are really two separate arguments here: that spirituality is, in fact, "not new," and that it is not "sufficiently different." Let me address them one at a time.

First, spirituality is "not new," therefore doesn't warrant serious consideration. Imagine posing this same objection during the Renaissance, or at the dawn of the Enlightenment! Is not the history of ideas indebted to periodic rediscoveries of older, perhaps even discarded or discredited notions? That spirituality has survived every material manifestion of culture, religion, ideology, war, pestilence, science, rhetoric, and suffering ought to speak to its centrality in human affairs. That it is "not new" simply deflects attention from its enduring value to humankind, reducing the beauty of its metaphorical complexities to the capital flicker of baser commodity values.

Which brings me to the second objection, that spirituality is not "sufficiently different." That we have constructed a dominant ideology

Afterword

of global capitalism that relies on consuming the "new" as its lifeblood is clear. That academic culture, too, suffers from this ideological commandment, is clear in the light of this second objection. If an idea is not "new" it ought to at least be "sufficiently different." So, some critics argue, how is the current recycling of spirituality different from Hegel's phenomenology of Spirit? Or from Thoreau's understanding of the transcendental? Or from "x's" theory of the cosmos?

The problem with these objections is not that they are raised, but that they are promoted as objections to less historical or critical approaches to using Spirit in inquiry. I don't think any of my colleagues would object to work done in the historical and or critical reconstruction of the ideas or themes in spirituality, but some of us prefer to do work that relies less on reconstituting the past than on reinventing the future. For us, "sufficiently different" refers to where we want to take the idea of Spirit, not to where it has already been.

SPIRIT IS POLITICALLY NAÏVE

The third objection raises the issue of the utility of Spirit in promoting pragmatic change, particularly in organizations and institutions. The charge is, baldly put, that the spirituality of organizations movement is politically naïve. Organizations and institutions are bottom-line places, sites of continuous political struggles between employees and managers, people of color and the dominant white race, and between women and men. These are strong cultures made up of hard-headed individualists who will only implement an idea if there is a real payoff for them, and given the rapidly escalating competition in the cut-throat global marketplace, there is simply no time to deal with, well, *mysticism*.

Although one could partially counter these objections with evidence from successful companies who have taken a spiritual turn (see chapter 8), the core political and change issues here cannot be so easily dismissed. The hard questions remain. Put simply, how can we use the lessons of spirituality, the teachings of Spirit, to reinvent work? How can we teach employees and managers alike, people of all races and both genders, to integrate their understandings of work into the larger questions about the work of our lives?

Naïveté is sometimes a good thing. To be a beginner, always, is to be naïve. It is to see the world anew. It is to approach a common problem

AFTERWORD

with the freshness that only a lack of prior knowing can facilitate. It is to ask the new question, perhaps the hard question, without an agenda.

But it is also to be put at risk. To be naïve in a political and economic world is to risk being crushed by the forces that cannot make money out of your freshness, your questions, your lack of an agenda. The bare fact is that when naïve optimism runs into headstrong pragmatism, naïve optimism seldom wins. Pragmatists, after all, usually have money and guns, in addition to favors, laws, status, and power.

Similarly, to be naïve in academic culture is to risk being marginalized, or worse—demonized by name-calling: unscientific; methodologically unsound; theoretically vacuous; ahistorical; merely entertaining. For some of us, it means to risk being sent away without tenure because we don't fit in, because our way of explaining persons and things is sufficiently different but too much so. In the name of the Order, we are policed by the obvious, rebuffed by those already thoroughly disciplined by editorial bureaucrats. These acts of academic righteousness are committed so that the similarly disciplined can enjoy rank and status within the academic community, which is to say that the study of communication is roundly considered fully doctoral and not any longer equated with academic dentistry.

But sometimes to be naïve is also to be dumb. To have been sucked into a scheme that is unworthy or untenable is to be unaware of the pragmatic politics of your own supposedly agendaless agenda. Viewed this way, to be naïve about the politics of spirituality is to reproduce the conditions of the struggle between Power and Other by metaphorical means. And by using the ineffable as a guise, aren't we just substituting a new term for an old con?

Perhaps the spiritual turn is merely the most recent byproduct of generalized American middle-class *ennui*, the well-educated white person's search for meaning in a world turned upside down. Is this the newest consumable "experience" for boom generation life explorers who now find in questions of Spirit a way to unite their lost youthful '60s idealism with the materialism of the '80s we have truly learned to love? Is Spirit just the newest Toy on the block, the latest cool thing to be into? Another cause for a bumper sticker on the Accord or the minivan?

Maybe. Surely this is the sad, ironic case for some of us. When my wife was researching spiritual healers there were certainly more false prophets than true sources of insight, and God only knows there are busi-

Afterword

ness leaders, educators, and politicians who rely on horoscopes, tarot cards, or flips of a coin to make major decisions. Everyone wants not just to win the lotto but to believe in the healing powers of sudden big money in our lives, right? How different is this quest for something, anything, to save us from the gray middle-class everydayness or the turmoils of organizational change from a spiritual quest to find our place, our meaning, in the Milky Way?

To quest is human. That much is clear. To want to believe in something—God, marriage, reincarnation, Science, the lottery, or semiotic meaning—is universal. To work is necessary.

> Quest
> Belief
> Work

How can these ideas be merged? Is there something—call it Spirit—that lives in between them that can pull them together? Pull all of us together? That seems to be the central question.

Or maybe just the question I've learned to ask in Central.

But I hope not.

Naïveté is itself problematic, isn't it? But let's turn away from the academic pursuit of the problematic and return to the real problems of people in these times of organizational and institutional change. That was, after all, the original question. Left unchecked, which is to say left unmediated by a new organizing metaphor, the end of our era will continue to be marked by persons and things coming apart and falling apart, by a generalized retreat to tribes, and by nations and states doing the bidding of powerful multinational corporations by engaging in localized varieties of economic and political Darwinism.

The rich will get richer; the poor will just stay poor. Sooner or later somebody will break out the big guns, and rebellions or riots will serve as the only available tactic against which those various Others denied access to their American dreams can continue the struggle against Power, because that is the symbolic name and narrative progression of the myth we are trapped within. Our requirement is its resolution.

This will happen if we lack the language to initiate a new, alternative vision for change. Without the new language, without the alternative organizing metaphor, we lack the myth—the storytelling and inspirational abilities—to counter Ventura's seductive menacing endarkenment or to

AFTERWORD

stop this century's headstrong rush toward the fulfillment of Hamill's Endgame. These are the terms of our narrative condition, and they are not negotiable.

Given this framework, *now* who is being naïve?

Killing Spirit: Mismanaged Narrative Transitions in Times of Organizational Change

Spirit is not a panacea. No metaphor can be. Mythically, it may offer a strong narrative counter to the struggle between Power and Other, but we should remember that this struggle is always with us and is never fully defeated or erased from earthly concerns.

As strong a narrative force as Spirit can be, we must remember that without our influence it is very fragile. In-between and ineffable, it can only inspire *us* to make the worldly connections and use our imaginations. It can teach *us* to interpret signs, but ultimately we are the ones who must act on those lessons. If we don't act on those teachings, don't interpret those signs, make the connections, or use our imaginations, Spirit's influences recede into that parallel world, and the struggle between Power and Other once again dominates the discourse, the community, the Earth.

This book has been, at least in part, a study of community in a place where Spirit has been alive. But as this writing project came to a close I witnessed firsthand how fragile Spirit can be in times of organizational or communal change, and how easily it can be displaced by the discursive struggle between Power and Other. Specifically, Clemson University—the Spirit that was so much a part of the allure and community of this region—underwent massive organizational restructuring. From my vantage, it was probably necessary but poorly done, and, in the two year-long odyssey required to do it, completely and thoroughly mismanaged. An academic culture that valued interdisciplinary study, open discussion and philosophical debate, evolutionary change, and collegial decision making by practices Karl Weick calls "loose-coupling" clashed dramatically with senior administrators and the board of trustees, who brought to this organizational change effort the rhetorical and strategic instruments of top-down corporate domination over decision-making and a preference for fast action over reasoned discussion and evolutionary change.

Afterword

What was sacrificed was Spirit. Everyone could feel it vanish. People talked about it, openly. During faculty meetings where open discussions were reduced to prepared statements that protected turf, when emotionally charged memos were issued that alternately blamed administrators or faculty members for misinformation or foot-dragging or outright deception, and when good people who had come here in good faith to build lives for themselves and their families found that the institution was not going to honor its contractual promises to them, something vital but ineffable disappeared. Like the gray ghosts rising from the warm lakes on a cool autumn morning, something vaporous and beautiful slowly but unmistakably left us.

Students noticed it too. Because there was much ambiguity about "where they would be" in the college restructuring as well as the future status of their degree programs, in many cases the students began to act like battered children in dysfunctional families: they retreated into themselves, focused on "getting out," and stopped entertaining what was left of the notion that there is much point in the more abstract or theoretical aspects of their educations. *Surviving* the change was foremost, for all of us, which meant surviving the sharper fragments of a broken narrative that had lost its center and its connection to the larger story of the meaning for our lives.

These were signs. Bad signs. They were signs of institutional failures to communicate and individual failures to understand the relationship between what we were saying (or not saying) and who we—as a commu-

---

[4] This story could be told differently. From published reports in the local newspapers, the board of trustees believed that the faculty was unnecessarily clinging to outmoded ways of doing things that were fiscally and managerially unsound, and that our recommenations about restructuring lacked vision. Phil Prince, the temporary president brought in by the board to manage the transition and whose background was solely corporate, expressed his belief that certain faculty groups were opposed to the change and were blocking it with misinformation and deception that challenged his well-intentioned efforts. Regardless of how this story is told—the "truth" is no doubt partial, partisan, and problematic in either case—the narrative point here is that this conflict reveals the classic struggle between Power and Other that, once brought to the forefront of a community's affairs, sacrifices Spirit.

[5] Students majoring in education, for example, discovered they were now in a college that merged business, education, and nursing. Similarly, students majoring in psychology, sociology, and political science—originally housed in liberal arts—found they were also in the College of Business, Education, and Nursing. Liberal arts majors were merged with architecture. Science majors discovered they were merged with the engineers; agriculture majors with textiles. In the end, nine colleges were reduced to four "megacolleges."

nity—were becoming as a result. Restructuring, reorganizing, combining, merging, downsizing, empowering—these are symbols that stand for vast territories of important conversations, exchanges of talk, communication in decision-making, and careful narrative nurturing. To think that bottom-line change can be mandated without serious and abiding attention to the emerging storyline is not simply bad judgment, it is a large cultural mistake. The change will come, what is mandated will indeed be implemented, but at a far more costly figure than any dollar can name.

What this experience teaches us is the importance of transitional narrative management in times of institutional, organizational, and communal change. What lies in-between vision and implementation are the true stories of the transition and change, and ultimately it is those stories that live in the hearts and minds of those charged with making the change happen. Narrowly focusing on strategic and material outcomes without attending to the needs of communicative processes is unlikely to work and will do a lot of spiritual and practical damage along the way. People who were deeply loyal to the institution, who were closely identified with the Spirit that defined their relationship to how they imagined the place, lost their communal sense of loyalty and personal sense of identification. What they imagined seems now like some distant dream, a dream that betrayed them.

It's a crash at the *nexus*. Perhaps of it.

The Afterlife of Sentences

Spirit can be sacrificed because it can be narratively killed. It is a death of the imagination, a dying off of that one true, ineffable connection between ourselves and each other, between each other and our communities, and between our communities and the stars. To kill Spirit is to murder what is holy, what is sacred, within us, and to reduce the marvelous narrative complexities of our existence and purpose to that age-old struggle between Power and Other.

---

[6]The point is not to blame any individual or individuals for these problems. Accountability for decisions, for participation in the process, for the imagination (or lack of it) and inspiration (or lack of it) needed to make productive change—these are all shared activities in any community. But what was clearly lacking throughout this process of change was a deep appreciation for the vital role of communication and story-building required to manage the transition. For that failure of management, for that singular lack of vision, responsibility belongs—as it always does—at the top.

Afterword

When Spirit vanishes, where does it go? Into the afterlife of sentences? Into a parallel world? Does it split narrative body from narrative soul and resurrect locally? If that can happen, who will tell this new story this time? Who among us is capable of bringing forth a new testament, some powerful explanatory tale capable of healing our wounds, of uniting this community again, of reassuring us that Spirit is, in fact, everlasting?

These are mysteries, questions without answers that speak to imagined possibilities for meanings. They are speculations about ways of reframing, which is to say only that they are metaphors within metaphors about metaphors. But they are true lines in a big story, I think. It's the story about who and what we are as speaking beings on this earth. And these lines ask whether what we say and how we say it are, indeed, the only real clues about who we are and where we are headed.

The lesson here is that we are the beings who communicate in order to survive; who imagine in order to communicate; and who use both imagination and communication to connect our individual puzzles to the puzzles of each other, to the riddles of our work and families, to the *nexus* of our communities, and ultimately to the meaning of that greater, that eternal, mystery. At the deepest level of our spiritual being, this sacred unity of what we can imagine and what we say is all we have to save us.

Appendixes   References   Index

Appendix 1: Power, Other, and Spirit

From insights offered by Janice Hocker Rushing, herein expanded and elaborated

Power	Other	Spirit
(The goal of modernism)	(The goal of postmodernism)	(Limits Power and Other by revealing interrelations among dominant and resistance groups, both of which are part of "the One in the Many.")
Social and political manifestation of a unity of modern philosophy, commodity capitalism, and scientifically driven technologies.	Social and political manifestation of antimodern, antitechnology sub- and countercultures who resist the domination of science and capitalism.	Transcends opposition by moving "in" and "out" of all social, philosophical, and political camps; unity of Self and Others, mediated by "Interbeing."
"Sovereign rational subject" (autonomous, disembodied, individualistic Self).	Decenters the conscious, rational subject by historicizing it and legitimating oppositions to Power by naming them as forms of "Other."	Does not require faith; can be experienced directly (noetic, prayer, meditation) or in mediated forms (poetic, perceptual, extrasensory).

APPENDIX 1

Power	**Other**	**Spirit**
Goal: Ahistorical certainty.	*Goal:* Historical pluralism.	*Goal:* Unity of diversities.
Method: Rational thought/sensory observation.	*Method:* Deconstruction of authority (e.g., Science, History, Culture).	*Method:* Awareness of differences and possibilities.
Logic: Scientific rationality.	*Logic:* Cultural, scientific, and social constructions of material realities are inherently political; they represent and advocate interests at the expense of Others.	*Logic:* Human potential and spiritual growth are interdependent.
Outcome: Produces binary oppositions or dualistic of structure.	*Outcome:* Produces critiques of commodity capitalism surfaces that underscore hegemonic reach of Power and deep nationalization of Others.	*Outcome:* Self-and-Other awareness mediated by Ultimate Purposes, understanding of which should be reflected in everyday choice-making and interaction.
Textual Authority: The Word (in religion); the Theory (in Science); the Dominant Western Narrative of Progress (History).	*Textual Authority:* Cosmic Abyss (anti-religion, Marxist existentialism); the Practice (material surfaces that counter explanatory Grand theories); multiple cultural critiques (New Historicism).	*Textual Authority:* Fullness of presence, and absence of Abyss in all persons, nature, and things. Personal experience of insight, imagination, ecstasy, possibility, rapture, immanence, and vision transcends all categories of Power and Other.
The Mind (philosophy).	The Body.	Souls inherit the actions of mind *and* body.
The Ruling Class (economics).	Working classes.	Rich *and* poor.

Power, Other, and Spirit

Power	**Other**	**Spirit**
Conscious ego (psychology).	Unconscious.	Unity of conscious and unconscious found in material manifestations of Consciousness.
Masculine (gender).	Feminine.	Male *and* female.
White (race).	Dark.	Light *and* dark.
Logos (texts).	Mythos.	Logos *and* mythos.
The Original (art and aesthetics).	Simulacrum (e.g., endless copies and reproductions).	"God is in the details" of all things.
The King who becomes a despot (myth).	The Fool who speaks truth to the King, thereby challenging him.	The Victim of the struggle between Power and Other.

Appendix 2: Modern, Postmodern, and Spiritual Communication

Modern Communication

The World:

Exists in material form and is knowable through observation, mediated by scientifically informed rational thought. Reality is composed of empirical, physical, and material forms. Language has referents in the empirical world; "good" language usage aims to describe reality "accurately."

THE REAL

Postmodern Communication

The World:

Exists as a social and cultural construction in which multiple versions of reality vie for political, aesthetic, and social power. The empirical world is real but (since Einstein and Heisenberg) is dependent upon our perceptions of it and is mediated (always) by language. Language is non-representational, mostly evocative, and always partisan. "Good" language usage depends on your political purpose and vested interests.

THE SURREAL

Spiritual Communication

The World:

Exists both as a material/empirical and political/social construction; knowledge should be not of an "objective IT" or a "subjective US" but a unity of IT *and* US. The aim of language is to shape moral and ethical conduct capable of offering "lessons" from everyday experience about our "spiritual" natures and destinies.

THE COSMIC

Modern, Postmodern, and Spiritual Communication

Modern Communication

Humans:

The human is a "soulless, jellital sack of behaviors suspended by a calcium skeleton and driven by cognitions." Respect the Mind/Body divisions of Descartes with attendant language associations in everyday speech; Mind represents "higher" orderly rational activities whereas Body represents "lower" emotional/genital urges and chaos. SPEECH is the embodiment of rationality (logos), is used to improve one's public character (ethos), and can use appeals to emotions (pathos) to work.

Our main game is to use speech to advance our material gain.

Postmodern Communication

Humans:

We are products (subjects) of material and commodity capitalism, class and racial politics, and are mediated (as well as driven) by the genetic forces of evolutionary biology. Our purpose is to consume material surfaces (including Others' surfaces) as commodities. *"S/he who dies with the most toys, wins."* SPEECH is the localized, conflicted site of social, cultural, and political constructions of reality. Our main game is a language game in which resistance to domination is not only fun but profitable.

Spiritual Communication

Humans:

We are spiritual creatures lost or purposefully adrift in a material world.

Our purpose is to evolve consciousness of this condition and its requisite influences on our choices and characters; we are also responsible for uniting ourselves and sustaining our planet.

SPEECH is the material manifestation of our consciousness. Our main game is spiritual awareness and—ultimately—transcendence.

APPENDIX 2

Modern Communication	**Postmodern Communication**	**Spiritual Communication**
Order:	*Order:*	*Order:*
Well-ordered world is the master work of a well-ordered, rational mind. Characteristics include bureaucratic organizing and capital control define occupations of public and private cultural space, surveillance of opposition (e.g., strategies deployed to counter tactics of resistance groups), divisions of labor and management, representative (rather than direct) democracy.	Social order is political and cultural, and therefore driven by commodity capitalism and vested interests; result is a highly conflicted yet open domination of public and private cultural space enforced by military and police might; this form of order must be resisted with antistructural tactics designed to poach or appropriate meaning and space, and to surveil the surveillance.	The purpose of life is to seek God's hand in all things (*Talmud*); image of order is ultimately Divine; because it is Divine, it is mysterious, not so much a problem to be solved as a "metaphorical mystery" to be engaged with unities of body and mind, consciousness and the unconscious, Self and Others.
Language seeks (through grammar and logic) and supports (through rhetoric) the social construction of hierarchies (e.g., "We are rotten with perfection") and the highest aim of language-order is the "machine metaphor" in all things.	All hierarchies are suspect and the best thing to do is reverse them, turn the well-ordered world constituted by them "upside down" through privileging what is supposed to be hidden through the "carnival metaphor." Absence of a presence is the mark of presence of absence. The body, talk, and public streets are the localized sites of these counter-constructions—tattoos, hairstyles, fashion statements; profanity, jokes, puns; graffiti.	

Modern, Postmodern, and Spiritual Communication

Modern Communication

Image/Icon:

Romantic, individualized Self as the localized site of cultural and material constructions. This Self is one-half mind, one-quarter heart, one-quarter libido, has something called "attitudes, values and beliefs" and responds to rational argument but is swayed by emotions. Archetype is the mythic person on an existential quest that requires overcoming early hardships and/or disadvantages to gain character and credibility, then advances to the "top" of all hierarchies: the noble King.

Theme:

POWER: earthly attainment is akin to spiritual attainment of place in the well-ordered Universe.

Postmodern Communication

Image/Icon:

Alienated, fragmented, largely materially co-opted being who depends on reading surfaces for a sense of who or what he/she is becoming. What you look like is more important than how you think or feel. The body is a secular temple and must be shaped, worked-out, contoured, fitted, plasticized, tattooed, hairdoed, and constantly reinvented to meet the increasingly commodity demands of fashionable appearances in a commodity-cultures as a critique and commentary on its themes. Wearing the clothes of the Other is making a political statement. The Fool who plays our nationalized truths for the King. The world is tragically comic; we are comically tragic.

Theme:

OTHER: earthly attainment of empathy for victims of power allows us to attain equity, sponsor diversity, and transcend the divisions Power has created.

Spiritual Communication

Image/Icon:

The Cosmos as a transformation unity of energy and information mediated by Spirit, in which all of our symbols (e.g., speech, activities, body art, and so on) should be read as signs of our spiritual consciousness.

Theme:

UNITY: earthly attainments have cosmic implications.

Appendix 3: Connecting Spirit to Community through Imagination and Communication

Questions	Explanatory Tensions	Sources of Communicative Transformation
Preface *What constitutes meanings in and for a community?*	Organizing Rhetorics versus Personal Experience: The various symbolic, semiotic, and rhetorical tensions operating in the *nexus* of public and private forms of communication, such as: 1. individuals and groups 2. race, class, and gender 3. homes and works 4. art, artifacts, and architectures 5. thoughts and actions and so on	Understanding the historical, mythic, and narrative struggles among Power, Other, and Spirit that vie for interpretive dominance and political power in and for a community.

Connecting Spirit to Community

How are those meanings suggested?	Symbolic Dominance versus Symbolic Resistance: Dominance of symbols, signs, and everyday rhetorics of explanation and resources for resistance through ineffable feelings, intuitions, experiences, and insights concerning what meanings may lie in between persons and things, beings and communities, communities and the cosmos.	Being open to alternative possibilities for explanations and meanings through extraordinary, imaginative, and extrasensory awareness and experiences.
How are communal meanings organized?	Empirical versus Analogic: Histories, narratives, conversations, and personal accounts that express or suggest empirical and analogic information and that vie for authority, power, and explanatory control.	Search for interconnectedness among the empirical and the analogic, among narratives, conversations, histories, and personal accounts, between signs and their interpretive linkages to purposeful, unifying themes.

Introduction

Why do we need a book that connects Spirit to community?	Power/Other: Dualities of Power and Other have led to the total collapse of all paradigms world-	Spirit offers explanatory narratives and imaginative experiences that unify diversities, thereby

APPENDIX 3

	wide: social, environmental, educational, and spiritual.	offering a new resource for transforming communities.
Why do we need a spirituality of communication?	*Modern/Postmodern:* Failure of Enlightenment project within the modern world and the rise of marginalized Others giving voice to the postmodern challenge have led to contradictory and a seemingly senselessness of everyday life.	Spirit offers a democratic and edifying corrective.
What is the relationship between communication and consciousness?	*Questions/Answers:* What we say and do constitutes the material manifestation of a discursive consciousness; our narratives and explanations are framed as solutions to problems within a modernist conception of rationality. *Human/Nature:* Western consciousness separates humans from nature, and the blue planet from its relation to the cosmos.	Spirit teaches us that we are part of a much larger mystery that is not ours to solve but depends on our imaginative participation through the achievement of a practical communicative consciousness. Practical communicative consciousness is not limited to Western conceptions of rationality, human/nature separations, but instead accepts extraordinary and extrasensory experiences and insights as signs of our spiritual natures, the human/nature unity, and our ultimate quest.

What does ethnography have to do with spirituality?

Representation/Evocation:
Traditional ethnography relies on a representational metaphor and values the objective, empirical relationships between symbols and what they claim to represent. Nontraditional ethnography relies on personal and cultural evocations that challenge the ability of symbols to represent what may be known or experienced and instead use symbols to explore imagined and analogic possibilities for interpretation.

Self/Others:
Traditional or modern ethnography attempts to understand Others in their native contexts, thus respecting a critical distance between the observer and the observed. Nontraditional or postmodern ethnography (in this case, the subcategory of autoethnography) blurs the self/Other distinction and writes of native experience as a native.

Person/World:
Traditional ethnography assumes that the world

Spirit offers the primacy of intimacy through the location of deeply meaningful connections that are communicated (however ordinarily or extraordinarily) between and among persons, nature, and things.
Spirit encourages a quantum vision of reality. Our actions and our imaginations are part of the ongoing construction of the cosmos; we are energy and information, just like the rest of the universe.
Our essential state is one of Being; Knowing is but one expression of our use of energy and information.

APPENDIX 3

	actions. Nontraditional ethnography assumes a subjectively constructed world codependent on our interpretations and actions for meaning.	
	Knowing/Being: Both forms of ethnography privilege Knowing over Being, al though nontraditional ethnography does so to a lesser extent.	
What is "communication"?	*Rhetorical/Poetic:* Modern and postmodern approaches to or analytical uses of communication are generally confined to the verbal and nonverbal exchange or transmission of messages whose rhetorical purpose is to influence, persuade, or control, and whose poetic uses are largely to make metaphors, images, and icons that represent or evoke the cultures producing and consuming them.	*Dialogue:* Communication is a connective spiritual pathway through which empirical, imagined, plural, and parallel worlds are symbolically and semiotically urged into existence.

Connecting Spirit to Community

| What should theories of human communication include? | *Modern/Postmodern:*
Modern:
Humans are soulless jellital sacks of behaviors suspended by calcium skeletons and driven by something called cognitions.
Through these cognitions our bodies produce words and actions we label "communication." Communication is composed of discrete components in something called a "process": source, message, channels, receiver, feedback, environment.
To understand "communication" means to focus on the meanings of messages within empirical, sensory (primarily optical and auditory) environments. Knowledge about communication is knowledge about messages, cognitions, and behaviors.

Postmodern:
To the above add a capitalist framework and report on the itemized "characteristics" of marginalized Others: race, class, language, personal experience, and gender. Recognize that all communication is mediated. | We are Beings who communicate, and our communication is purposeful. We study and use communication to make progress on our spiritual journeys, not just to understand the process of communication. Communication is best approached not as discrete components but as "life coaching," in which the purpose of communicating is to connect us to each other, to nature, and to the cosmos. Fundamental analytical questions include: Who am I? How can I know you? Why am I here? Why are we here together? What is the meaning our lives? What are we communicating for? How is communicating connected to that meaning? How can I help you? How can I ask you for help?
Spirit accepts ordinary and extraordinary, sensory and extrasensory, "real" and "imagined" information and energy as data for our quest. Being is achieved through fully lived experience, and the purpose of our communicative experiences is to help us achieve our purposes and help others achieve theirs. |

APPENDIX 3

What is the relevance of this study to other communities?	*Difference/Similarity:* Derived from empirical manifestations of culture and consciousness.	Central is a place and a metaphor; imagination shows us the spiritual basis for reading this community as a particular of the universal.
What is Spirit?	*Modern/Postmodern Mythic Narrative:* Power is the social manifestation of modern philosophy that articulates the sovereign rational subject; the Other represents the postmodern challenge and anti-philosophical opposite of Power, which is achieved by decentering the sovereignty of the rational subject and categorically deconstructing its world.	Spirit is victimized by this struggle between Power and Other although it transcends opposition by working in and out of as well as between both characters, thereby limiting Power by showing the interrelations among all things and erasing the symbolically constructed separation (taken-for-granted boundaries) between Self and Other. Spirit is, therefore, the spiritual pathway capable of uniting diverse communities.

Chapter 1

What is the nature of a spiritual journey?

Destination and Arrival: All journeys outward really begin with an arrival or destination that happens within you. Humans exhibit "thrownness" (Heidegger), wherein we experience a feeling of being lost, or the deep emptiness that comes from knowing something is missing.

The root metaphor of this tension is *dissatisfaction*, and because we are trapped within a narrative frame that emphasizes machine-like cognitive rationality, we treat the "problem" of dissatisfaction as something wrong that can be corrected by application of the proper rule, etiquette, behavior, therapy, or drug that allows us to "gain control" over our minds and bodies.

What is "lost" is Spirit.

By reframing our "problem" as a loss of Spirit we learn to accept our state of "thrownness" as an inherent part of human Being; we are experiencing loss because we are on a journey to recover Spirit in our souls, and in our lives. Viewed this way, our feelings of emptiness are extraordinary opportunities for spiritual engagement.

What is "ordinary" experience?

Ordinary/Extraordinary or Constraint/Creativity: This tension expresses the differences between empirical and analogic experience, as well as between routine performances of communicative behavior/cognition and inventive playfulness that seeks creativity and thrives on imagination. "Doing the business of

Seize extraordinary opportunities in the everyday, particularly in conversations and readings of signs. Learn to listen "between the lines" and to see "in between the appearances" of persons and things. Work on alternative explanations that are derived from extraordinary sources, extrasensory perceptions,

APPENDIX 3

	being ordinary" (Sacks) is hard work because we use it to frame all of our everyday experiences and expectations. We become "preoccupied" with normalcy and routine, with rules for behavior and thinking and arguing, with following traditions for social etiquette, with what is "ordinarily" expected of us. Communicative rituals (phatic communion) versus creative talk, joke-telling, imagined scenes, conversational playfulness, poetics of expression, exploring riddles, and accepting or engaging in ambiguity.	and interconnected narratives.
What are signs?	*Intentional Messages/Interpretive Opportunities:* Signs provide contexts for interpretation, either evoking or representing communicative territories. Signs can be about Power (domination) or Other (resistance).	Signs are openings for dialogues, for creativity, for playfulness, for entertaining oppositional or alternative readings. Signs can be about spiritual direction or can ask spiritual questions. To ask questions about the possible or alternative meanings for signs is to give voice to Spirit, to the work of intimate imagination.

Chapter 2

What are the extraordinary borders of lived experience?

Boredom and Ecstasy:
This continuum frames our experiencing of everyday events and talk and may be interpreted as the *emotional architecture* of human states of Being. Central or Zentral? To be "in public" in Central means using communication to bridge our emotional architectures within specific environments or contexts that call for particular forms of talk. Dominant forms are governed by politeness rituals, cordiality, and gracefulness that also bespeak power, status, and social hierarchy. Resistance forms include rudeness or profanity, put-downs, and carnivalizing or turning upside down the routine expectations for talk. Resistance in talk is *always* resistance to power, status, and hierarchy.

Boredom is a sign of possibilities, of opportunities, of the need or desire to seek ecstasies. As such, experiencing boredom is a spiritual reminder that our real work is elsewhere, waiting for us.
Zen Trail.
Spirit encourages grace over graciousness, creativity over constraint; Spirit arising through boredom prepares us *for* or is leading us *into*.

What is boredom about?

Risking Boredom and Being Held in Suspense:
In the experience of boredom we secretly negotiate absurd desires, which is emotionally equivalent to "being held" in a state of suspended consciousness. If we are held too long, we never learn how to get what we want, or to go

Boredom may be a wellspring for building community when communication is instrumentally and expressively linked to it.
We alleviate boredom by telling new stories, by venturing out into public places, by learning to use own imaginations and to worry about Others. In

261

APPENDIX 3

	where we need to go. Phatic communion constructs meaninglessness as the soul of boredom in everyday encounters. From a postmodern perspective, it is a sign that we have given in to the velocity of postmodern living (Baudrillard) and to a vanishing sense of self. It is therefore both giving into Power and giving up to Other at the expense of Spirit. Bored people often victimize themselves by avoiding risk, particularly in conversation. They teach themselves to dull down the talk by daily engaging in meaningless exchanges. In so doing, they lose the capacity for creative talk, playfulness, and making their lives interesting. They also lose the skill of making dialogue meaningful, which is the cornerstone of building community.	this way, boredom sets free the capacities for wonder, for possibility, for freedom. It is to take the "here and now" *out there*, away from the known territories of the lonesome self. To take risks in communication is to invite Spirit.
What is ecstasy?	*Structured/Unstructured Rituals or Experiences*: Difference between symbolically ordered and community-organized events (Huichol) and spontaneous (Woodstock) occurrences.	Recognize ecstatic experience as a communicative pathway to (perhaps) a parallel world (McKenna), certainly to reenvision relationships of individuals to communities.

Chapter 3

How are communities organized semiotically?	*Difference/Possibility:* Signs induce communicative meanings rooted in the contexts of a community's social imagination. These imaginings are always plural and political, thus suggesting the need for dual readings and complex texts. Traditionally, even oppositional readings are rendered through traditional methods and respect traditional boundaries: the known senses (privileging the optical and auditory), rational argument, and problem/solution formats for applications of reasoning.	Learn to read signs in communities as signs of Spirit, as communicative pathways to alternative interpretations of the relations between persons and their meanings. To accomplish this, bring to the forefront extrasensory, extraordinary, or mystical explanations for signs, feelings, "coincidences," and intuitions. Learn to see interrelationships, not distinctions between or among phenomenon. Learn to appreciate participation in the larger mystery, ask questions about your purpose in the scenes you examine.
What would a "communication study" of dominant signs and spiritual readings in Central look like?	*Context/Interpretation:* By privileging solely intentional contexts for interpretations of signs, we remain bounded by traditional rationality and narrowness of purpose. We also evoke dualities through the interpretation: good/bad; right/wrong; fact/fiction, and so forth.	By alternatively privileging ourselves as the conjurers of meanings, we engage signs as clues to alternative contexts or frameworks for interpretation. In so doing, the known dualities are transcended and the playfulness of the engagement invites Spirit as a teacher of alternative possibilities for the meaning of our relationship to acts of creation, interpretation, and purpose.

APPENDIX 3

What might the implications of doing this sort of study be?

Power/Other/Spirit: Privileging any of these resources for narrative or mythic interpretation provides a resource for our understanding of the historical struggle.

Actually using Spirit as an interpretive guide to contexts for signs opens up imaginative possibilities and enlivens everyday experiences. To surrender to wonder is to see the extraordinary as a permeable border through which the boredom and rituals of everyday life may be transcended. The experiential results of seeking wonder and ecstasy pay off in an enlarged appreciation for how asking new questions and reframing ordinary meanings can lead to interconnectedness and interbeing.

What is communication a sign of?

Information Processing/Expressive Ways to Act on Our Need for Creative Activities: Communication is commonly understood as a tool, an instrument, a way of processing information in order to make and keep social relationships; constitute families, organizations, and institutions; and build communities. It may also be conceptualized as the poetic or expressive capacity humans possess. This sort of duality leads to the problems of splitting the rational from the emotional, the mind from the body, and "self"

Spiritual Growth: Learn to use communicative powers for the further nature of human reaching, not simply the further reaches of human nature. Communication is how we attain what we are here for in material, relational, and spiritual ways. The connectedness of all persons and things that emerges from this insight allows us to transcend the rational/emotional, mind/body, or self and Other categories by finding the unities among apparent diversities.

Connecting Spirit to Community

What might a Zen of communication alternative offer us?

Epistemic/Ontic:
Should the point of learning or studying communication be more and more knowledge for better prediction and control, more elaborate theories, better problem-solving, more eloquent research methods and procedures? Or should it be enriched experiential Being and the ability to help each other achieve human fulfillment and happiness? Either way, constructed this way we tend to value beliefs over practices and accord intellectual high ground to theory makers.

By learning to ask new questions about the assumed purposes and outcomes of communication inquiry, we develop alternative visions for what communication, and the study of it, might be *for*. By unifying the quest for knowledge with the experiences of Being, we combine where once we divided. Payoff should be in practices, not beliefs.

Chapter 4

What is the relationship between religion or spirituality and college football?

Rapture/Ecstasy:
Using a set of rules for behavior in a game whose purpose is to achieve victory (religion) or finding in the chaos of the everyday the deeper ordering required to achieve ecstatic experience (spirituality) are dualities that exist side-by-side in our American culture; football is just a metaphor for American culture.

Mystic Football Can Be Read as a Transformational Stage:
Viewed this way, football is about humans as spiritual beings who seek—through communion, ritual, solitude, symbolism, freedom, communication, coordinated actions, interpretive accounts, and storytelling—deeply personal transformations from their felt status as isolated, incomplete souls to a sense of connectedness, completion, and meaning that transcends ordinary life and establishes contact with Creation.

APPENDIX 3

Why do opposites attract?	*Good versus Evil:* Also right versus wrong, women versus men, appropriateness versus inappropriateness, lighter versus darker, richer versus poorer, them versus us, self versus Other(s), aliens versus natives, Heaven versus Hell, and so on.	Consider that perhaps they are part of a larger Unity. If so, are not our categories false?
What is the common language of a spiritual community?	*Individuality versus Community:* The tension here is one communication theorists are fond of attributing to problems of shared meanings. The idea is that the more we rely on individuality, the less meaning we are likely to share within communities; conversely, the more communal meanings we share, the more likely we give up aspects of individuality (e.g., "Groupthink" or cults).	In the real and imagined ecstatic connections we make or find, we organize our diversities through shared activities, unify our opposites and identify with each other through coordinated rituals, rites, and games *without* relying on shared meanings. We are "in the flow" (Csikszentmihalyi) or we are "jamming" (Eisenberg).

Chapter 5

What are the immanent characteristics of a community?	*Immanence and Angels:* We too often assume that Big Reality divides us from the stars in the same way that we assume individuals are "naturally" divided from each other. This view of divisions too often prevents us from building communities out of difference.	In what sense is Sibyl's a "Beauty Shop?" Or is it more of a spiritual community center where healing practices pass for "permanents," for "changes," and for "tips?" How we frame a context determines what we find in it; we must learn to hear in the twists, turns, and

		metaphors of everyday conversation the resources for spiritual and communal transformations.
What is the nature of sacred places?	*Religion versus Spirituality:* Too often we assume that sacred places are found only in traditional sites of religious value or practice without taking into account that many religious sites became such because something extraordinary or extrasensory happened there. Similarly, we think of spiritual sites as having already been defined by some ancient group or tribe. In either case, we rob ourselves of the immanence of the present by avoiding reading local signs and practices as sacred.	Think of the sacred as located squarely *within* the everyday, *within* contemporary experiences, *within* communities that we are living in and through. Search these sites for crossings, for angels.
What is the relationship of the imagination to the immanent?	*Facts versus Fictions:* By dividing what our senses tell us (and what traditional rationality frames for us) from imaginative interpretive accounts, we disconnect the yearnings of soul from obeyance of the ordinary. Yet the human condition is always part fact, part fiction, and where those lines blur are resources for connections to purposes larger than mere rationality can catch.	Teach yourself and others to construct metaphorical-language maps of local communities; connect places and persons by their shared activities and purposes rather than by their categorical adherence to ordinary divisions.

APPENDIX 3

How can we have a conversation without sharing meanings?

Shared Meanings = Signs of "Real" Connections; Ambiguous or Non-Shared Meanings = Signs of Conversational Chaos and a Loss of Community:
Assumes, of course, that we "have" meanings in our heads that then our bodies somehow act on, when instead we act first and then figure out what it meant later. Assumes also that we can share meanings, which has never been adequately demonstrated beyond simple routines. Hence, how can we lose a community when what we base its construction on is faulty?

Think of conversations as the simultaneous arrival of parallel worlds between or among beings whose meanings only occasionally intersect; learn to listen to "that little man inside" or intuitions; trust your feelings and doubt the unearned sanctity of your surface verbal agreements; decide to use those rare intersections as crossings, as resources for learning intimacy and higher purpose.

What are angels?

Reality/(Im)Possibility:
Privileging traditional sensory experiences as the basis for knowing excludes ordinary interventions or punctuations of other explanatory possibilities. Angels therefore exist as religious phenomenon or metaphors for those who believe in heavenly messengers or narratives that contain otherwise inexplicable events or episodes. There is no reality apart from the (culturally dominant)

Immanent ecstatic experiences contain the angelic heart of unifying communication practices and contain the soul of inter-being; learn to trust your instincts, your inner voices, the inexplicable intimate teachings of friends and strangers, the ineffable lessons of sacred places.

Chapter 6

How is a misspelled word a sign of a deeper riddle?

Awareness/Imagination:
The alphabet and numerical systems we have created are representational signs of all Order, which is to say of rationality itself. Altered states of syntax may be clues to alternative or deviant cultural logics, which in turn may be part of the defining riddles of cultures and sub- or countercultures within communities.

Speech and writing are rational activities; their ideal form (in the West) is reasoned argument, which is persuasive because of the weight of impersonal empirical evidence given in support of clearly articulated claims.

There are no coincidences or mistakes in the transformational grammar that defines the nature of universal consciousness. Every sign is a clue to part of the mystery; learn to think of signs as directed at you, for a reason. We can dismiss misspelled words or misspoken acts as "mistakes" or we can use them as semiotic resources for alternative explanations that might help us understand the truly parallel nature of communities and perhaps of all existence. Speech is a spiritual instrument; well-reasoned argument is useful in some applications but also robs the human voice of Spirit, which is personal, highly imaginative, supra-rational, humorous, imagistic, and playful.

What is the relationship between altered states of consciousness and altered states of syntax?

Normal/Deviant:
Anything—especially consciousness—that is "altered" is by definition a deviation from cultural norms. In the West, most deviations from what is normal are considered wrong, abnormal, dangerous, ridiculous, stupid, illegal, or crazy.

Altering consciousness can be used as a spiritual pathway to enlightenment, or to an appreciation for parallel worlds, or perhaps to evolutionary progress. Viewed this way, altered states of syntax—misspellings, misspeakings, riddles, puns—offer openings to alternative readings of

APPENDIX 3

How should we communicate in communities of difference, or how do we accomplish plurality?

Monologue/Dialogue and Rules/Improvisation: Traditional lessons in communicating are based on rule-governed systems in which shared meanings are the basis of community; the emphasis is always on creating useful scripts, routines, phatic communions, or monologues that carry very little creative information but contain a lot of obvious cultural redundancy. By contrast, artful communication relies on improvisation of dialogues and an empowering ambiguity that denies power to the redundancy and relative meaninglessness of culturally shared meanings. Too much ambiguity, however, is frustrating, and too much rule-governance is boring.

realities, of life-worlds, of imagined possibilities. They are signs of difference and of complexities.

Balancing our inherent constraints for making cultural meanings within a community with our need for improvisational, dialogic plurality. Recognizing that liminality is the ordinary state of cultural consciousness in diverse communities constructed out of differences makes dialogic improvisation and tentativeness a better guide to making spaces for unities.

Connecting Spirit to Community

What is the point of a dialogue?

Ends/Means:
If we are to embrace improvisational dialogue as a "better" model for communities of humans communicating, there must be some empirical end or clearly articulated benefit to be gained from the embrace. The fear is that dialogue doesn't accomplish anything beyond itself. Viewed this way, dialogue may simply be a way of taking a wrong turn in an otherwise rational and orderly historical construction of conversation that is best composed of (mostly) polite monologues that are aimed strategically at each other's brains. Dialogue may be a big, irrational mistake, another wrong turn in our common spelling of community.

To see the ends of everyday conversations and cultural dialogues as *continuance* of our interconnected spiritual growth, and a way of participating in a unified consciousness of the vagaries and complexities of community. To engage in dialogue is to substitute the ideal of interdependence for the assumption of the sovereignty of the rational subject. It is to learn that strategy is not the point of spiritual evolution; harmony is.

Chapter 7

How should instructions be written or spoken?

Vision and Reason:
Modernists believe in straightforward claims supported by empirical evidence or the testimony of experts or witnesses. Postmodernists see all instruction-giving as politically charged and seem to favor oppositional readings that challenge Power. Both Power and Other see reason as

Unifying visions are produced through the discovery and use of empowering ambiguities, not certainties or clarities. The best instructions are those that coordinate our actions without relying on shared meanings.

APPENDIX 3

	the product of shared *a priori* understandings and meanings.	
Why do instructions seem to be strange forms of communication?	*Clarity versus Ambiguity*: Instruction-giving assumes that one right way is known and should be reasonably followed whereas most communicative events and understandings in life challenge that assumption. Instructions value verbal directions and ignore the value of silence (particularly spiritual) in the interpretations of messages. Where humans are inspired to make choices they seem to believe they are freer and happier than when told what, specifically, to do. Hence, choice-denying or limiting instructions are often ignored (particularly by men), just as any form of domination through communication tends to inspire immediate and often forceful resistance.	Inspire choice through ambiguity and silence. Allow others to learn from taking responsibility for their choices. Recognize that in silence a lot of interpretive space is opened up and freedom acknowledged. Prayer and meditation are but two silent resources capable of unifying the chaos of words.
How are we prepared for this strange life?	*Knowing/Not Knowing*: Most of our modern and postmodern histories are accumulations of knowledge of and about Power and Other; the idea is that we are best prepared for dealing with the strangeness—the	Appreciate the paradoxes of knowledge: we learn, but it is never enough. This paradox teaches us that simply relying on knowledge to guide spiritual growth and experience—much less everyday choices—is

What is the relationship between reason and lessons?

Rational Knowing/Intuited Experience:
Life is only partially explained by rationality and reason-giving, yet most people doubt the validity of their own intuited knowledge or felt experiences without being able to attribute empirical or scientific reasons to them. The idea here is that lessons are reasonable responses humans make to evolutionary situations and progressive challenges to our environments: reasonable humans learn how to adapt to the world. The postmodern challenge is primarily political: who gets to construct the master narrative? Perhaps the real lessons of history are gendered or racial, not scientific and certainly not rational.

thrownness—of life by learning master explanatory narratives that help us cope with life's verbal and nonverbal irregularities. Not to seek out ways of knowing is a social problem as well as a sign of personal ignorance.

foolhardy. There are many sources of lessons in life, many of which are ineffable and some of which are borne only in spontaneous, intimate dialogue.

Perhaps there is wisdom in reversing the terms of our rationality: we should try to get the world to adapt to us. Particularly in spiritual matters, what would be privileged would be the primacy of our quest rather than the reasonableness of it. At any rate, human progress in all areas of endeavor tends to depend on challenging what reason teaches us ought to be taken for granted.

APPENDIX 3

What are the politics of instruction?

Liberal versus Conservative:
Political battles divide us according to economics, class, gender, and race. They also follow the same cultural logic as any other struggle between Power and Other: the more oppressive one side seems to the other side, the more resistance the other side demonstrates. Hence, we are caught in a repetitious circle of unrelenting and escalating argument that further stretches and ultimately divides right from wrong with little or no hope of resolution.
Forms of argument deteriorate to name-calling, innuendo, slander, and noncreative profanity; medium of exchange increasingly becomes mediated. The politics of religion replaces a cultural logic of good reasons as source of authority.
Community is destroyed by the righteous in the name of salvation.

Organizing for democracy is predicated upon acceptance of diversity and tolerance for difference as well as for producing an informed electorate and making public space for the free exchange of ideas.
Public imagination must be engaged through creative communication that invokes Spirit to counter trashed rationality and mediated religious politics.
Traditional forms of reasoning have lost their transformative powers; we must reinvent public communication on principles of dialogue to forge new, sustainable communities based on interconnected complexities.

Chapter 8

What is insight?

Insight and Complexity: Insight confounds traditional forms of Western rationality because it transcends all argument forms and subverts the very processes of reasoning that are believed to be the communicative cornerstones of community.

Complexity is generally considered to bederived from empirical or politicalcategories; even the postmoderns assumethat complexity can be reduced to issues ofvoice among marginalized groups occupyingeconomic, race, class, and gender categories.

Think of insight as the multichannel communicative pathway between complexity and interpretation.

Complexity and insight work together in dialogue by producing interpretive collisions of otherwise disparate ideas and forms of talk or silence. The clue is always about the permeable borders of otherwise fixed boundaries and the need to understand and deal with interconnectedness as sign of human divinity.

How do we learn to read ourselves into the texts and contexts of Others?

Intending/Negotiating: We are taught to go through life with the basic attitude that what we think is going on is really going on, but that we must be willing to change our interpretations when presented with better evidence. The modern problem is always with questions of admissable evidence in relation to the dominant narrative of Power. Extraordinary, extrasensory, or imaginative evidence is discounted in favor of that which can be empirically verified.

How do we learn how to drive on freeways? We privilege feedback over intentional messages and recognize the interconnectedness of everyone and everything.

To grant voice to Spirit is to engage the full range of communicative possibilities as a natural precondition of our interbeing.

APPENDIX 3

We learn, as a result, not to read ourselves into the contexts of Others but to assert intentional narratives in their faces. Negotiation is the last refuge of the verbally defeated.

The postmodern challenge is not derived from issues of evidence but from the sanctity of Others' authority to tell their own tales. As as result our communities are further dispersed across multiple narratives and opportunities for finding common ground materially reduced.

Negotiation must be premised upon acceptance of one's identity and purpose.

Negotiation is superseded by dialogue.

What are the implications of embracing a spiritual foundation for life at work?

Rationality/Spirituality: Here we confront the tension that defines and thereby informs our understanding and experience of reality. Is it empirical or ineffable? Is it a problem to be solved or a mystery to be engaged? Is it practical within a capitalist framework to sponsor a view that treats all people with dignity, respect, and care? Does this perspective actually negate the advances made by people of color, women, and other disadvantaged groups?

Spirit offers a new perspective on the historical narrative of the struggle between Power and Other. Reality is both empirical and ineffable, life consists both of problems to be solved and mysteries to be engaged. Perhaps we should learn to ask what the real "work" of our lives is. Perhaps if we asked this question we would reinvent and thereby reconstitute our priorities at work.

Perhaps a spiritual perspective is incompatible or at least conflicts with a rational business mentality. Can the search for excellence and competitive advantage in global markets accord with a world view that sees every action as having cosmic consequences?

| What are the lessons of Spirit? | *Power/Other:* The real world is a struggle between historically opposed forces and peoples. Spirit is a kind of fiction, a story about human evolution that tries to account for mysteries of human experience. Communities are constructed out of shared values, shared understandings, and shared meanings. Perhaps what we should be doing is learning how to exclude unwanted Others to ensure the likemindedness of our tribe, group, race, economic class, gender or nation. | All Power/Other narratives dichotomize the world and thereby deflect attention from our spiritual nature and quest. We need to link questions about what we feel is missing in ourselves, in our communities, and in our communication with issues that transcend the material concerns of Power and the power concerns of Other.
We need to learn to read signs as reminders about arrivals and destinations, immanence and transcendence, rapture and ecstasy, and so forth, as expressions of empirical tensions that have analogic content and purposes.
The purpose of our experience of the complexities of human communication is to make dialogic communities worthy of our abilities to organize diversity, much as the universe that created us does. |

APPENDIX 3

How do we act on these lessons?

Truth/Falsity:
As modernists we would have to rationally believe in the spiritual nature of the human condition, which may be a logical contradiction.
As postmodernists we would have to devalue the importance and defining power of Power in this historical struggle to make any room for Spirit; to make room for Spirit would mean devaluing the advances made of Others. Herein lies the contradiction.

We must learn to improve our world by being receptive to it.
We must learn to experience fully and to express fully what we feel, think, intuit, need, want, imagine, and believe.
We must share responsibility for the planet and for each other.
We must learn to use communication to dialogically explore the everyday possibilities of expanding consciousness.
We must recognize that communication perceptions and abilities improve with daily use. Communication is *divine*.

References

Agee, J., and Evans, W. 1941, 1984. *Let us now praise famous men*. Birmingham, AL.: Southern Living Galleries.
Allen, M. M. M. 1973. *Central: Yesterday and today*. Taylors, SC: Faith.
Anderson, J., and Goodall, H. L. 1994. Writing the body ethnographic: From a rhetoric of representation to a poetics of inquiry. In *Building communication theories*, edited by F. Casmir. Hillsdale, NJ: Lawrence Earlbaum.
Aronowitz, S., and DiFazio, M. 1994. *The jobless future*. Minneapolis: University of Minnesota Press.
Atkinson, P. 1990. *The ethnographic imagination: Textual constructions of reality*. London: Routledge.
Bakhtin, M. 1981. *The dialogic imagination*. Trans. C. Emerson and M. Holquist. Austin: University of Texas Press.
Baldwin, D. 1994. As busy as we wanna be. *Utne Reader* 61 (Jan./Feb.): 52–58.
Banks, S., and Riley, P. 1993. Structuration theory as an ontology for communication research. In *Communication yearbook 16*, edited by S. Deetz. Newbury Park, CA: Sage. 167–96.
Barnet, R. J., and Cavanagh, J. 1994. *Global dreams: Imperial corporations and the new world order*. New York: Simon and Schuster.
Barnoux, E. 1975. *Tube of plenty*. New York: Oxford University Press.
Bateson, G. 1972. *Steps toward an ecology of mind*. San Francisco: Chandler.
Bateson, G., and Donaldson, R. 1991. *A sacred unity: Further steps toward an ecology of mind*. New York: HarperCollins.
Bateson, M. C. 1993. Joint performance across cultures: Improvisation in a Persian garden. *Text & Performance Quarterly* 13: 113–21.
Baudrillard, J. 1988. *America*. Trans. Chris Turner. London: Verso.
Becker, C. B. 1993. *Paranormal experience and survival of death*. Albany: State University of New York Press.
Best, S., and Kellner, D. 1991. *Postmodern theory*. New York: Guilford Press.
Block, P. 1993. *Stewardship: Choosing service over self-interest*. San Francisco: Berrett-Koehler.
Bloom, A. 1987. *The closing of the American mind*. New York: Simon and Schuster.
Bloom, H. 1992. *The American religion*. New York: Simon and Schuster.
Bochner, A. 1994. Perspectives on inquiry II: Theories and stories. In *Handbook of interpersonal communication*, edited by M. Knapp and G. R. Miller. Newbury Park, CA: Sage.
Bormann, E. 1985. *The force of fantasy: Restoring the American dream*. Carbondale: Southern Illinois University Press.

REFERENCES

Bradley, B. 1991. *Death Valley days: The glory of Clemson football.* Atlanta: Longstreet.

Branham, R., and Pierce, W. B. 1980. The "ineffable." *Quarterly Journal of Speech* 67: 11–12.

Burke, K. 1966. *Philosophy of literary form.* Berkeley: University of California Press.

———. 1989. *Symbols and society.* Chicago: University of Chicago Press.

Callenbach, E., Capra, F., Goldman, L., Lutz, R., and Marburg, S. 1993. *EcoManagement: The Elmwood guide to ecological awareness and sustainable business.* San Francisco: Berrett-Koehler.

Capra, F. 1975. *The Tao of physics.* Berkeley: Shambhala.

———. 1982. *The turning point: Science, society, and the rising culture.* New York: Simon and Schuster.

Chappell, T. 1993. *The soul of a business: Managing for profit and the common good.* New York: BDD Audio.

Chopra, D. 1993. *Ageless body, timeless mind.* New York: Random House Audio Publishing.

Clifford, J., and Marcus, G. 1986. *Writing culture.* Berkeley: University of California Press.

Coffin, W. S. 1993. *A passion for the possible: A message to U.S. churches.* Louisville, KY: Westminster/John Knox Press.

Coles, R. 1989. *The call of stories.* Boston: Houghton Mifflin.

Conquergood, D. 1993. Homeboys and hoods: Gang communication and cultural space. In *Communication in context: Studies of naturalistic groups*, edited by L. Frey. Hillsdale, NJ: Lawrence Erlbaum.

Connor, S. 1989. *Postmodern culture: An introduction to theories of the contemporary.* London: Basil Blackwell.

Crapanzano, V. 1992. *Hermes' dilemma & Hamlet's desire: On the epistemology of interpretation.* New York: Columbia University Press.

Csikszentmihalyi, M. 1990. *Flow: The psychology of optimal experience.* New York: HarperPerennial.

———. 1993. *The evolving self: A psychology for the third millennium.* New York: HarperCollins.

Daniel, A., Wyllie, T., and Ramer, A. 1992. *Ask your angels.* New York: Ballantine.

DeCerteau, M. 1984. *The practice of everyday life.* Berkeley: University of California Press.

Deetz, S. 1992. *Democracy in an age of corporate colonization.* Albany: State University of New York Press.

Derrida, J. 1976. *Of grammatology.* Trans. G. Chakravorty. Baltimore: Johns Hopkins University Press.

Dunn, Stephen. 1989. *Between angels: Poems by Stephen Dunn.* New York: W. W. Norton.

Durckheim, G. 1991. Dialogue on the path of initiation. *Mindfield* 1: 49–55.

Eadie, W. R. 1992. Spirituality and *praxis* in monologue and dialogue: A meditation on themes by Barnett Pearce. Presentation at the Wichita Symposium, September, at Wichita, KS.

Edelman, J., and Crain, M. B. 1993. *The Tao of negotiation.* New York: HarperBusiness.

Eisenberg, E. M. 1984. Ambiguity as strategy in organizational communication. *Communication Monographs* 51: 227–42.

———. 1990. Jamming: Transcendence through organizing. *Communication Research* 17: 139–64.

---. 1993. An honest man. Paper presented at the Speech Communication Association annual meeting, November, at Miami, FL.
Eisenberg, E. M., and Goodall, H. L. 1993. *Organizational communication: Balancing creativity and constraint.* New York: St. Martin's Press.
Etzioni, A. 1993. *The spirit of community: Rights, responsibilities, and the Communitarian agenda.* New York: Crown.
Ewen, S. 1989. *All consuming images.* New York: Basic Books.
Fisher, W. 1987. *Human communication as narration.* Columbia: University of South Carolina Press.
Fiske, J. 1990. Ethnosemiotics: Some personal and theoretical reflections. *Cultural Studies* 4: 85–98.
Fox, M. 1994. *The reinvention of work: A new vision of livelihood in our time.* New York: HarperCollins.
Frentz, T. S. 1993. Reconstructing a rhetoric of the interior. *Communication Monographs* 60: 83–89.
Geertz, C. 1973. *The interpretation of cultures.* New York: Basic Books.
---. 1983. *Local knowledge.* New York: Basic Books.
---. 1988. *Works and lives: The anthropologist as author.* Stanford: Stanford University Press.
Gergen, K. 1992. *The saturated self.* New York: Basic Books.
Giddens, A. 1979. *Central problems in social theory.* Berkeley: University of California Press.
Goffman, E. 1959. *The presentation of self in everyday life.* Garden City, NJ: Anchor/Doubleday.
Goldman, K. 1992. *The angel handbook: A handbook for aspiring angels.* New York: Simon and Schuster.
Goodall, H. L., Jr. 1983. *Human communication: Creating reality.* Dubuque, IA: Wm. C. Brown.
---. 1983. The nature of analogic discourse. *Quarterly Journal of Speech* 69: 171–79.
---. 1989. *Casing a promised land: The autobiography of an organizational detective as cultural ethnographer.* Carbondale: Southern Illinois University Press.
---. 1991. *Living in the rock n roll mystery: Reading context, self, and others as clues.* Carbondale: Southern Illinois University Press.
---. 1992. Empowerment, culture, and postmodern organizing: Deconstructing the Nordstrom Employee Handbook. *Journal of Organizational Change Management* 5: 25–30.
---. 1993. Mysteries of the future told: Communication as the material manifestation of spirituality. *World Communication Journal* 22: 40–49.
---. 1994. Living in the rock n roll campaign: Myth, media, and the American public imagination. In *Bill Clinton on stump, state, and stage: The rhetorical road to the White House,* edited by S. Smith. Fayetteville: University of Arkansas Press.
---. 1995. Work-Hate: Narratives of mismanaged transitions in times of organizational change. In *Hate Speech,* edited by R. K. Whillock and D. Slayton. Thousand Oaks, CA: Sage.
Goodman, F. D. 1988. *Ecstasy, ritual, and alternate reality: Religion in a pluralistic world.* Bloomington: Indiana University Press.
Gorer, G. 1948. *The Americans: A study in national character.* London: Cresset Press.
Gottlieb, A., and Graham, P. 1993. *Parallel worlds: An anthropologist and a writer encounter Africa.* New York: Crown.

REFERENCES

Gramsci, A. 1971. *Selections from the prison notebooks*. London: Lawrence and Wishart.
Greeley, A. 1974. *Ecstasy: A way of knowing*. Englewood Cliffs, NJ: Prentice-Hall.
Greenhouse, C. 1986. *Praying for justice*. Ithaca: Cornell University Press.
Griffin, D. R., ed. 1988. *Spirituality and society*. Albany: State University of New York Press.
Hamill, P. 1994. Endgame. *Esquire* 122, no. 6: 85–92.
Hannah, B. 1993. *Bats out of hell*. Boston: Houghton Mifflin/Seymour Lawrence.
Harrison, J. 1991. *Just before dark*. Livingston, MT: Clark City Press.
Harvey, D. 1990. *The conditions of postmodernity*. London: Basil Blackwell.
Hawken, P. 1994. *The ecology of commerce*. New York: HarperCollins.
Hawley, J. 1993. *Reawakening the spirit in work: The power of Dharmic management*. San Francisco: Barrett-Koehler.
Heider, K. G., ed. 1993. *Images of the South: Constructing a regional culture on film and in video*. Athens: University of Georgia Press/Southern Anthropological Society.
Hillman, J. 1991. *Blue fire: Selected writings of James Hillman*. New York: HarperPerennial.
Hodge, R., and Kress, G. 1988. *Social semiotics*. Ithaca, NY: Cornell University Press.
Holquist, M. (1991). *Dialogism*. Austin: University of Texas Press.
Jackson, M. 1989. *Paths toward a clearing: Radical empiricism and ethnographic inquiry*. Bloomington: University of Indiana Press.
James, J. 1992. The future of education. Speech given to the South Carolina Vocational Education Association at Columbia, SC.
Katz, S. T. 1992. *Mysticism and language*. New York: Oxford University Press.
Kellett, P. 1994. Superstitious organizations: Resisting organizational change. Paper presented at the Speech Communication Association annual meeting, November, at Miami, FL.
Kelly, M. 1994. You can't always get done what you want. *Utne Reader* 61 (Jan./Feb.): 62–66.
Kristol, I. 1992. Economic success, spiritual decline, the capitalist future. *Current* 43: 9–11.
Limbaugh, R. 1992. *The way things ought to be*. New York: Pocket Books.
———. 1993. *See, I told you so*. New York: Pocket Books.
Lyotard, J.-F. 1979. *The postmodern condition: A report on knowledge*. Minneapolis: University of Minnesota Press.
McKenna, T. 1991. *Food of the gods: The search for the original tree of knowledge, a radical history of plants, drugs, and human evolution*. New York: Bantam.
———. 1993. *Omni* interview. *Omni* 14 (April): 69–74, 90–92.
McKeon, R. 1970. Communication as an architectonic, productive art. In *The prospect of rhetoric*, edited by L. F. Bitzer and E. Black. Englewood Cliffs, NJ: Prentice-Hall.
McLuhan, M. 1964. *Understanding media*. New York: McGraw-Hill.
Manganaro, M. 1991. *Modernist anthropology*. Princeton, NJ: Princeton University Press.
Marcus, G. 1990. *Dead Elvis*. New York: Doubleday.
Mills, C. W. 1959. *The sociological imagination*. London: Oxford University Press.
Moore, T. 1993. *Care of the soul: A guide for cultivating depth and sacredness in everyday life*. New York: HarperCollins.

References

———. 1994. Soul mates. *New Age Journal* (February): 56–59; 129–31.
Moran, R. 1995. *Teaching the body to dance again.* Johnstown, OH: Pudding House.
Morgan, M. 1993. Spirit in the workplace: A movement on the verge of taking off. *At Work: Stories of Tomorrow's Workplace* 2 (September/October): 7–9.
Murakami, H. 1990. *A wild sheep chase.* New York: Plume.
Murphy, M. 1992. *The future of the body.* Los Angeles: Jeremy Tarcher.
Myerhoff, B. 1975. Organization and ecstasy: Deliberate and accidental communitas among Huichol indians and American youth. In *Symbol and politics in communal ideology*, edited by S. Moore and B. Myerhoff. Ithaca, NY: Cornell University Press.
Needleman, J. 1986. *The heart of philosophy.* San Francisco: Harper and Row.
Nelson, S. 1994. Sex, love, and ethnography. In *A world made out of margins: Writing the personal experience of communication and culture*, edited by H. L. Goodall, Jr. Unpublished manuscript.
Nisker, W. S. 1990. *Crazy wisdom.* Berkeley, CA: Ten Speed Press.
Okely, J., and Callaway, J. 1992. *Anthropology & autobiography.* London: Routledge.
Ong, W. G., S. J. 1971. *Rhetoric, romance, and technology.* Ithaca, NY: Cornell University Press.
———. 1977. *Interfaces of the word: Studies in the evolution of consciousness and culture.* Ithaca, NY: Cornell University Press.
———. 1982. *Orality and literacy: The technologizing of the word.* London: Methuen.
Opt, S. 1993. The development of rural wired radio systems in upstate South Carolina. *Journal of Radio Studies* 1: 71–82.
Orsborn, C. 1992. *Inner excellence: Spiritual principles of life-driven business.* San Rafael, CA: New World Library.
Pearce, W. B. 1992. Achieving dialogue with 'the other' in the postmodern world. Presentation at the Wichita Symposium, September, at Wichita, KS.
Percy, W. 1959. *The moviegoer.* New York: Farrar, Straus, Giroux.
———. 1983. *Lost in the cosmos: The last self-help book.* New York: Farrar, Straus, Giroux.
Phillips, A. 1993. *On kissing, tickling, and being bored: Psychoanalytic essays on the unexamined life.* Cambridge, MA: Harvard University Press.
Phillips, W. G. 1994. *Tuscaloosa.* New York: Morrow.
Postman, N. 1986. *Amusing ourselves to death.* New York: Penguin.
Rabinow, C., and Sullivan, W. 1987. *Interpretive social science: A reader.* 2d ed. Berkeley: University of California Press.
Rifkin, J. 1995. *The end of work.* New York: Tarcher/Putnam.
Ronell, A. 1989. *Telephone book: Technology, schizophrenia, electric speech.* Lincoln: University of Nebraska Press.
———. 1992. *Crack wars: Literature, addiction, mania.* Lincoln: University of Nebraska Press.
Rorty, R. 1979. *Philosophy and the mirror of nature.* Princeton, NJ: Princeton University Press.
Rose, D. 1989. *Patterns of American culture: Ethnography and estrangement.* Philadelphia: University of Pennsylvania Press.
Rushing, J. H. 1993. Power, Other, and Spirit in cultural texts. *Western Journal of Communication* 57: 159–68.
Sacks, H. 1984. On doing being ordinary. Edited transcript of Lecture 1, Spring 1970. University of California.

REFERENCES

Scott, J. C. 1990. *Domination and the arts of resistance.* New Haven, CT: Yale University Press.
Scott, R. L. 1993. Dialectical tensions of speaking and silence. *Quarterly Journal of Speech* 79: 1–18.
Sennett, R. 1978. *The fall of public man.* New York: Vintage.
Sennett, R., and Cobb, J. 1972. *The hidden injuries of class.* New York: Knopf.
Shimanoff, S. 1980. *Communication rules: Theory and research.* Newbury Park, CA: Sage.
Shotter, J. 1993. *Cultural politics in everyday life.* London: Open University Press.
Smith, D. 1972. Communication research and the idea of process. *Speech Monographs* 39: 174–82.
Smith, S. 1993. Political vision and envisioning political space. Keynote address at Carolinas Speech Communication Association Conference, October, at Browns Summit, NC.
Spretnak, C. 1991. *States of grace: The recovery of meaning in a postmodern world.* New York: HarperCollins.
Stallybrass, P., and White, A. 1986. *The politics and poetics of transgression.* Ithaca, NY: Cornell University Press.
Stoller, P. 1989. *The taste of ethnographic things: The senses in anthropology.* Philadelphia: University of Pennsylvania Press.
Stoller, P., and Olkes, C. 1987. *In sorcery's shadow.* Chicago: University of Chicago Press.
Thomas, L. 1975. *Lives of a cell.* New York: Viking Press.
Turner, V. 1969. *The ritual process.* Ithaca, NY: Cornell University Press.
Van Maanen, J. 1988. *Tales of the field: On writing ethnography.* Chicago: University of Chicago Press.
Ventura, M. 1992. *Letters at 3 a.m.* Dallas, TX: Spring Press.
Ventura, M., and Hillman, J. 1992. *We've had one hundred years of psychotherapy and the world is getting worse.* San Francisco: HarperSanFrancisco.
Verenne, H. 1984. Collective representation in American anthropological conversations: Individual and culture. *Current Anthropologist* 25: 281–300.
Vonnegut, K. 1990. *Hocus Pocus.* New York: Putnam.
Warner, W. L. 1952. *Structure of American life.* Edinburgh: Edinburgh University Press.
Warren, C. A. B. 1987. *Madwives: Schizophrenic women of the 1950s.* New Brunswick, NJ: Rutgers University Press.
Watson, L. 1973. *Supernature: A natural history of the supernatural.* London: Coronet Books.
Wheatley, M. 1992. *Leadership and the New Science: Learning about organization from an orderly universe.* San Francisco: Berrett-Koehler.
White, M. 1992. *Tele-Advising: Therapeutic discourse in American television.* Chapel Hill: University of North Carolina Press.
Whyte, W. 1955. *The organization man.* New York: Doubleday.
Winograd, T., and Flores, F. 1985. *Understanding computers and cognition: A new foundation for design.* Norwood, NJ: Ablex.
Winokur, J. 1989. *Zen to go.* New York: New American Library/Penguin.

Index

ABCs, of ecstasy, 152
Agee, James, 106
age of endarkenment, 229
Allen, Mattie May Morgan, 80
alphabet, riddle of, 159
ambiguity, 42, 86
  and character, 218
  first technology, 179
  human preference for, 179–80
  of language, 179–80
Amtrak, 59, 150
Anderson, James A., 16
Anderson (SC), 27, 127, 209
angels, 136, 151, 151n
  taking human form, 151n
architecture, 47, 48
argument, warrantable
  and loss of transformative powers, 206
  problems of, 192n
Aronowitz, Stanley, 230n
arrival, 27, 28, 34, 101, 152
Atkinson, Paul, 8n
autoethnography, xiii, 9n
awareness, 157, 159
  and imagination, 157–70

Bakhtin, Mikhail, 13n, 170
Baldwin, Debra, 128n
Barnet, Richard J., 229
Barnoux, Eric, 201
Bateman, Claire, 38
Bateson, Gregory, 8, 89, 122
Bateson, Mary Catherine, 173
Being, 30, 49, 72, 212
  spiritual, 147
  textual, 212
Big It, 100, 116, 131
  theories of, 115
Block, Peter, 217n

Bloom, Allan, 161n
Bloom, Harold, 131, 132
Blumer, Herbert, 112
Bochner, Art, 218
body, lower and upper, 19
Bonneville Salt Flats (UT), 109
"Book, The" (Holy Bible), 179–83
boredom, 47, 55, 57, 60, 63, 65, 66
  and ecstasy, 67
  and modern, 56
  as opportunity, 56
  and phatic communion, 62
  as sign, 56
  and silence, 51
  and surrender, 58
  and weather/whether, 61
  as wellspring for community, 57
Bormann, Ernest, 211n
Bradley, Bob, 106
Branham, Robert J., 8n
Brooks Center (Clemson University), 142
Bryan, Wright, 120
Buddha, Siddhartha, 30
  story of wisdom, 157
Bullis, Connie, 8n
Burke, Kenneth, xii, 22, 49, 54, 92, 100, 112, 166, 204, 206, 224
By-Pass 76/123, 143

Calloway, Helen, 9n
Campbell, George, 73n
Campbell's Healthy Choice Soup, 182n
Camp Creek Baptist Church, 130
Cannon Memorial Baptist Church, 8, 46, 48, 50, 62, 82, 85, 106, 113, 123, 125, 130
cap, baseball, 209–10
Capra, Fritjof, 10n

INDEX

Carroll, Christa "C. J.," 138n, 141
Castenada, Carlos, 147n
Cateechee Beach, 79
Central (SC) 19–21, 23, 34–36, 39–40, 42, 46–50, 54–56; 59, 62, 64, 66, 68, 76, 77, 80, 83, 99, 101, 113, 127, 157, 163, 182, 189, 200, 237
  and night court, 50
Chappell, Tom, 215
Chopra, Deepak, 10, 11, 156n
Clemson (SC), 19–21, 23, 28, 34–35, 77, 80, 104, 106–35, 139, 143–46, 163, 182, 200
Clemson House, 136–37
Clemson University, 35, 40, 52–53, 80, 146–47, 148, 194, 238–40
  football, 104–35
  and killing Spirit, 238–40
  Marching Band, 116
Clifford, James, 16, 232n
Clinton, Bill, 189, 189, 197
Clock Drive-In, 51
Coffin, William Sloan, 146, 208
Coles, Robert, 218
communication, 13–14, 20, 69, 71–72, 73, 116, 125, 131, 220–23
  with angels, 152
  and business, 121–22
  and change, 205
  and cognition, 90
  as connective pathway, 13–14, 21, 208
  directive, 179
  and disciplined imagination, 95–100
  and dualities of vision and reason, 184
  and life coaching, 131, 220
  mass, and influence on local community, 196
  modern, 73–74, 94, 221
  and parallel worlds, 183
  and peak experiences, 90
  postmodern, 73–74, 94, 222
  and power, 221–22
  as practical consciousness, 4–5
  as responses to messages, 89
  and signs, 83–84, 89–91
  and spirituality, 4, 14, 46, 166
  and survival, 71
  theories as stories, 218
  and Zen, 91–95
community, ix, 21, 23, 108, 113, 126–28, 130, 139, 142, 223–26, 232
  as calling, 127
  dialogic, 223–26
  and football, 121
  limited by rationality, 206
  loss of, 240
  mediated, 194
  and power struggles, 76
complexities
  interconnected, 208
Connor, Steven, 16
Conquergood, Dwight, 188
  and the Latin Kings, 188
consciousness, 34, 122–23, 221
  altered, 158, 166
  and culture, 124
  dialogic, 167
  and immanence, 137
  as the next step, 165
  universal, 159
context(s), 1, 44, 75, 88–89, 140, 150, 170, 211
  and interpretation, 77–78, 84, 153, 170
conversation, 148–50
  and liminality, 150n
  and politics of, 53
  and put-downs, 54–55
Corinth Baptist Church, 130
Crain, Mary Beth, 215
Crapanzano, Vincent, 105
crossings 152–56
  and coincidences, 152–56
Csikszentmihalyi, Mihaly, 114n
culture
  American, 27
  Central, 50
  first principle of, 170
  Greek and Roman, 23n
  as masterpiece, 173
  riddles, 158
  strong, and superstitions, 220n
  struggle, between Power and Other, 230

Daniel, Alma, 136
Daniel High School, 142
Dante, 29
death, 112, 141
  as "Other Side," 141n
Death Valley, 107, 116–17, 124, 126, 128, 129, 132, 133
DeCerteau, Michel, 75, 160n, 163n
democracy
  and democratic consciousness, 4
  festering soul of, 199
Derrida, Jacques, 33

Index

Descartes, René, 161
destination, 27–28
dialogue, 13, 45–46, 76, 122, 132, 152–53, 172–73, 207, 213, 220, 223–26
  absence of, in Rush Limbaugh, 191
  aim of communication practices, 99, 132
  and architecture, public, 192
  and dialogics, 13, 223–24
  and difference, 172
  and lessons, 186–87
  and poetics, 213
DiFazio, Michael, 230n
difference, 33, 84–89, 171–73
  work of, 171–73
diversity, promotion of, 234
Dole, Bob, 198n
Double Indemnity, 151n
drugs
  as hallucinogens, 18, 69, 165–67
  lexical, 166
dualities, unifying, 220–23
Dunn, Stephen, 177

ecstasy, 58n, 68
  ABCs of, 152
  and communication, 70
  as communicative pathway, 69
  as desire for, 68
  and experience, 68
  as freedom, 114
  and insight, 208
  as metaphor, 69
  and rapture, 114
Edelman, Joel, 215
Eisenberg, Eric M., 68, 114n, 218, 219n, 230n
  and peak experiences, 114n
  and "work" of communication story, 218–19
Endgame, 230, 238
Enlightenment
  as project, 1, 2
  and Western rhetoric, 73n
ennui, 29, 32, 67, 71, 236
Esalen Institute, 18
ethnography, 8
  as attitude, 16
  and imagination, 10
  and intimacy, 9
  as method of experience, 8, 15, 156
  and writing, 16, 20
Evans, Walker, 106

evolution, exosomatic, 165
existential, 109–10, 112
  and raw categories for behavior, 88
experience, 15, 16, 100–101
  and being human, 94
  consumable spirituality, 236
  as the end of engaging mystery, 96
  peak, 114n, 119, 137
extrasensory, 17–18;

Fisher, Walter, 17, 184n
Fishman, Teddy, 210n
Fiske, John, 9n
Fitzgerald, F. Scott, 150
football, 103, 119
  and Christian teleology, 109
  college, 108
  frameworks for understanding, 108
  mystic, 108
  and peak experiences, 119
  as purposeful sign, 123
  and religion, 108
Fox, Matthew, 217
Frentz, Tom, 9–10n, 31n
Freud, Sigmund, 212n

Gallagher, Mike, 190
Geertz, Clifford, 16, 54, 74
Gergen, Kenneth, 112, 184n
Giddens, Anthony, 4, 220
Gingrich, Newt, 198n
Glaser, Hollis, 8n
Goffman, Erving, 166
Goldman, Karen, 136
Goodall, H. L., Jr., 9n, 13n, 89, 158, 220n, 221n, 222n, 230n
Gottlieb, Alma, 147n
Gorgias, 74
grace, 53, 232
  as graciousness, 52–53
Graham, Phillip, 147n
Gramsci, Antonio, 189
Greeley, Andrew, 58n
Greenhouse, Carol, 23
Greenville (SC), 127, 190

Hamill, Pete, 229–30; 238
Hannah, Barry, 103, 150
Harrison, Jim, 45
Hate speech, 190n
Hatfield, Kenny, 116n
Hawken, Paul, 217n
Hawley, Jack, 205

287

INDEX

Head, John
 and "Headtown," 36n
Hegel
 and phenomenology of spirit, 235
Heidegger, Martin, 29, 36, 39
Heisman, John, 106
Hell, 129
Hendrix, Jimi, 223
Hermes, 105
highways, 211
Hillman, James, 27
Highway 93 (SC), 35, 139
Highway 133 (SC), 139, 142
Hodge, Robert, 75
Holquist, Michael, 13n
Homecoming, 117–18, 133
Huichol Indians, 68

I/me, 112
imagination, x, 20, 22, 29, 142, 154, 173–75, 222, 241
 as alternative reality, 149
 and awareness, 157–70
 and communication, 93–99
 and community, 126
 and context, 9–10
 dialogic, 171–73
 and improvisation, 173
 and knowing, 175
 and spirit, 21
 and worlds, 20
immanence, 107n, 136, 137, 139, 144
improvisation, and culture, 173–75
Ingram, Hootie, 120
inner voice, 151–52
instructions, 179–81
 and radio in America, 193
 resistance to, 187
 and Saifun (bean threads), 181n
 as strange communication, 181–87
 and technical manuals, 180n
 televised, 200–205
interbeing, 31, 132, 213
 of Spirit, 142
interconnectedness
 complexities, 208
 and life, xii
interpretation, 44
 and imagination, 44
 and meanings, 97–99
 and signs, 83–84
intimate, 9–10, 15, 46
 intimacy, root in Latin, 31

IPTAY, 116n, 133, 163
 history of, 117n

Jackson, Michael, 15
James, Jennifer, 97n, 124
Jesus Christ, 30, 78, 131
 as celebrity, 43
 as legend, 43
 as Superstar, 43
Jurassic Park, 187

Kellett, Pete, 53, 220n
Kelly, Majorie, 161
Kerouac, Jack, 74
Knapp, Ann, 142
knowledge
 local, in Geertz, 74
 as supporting narrative motif, 96
Koans, Zen, 51, 184
Kress, Gunther, 75
Kristeva, Julia, 2n, 3n

language, xii, *19*, *124*, *154*, *160n*, *237*
 and change, 237–38
 and order, 19, 160n
 and resistance, 188–89
 and vision, 19
Lao-tzu, 50
LA Story, 42
leaders
 with spirit, 215
lessons, 184–87
 and constructions of reality, 185
 and dialogue, 186
 and learning, 184
 in *Oxford English Dictionary*, 186
 paradox of, 184
 and shape-shifting strangeness, 185
 types, 185
 and The Way, 184
Liberty (SC), 80, 113, 127
Limbaugh, Rush, 161n, 189–93, 195, 197, 198
 and instructions, 190
 and 1994 election results, 189n
 and public imagination, 191–92
Lindsley's story, 153–54
literature, academic
 as bifurcated by lay semioticians, 233–34
 and gang rhetoric, 233–34
Long, John, 214
Lovitt, Carl, 148–50, 157
Lyotard, Jean-François, 16

Man
  sexist noun, 85
Manganaro, Michael, 8n
Marx, Karl, 92, 212n
McKenna, Terrance, 68–69, 164–67, 169, 173
McKeon, Richard, 7
McLuhan, Marshall, 159n, 179
Mead, George Herbert, 112
medicine, 6
metaphor, 18, 23, 106n, 125–26, 147, 152, 165–66, 231–32, 232n
  detective, 24
  intersections as, 147
  machine and systems, 30
  Milky Way, 120–21, 131
  as moon *deluxe* of human language, 174
  Persian garden, 173
  religious, 31
  tails and horns, 183
Mills, C. Wright, 8n
misspelling, 157–70
  as code-breaking, 164
  as misspeaking, 163, 166–67
  as mistakes, 167–69
  as resistance to domination, 159, 163
  and Rush Limbaugh, 191
  as sign of extraordinary experience, 169
modern, the
  and modernity, 2
  and rationality, 206–7
  and surrounds, 211
Monty Python, 91
Moore, Thomas, 31
Morgan, Marie, 213, 215
Moyers, Bill, 6
Murakami, Haruki, 106
Murphy, Michael, 18
Myerhoff, Barbara, 68
mystery, 31, 93, 156, 241
  about afterlife of sentences, 240–41
  and boredom, 58
  and explanation, 93
  as research method, 92, 93
  sources in misspelled signs, 157
mythos, 10, 24, 162
  and logos, 24
  and narrative, 212, 237
  and time, 162
  Western cultural, 21

naïve
  in academic culture, 236
  and dumb, 236
  as good thing, 235–36
  Spirit as, 235–38
narrative, 17
  age, end of the, 231
  management of, in times of transition, 240
  and organizational change, 238
  and rationality, 17
National Public Radio, 198–99
Needleman, Jacob, 138n
Nelson, Stephanie, 9n, 199
Neumann, Mark, 189n
New Age, 18, 39, 39n, 167
Newton, Isaac, 161
nexus, ix, 4, 15, 232, 240
Nick's (bar), 142
Nietzsche, Friedrich, 212n
Nordstrom Employee Handbook, 222n
Norris (SC), 35, 79–80, 113
  speech in, 78

Okely, Judith, 9n
Olkes, Cheryl, 147n
Omega Institute, 18
Ong, Walter, 159n
oppositional readings, 110–24
Opt, Susan, 194–96
Order, 19
  and disorganization, 232
  and the obvious police, 236
ordinary, 34, 36, 39, 45
  as argument, 39
  as intertwined with extraordinary, 88
  and miracles, 217
  as preoccupation, 36–37
organizational age, end of, 230–31
Orsborn, Carol, 216
  principles of life-driven business, 216–17
Other(s), 45, 57, 152, 161, 222
Otherness, 33, 43, 222
Other's songs, 117n
postmodern, 212
  reading myself into texts of, 211

Payne, Elizabeth, 219n
Pendleton (SC), 113, 127, 139
Penn State University, 41
Percy, Walker, 30, 41, 65–67
Peters, Tom, 214n
phatic communion, 37–38, 61–64, 67, 69, 76
  as constraint on creativity, 38, 76

289

INDEX

and danger, 63–64
as replacement for dialogue, 64, 76
as vain repetition, 38
Phillips, Adam, 56
Phillips, W. Glasgow, 123n
Pickens (SC), 113
Pickens Church of Christ, 130
Pierce, W. Barnett, 8n
place, 23, 34, 47
  "plural present," 158
  and storytelling, 141
Plato, 2n, 9n, 161, 166
postmodern, the
  Hell, 129
  mediated worlds, 109, 207
  societies, 112–13
  and surrounds, 211
  and the velocity of living, 63
Power, 21, 42, 183, 232
  and communication study, 74, 92–93
  as earthling obsession, 124
  and modern signs, 41
  and Other, 21, 183, 232
  and Spirit, 21, 232
practices
  and beliefs, 97–98
Presley, Elvis, 141
  as dead, 43
  stamp, free with haircut, 138, 142
Prince, Phil, 239n
Pro-Logic, stereo, 89–90
public
  greeting, 54
  as imagined, 54, 207
  space, 47, 53, 75–77
  talk, 54
purpose, x, 116, 137
  and communication, 14
  and communication study, 77
  and lessons, 187
  misreadings of, 32
  and peak experiences, 119, 137

Quest
  and belief, 237–38
  and work, 237–38

Rabinow, Paul, 16
radio talk, 189–96
  past, in the region, 193–96
  and Rush Limbaugh, 189–93
railroad, 59
  in American South, 59
  annual celebration in Central, 60
  tracks, as metaphor, 59, 60, 63
Ramer, Andrew, 136
Rapture, 106, 107n, 110–11, 114, 133, 135
reality, 138n
  mechanical, 12
  quantum, 11, 156
reason
  and unreasonableness, 188
  and vision, dualities of, 205–7
relationships
  digital and analogic, 171n
religion, 14
  American, 130–31
  and college football, 108
  legalistic, and written codes, 160–61
religious persons, 123n
Revelation, 42, 43
  and authority, 85
rhetoric, 73n, 162
  and enchantment, 84, 162
  and poetics, 213
  modern, 73n
  oppositional, 114
  persuasive human speech, 162
  postmodern, 113
  "third kind," in Shotter, 184n
riddle(s)
  cultural, 157, 158
  Grand, 175
  of the Sphinx, 159
Rifkin, Jeremy, 230n
rock n roll music, 170
  and narrative communities, 170–71
Rogers, Gordon, 194
Rorty, Richard, 90
Rushing, Janice Hocker, 212n

Sacks, Harvey, 36–39, 85
Salvation, 85
Saxon, Allan, 188
SCA (Speech Communication Association) convention, 233
Scott Robert, 8n
Self, the, 112–13
  and boredom, 66
  and coding, through television, 202
  and community, 108
  existential, 109–10
  in public, 64
  romantic, 112
  spiritual, 24

Index

Seneca (SC), 127
sense(s)
  and knowing, 17
Shotter, John, 13n, 184n
Sibyl's (beauty shop), 138–42
signs, x, 41, 49, 80–91, 125
  and ambiguity, 180
  and beliefs, 98
  commercial and Christian appeals, 82
  as communication, 83–84
  as contexts, 41
  and immanent imagination, 142
  and insight, 208
  misspelled, 157–70
  and misspelling, 186
  and participative democracy, 197
  and possibilities, 86–87
  as postmodern, 43
  as puns, 157
  as representational surfaces, 41
  as riddles, 157
  and semiotics, 75, 77, 144
  as signage, 80, 82
  and strangeness, 182
  and toys, 229
Simpsons, The, 201
Six Mile (SC), 77, 80, 113, 125, 127, 139
Socrates, 162
soul, 27, 29, 110, 112, 129
Southern
  politeness in conversation, 51
  women's speech, 52n
spelling, correct, 159–60
Spielberg, Steven, 187
Spirit, ix, 21, 30–32, 45–46, 56, 58, 72, 211–20, 232–38, 241
  and community, 212
  distinct from spirituality, 213–14n
  as ghost in alphabet machine, 161
  Holy, 111, 112
  induced spiritual mystery, 87
  killing, through mismanaged transitioanl narratives, 238–40
  living, in the human voice, 160
  as metaphor for Grace, 232
  and mythic narrative, 212n
  and *nexus*, 232–33
  as "not new," 234–35
  as playful, 213
  as politically naïve, 235–38
  problematizing, 229–38
  role of, 212
  as sign, 213
  and storytelling, 218–20
  and transformative power, 213–14
  as unifying force, 212
  and unscientific, 233–34
  and work, 213–18
spirituality
  and college football, 108
  and communal voice, 129
  as ghost in alphabet machine, 161
  and organizational change, 235
  and organizational democracy, 233
  and organizing business practices, 121–22
  mediated, 203–5
  and mysticism, 235
Springsteen, Bruce, 205
Stallybrass, Peter, 19
stewardship, 217n
St. Joseph Hospital, 214
Stoller, Paul, 17, 147n
storytelling, xii
  and Spirit, 218–20
strangers, 48, 54
Sullivan, William, 16
superstition, 154n
surrender
  to dreams, 88
  to wonder, 87
sustainability, and organizational ecology, 217n
symbols, 112
  construction of opposites, 113–14
  gang, 188
  symbolic convergence, 211n
syntax, 157–73
  altered states of, 157–58; 164
  visible, on DMT, 165

talk
  good, 65
  ordinary public, 54–55
  radio, and public imagination, 193
  ritualized, 61
Talmud, 17
Tao Te Ching, 215, 216
  and negotiation, 216
TD's (bar), 142, 148–50
television, 128n
  and instructions, 200–205
  and loss of community, 128
  and modernist textual strategy, 200
  and spirituality, 199
  programming, 199

291

INDEX

Ten Commandments, 186, 203
text(s)
 and settings, 75
Thomas, Lewis, 180
Thoreau, Henry David,
 and transcendental, 235
Tiger, the (Clemson)
 Clemson symbol, 104, 117, 120–21
 paws, on clothing, 145
Tiger Boulevard (Clemson), 144
time, 161–62
toys, as signs, 229
TQM, 215
transcendence, 107n
transcendentalism, 3
translations, and instructions, 181n
thrownness, 28–29, 31
Turner, Victor, 150n, 172
 and liminality, 150n, 172
Tuscaloosa (AL), 23

unconscious, the, 212
unhymnal, the, 116n
unities, 208
 sacred, 241
University of Alabama in Huntsville, 41
University of North Carolina at Chapel Hill, 40

vanity (license) plates, 163
Van Maanen, John, 8n, 16
Ventura, Michael, 103, 124, 229, 237
verbs
 absence in talk, 65
vision
 logic of, 180n
 and new logic, 207
 and reason, dualities, 205–6
 and spiritual phenomena, 205

voice, 211–13
 and Spirit, 211–13
 transformative, 224
Vonnegut, Kurt, 32n

Wal-Mart, 209
Warren, Carol A. B., 220n
Watson, Lyall, 6–7
Wayne's World, 150
Weick, Karl, 238
Welcome Baptist Church, 34, 46
Wheatley, Margaret, 10n, 217n
White, Aron, 19
White, Mimi, 203n
Whyte, William, 230n
Wirikuta, 68
Wittgenstein, Ludwig, 170
WJEJ/WWMD, 193n
Wolf, Fred Alan, 162
Wolfe, Thomas, 41
Woodbury, Marsha, 188
Woodstock, 68
word(s)
 angel aspect, 27
 misspelled, 158
 as signs, 44
work
 as classroom, 225
 reinvention of, 217
 and workplace, 217
world(s)
 parallel, 12, 137–38, 142, 146–47, 147n, 149–50, 155, 158, 193
Wyllie, Timothy, 136

Zen, 50, 51, 56, 74, 91
 of communication, 91–95
Zentral, 50, 51
Zhaozhou Congshen, 51

About the Author

H. L. Goodall, Jr., a professor of communication and the head of the Department of Communication at the University of North Carolina at Greensboro, is the author or coauthor of twelve other books. *Divine Signs: Connecting Spirit to Community* is the third volume of an auto- and ethnographic quest exploring the communicative and cultural tensions of contemporary American organizing and sense-making. The series includes *Casing a Promised Land: The Autobiography of an Organizational Detective as Cultural Ethnographer* (1989, 1994) and *Living in the Rock n Roll Mystery: Reading Context, Self, and Others as Clues* (1991). He conducted research for this book while teaching at Clemson University from 1991 to 1995. In 1995, he received the Gerald M. Phillips Award for mentoring from the American Communication Association.